World Wisdom
The Library of Perennial Philosophy

The Library of Perennial Philosophy is dedicated to the exposition of the timeless Truth underlying the diverse religions. This Truth, often referred to as the *Sophia Perennis*—or Perennial Wisdom—finds its expression in the revealed Scriptures as well as the writings of the great sages and the artistic creations of the traditional worlds.

Esoterism as Principle and as Way appears as one of our selections in the Writings of Frithjof Schuon series.

The Writings of Frithjof Schuon

The Writings of Frithjof Schuon form the foundation of our library because he is the pre-eminent exponent of the Perennial Philosophy. His work illuminates this perspective in both an essential and comprehensive manner like none other.

English Language Writings of Frithjof Schuon

Original Books

The Transcendent Unity of Religions
Spiritual Perspectives and Human Facts
Gnosis: Divine Wisdom
Language of the Self
Stations of Wisdom
Understanding Islam
Light on the Ancient Worlds
Treasures of Buddhism (In the Tracks of Buddhism)
Logic and Transcendence
Esoterism as Principle and as Way
Castes and Races
Sufism: Veil and Quintessence
From the Divine to the Human
Christianity/Islam: Essays on Esoteric Ecumenicism
Survey of Metaphysics and Esoterism
In the Face of the Absolute
The Feathered Sun: Plains Indians in Art and Philosophy
To Have a Center
Roots of the Human Condition
Images of Primordial and Mystic Beauty: Paintings by Frithjof Schuon
Echoes of Perennial Wisdom
The Play of Masks
Road to the Heart: Poems
The Transfiguration of Man
The Eye of the Heart
Form and Substance in the Religions
Adastra & Stella Maris: Poems by Frithjof Schuon (bilingual edition)
Autumn Leaves & The Ring: Poems by Frithjof Schuon (bilingual edition)
Songs without Names, Volumes I-VI: Poems by Frithjof Schuon
Songs without Names, Volumes VII-XII: Poems by Frithjof Schuon
World Wheel, Volumes I-III: Poems by Frithjof Schuon
World Wheel, Volumes IV-VII: Poems by Frithjof Schuon
Primordial Meditation: Contemplating the Real

Edited Writings

The Essential Frithjof Schuon, ed. Seyyed Hossein Nasr
Songs for a Spiritual Traveler: Selected Poems (bilingual edition)
René Guénon: Some Observations, ed. William Stoddart
The Fullness of God: Frithjof Schuon on Christianity,
ed. James S. Cutsinger
Prayer Fashions Man: Frithjof Schuon on the Spiritual Life,
ed. James S. Cutsinger
Art from the Sacred to the Profane: East and West,
ed. Catherine Schuon
Splendor of the True: A Frithjof Schuon Reader,
ed. James S. Cutsinger

Esoterism as Principle and as Way

A New Translation with Selected Letters

by

Frithjof Schuon

Includes Other Previously
Unpublished Writings

Edited by
Harry Oldmeadow

World Wisdom

Esoterism as Principle and as Way:
A New Translation with Selected Letters
© 2019 World Wisdom, Inc.

Translated by Mark Perry and Jean-Pierre Lafouge

Published in French as
L'Ésotérisme comme principe et comme voie,
Éditions Dervy, 1978, 1997

Library of Congress Cataloging-in-Publication Data

Names: Schuon, Frithjof, 1907-1998. | Oldmeadow, Harry, 1947- editor. |
Perry, Mark, 1951- translator. | Lafouge, Jean-Pierre, 1944- translator.
Title: Esoterism as principle and as way : a new translation with selected
letters / by Frithjof Schuon ; edited by Harry Oldmeadow.
Other titles: Esoterisme comme principe et comme voie. English
Description: Bloomington, Indiana : World Wisdom, Inc., [2019] | Series:
The library of perennial philosophy | Series: The writings of Frithjof Schuon
| "Includes other previously unpublished writings." | Includes
bibliographical references and index. |
Identifiers: LCCN 2019009740 (print) | LCCN 2019012901 (ebook) |
ISBN 9781936597659 (epub) | ISBN 9781936597642 (pbk. : alk. paper)
Subjects: LCSH: Religion--Philosophy.
Classification: LCC BL51 (ebook) | LCC BL51 .S463513 2019 (print) |
DDC 200--dc23

Cover:
Plains Indian feathered sun

Printed on acid-free paper in the United States of America

For information address World Wisdom, Inc.
P.O. Box 2682, Bloomington, Indiana 47402-2682
www.worldwisdom.com

CONTENTS

Appendix

EDITOR'S PREFACE

In recent times the terms "esoteric" and "esoterism" have become somewhat elastic and imprecise. In popular usage "esoterism" loosely refers to a field of "spiritual" knowledge and practice that is secret, arcane, and initiatory; the term encompasses movements as diverse as hermeticism, alchemy, Rosicrucianism, theosophy, freemasonry, spiritualism, shamanism, Christian mysticism, Kabbalah, and Sufism as well as a plethora of modern occult and para-psychological movements gathered around disparate and often bizarre charismatic figures. However, many modern movements that claim access to esoteric knowledge are in fact concerned only with the study and manipulation of psychic and extra-sensory phenomena and have no necessary connection with religion or the spiritual life properly speaking. A vast spiritual wasteland is populated by self-styled "esoteric" groups that concern themselves with auras, astral bodies, ectoplasmic apparitions, vibrations, mind waves, death lights, and, in Whitall Perry's words, "sundry other emergences and extravagances of hideous nomenclature".[1]

The esoterism with which Frithjof Schuon is concerned is of an altogether different order: it is in fact nothing other than the *sophia perennis* itself, the timeless wisdom that lies at the heart of the diverse religions and behind the manifold forms of the world's integral traditions, not only those of East and West but also from the primordial worlds of non-literate and nomadic peoples. As Schuon has written elsewhere, "In all epochs and in all countries there have been revelations, religions, wisdoms; tradition is part of mankind just as man is part of tradition".[2]

Schuon is the pre-eminent exponent of what has been called the traditionalist or perennialist school, which includes such luminaries as René Guénon, Ananda Coomaraswamy, and Titus Burckhardt. However, unlike some of those who have sought to popularize the perennial philosophy, these writers are also dedicated to the preservation and

---

[1] Whitall N. Perry, *A Treasury of Traditional Wisdom* (London: George Allen & Unwin, 1971), p. 437.

[2] Frithjof Schuon, *Light on the Ancient Worlds* (Bloomington, IN: World Wisdom, 2006), p. 25.

illumination of the traditional forms that give each religious heritage its *raison d'être* and guarantee its formal integrity and, by the same token, ensure its spiritual efficacy. They have no interest in any sort of syncretism that seeks some kind of supra-religion on the basis of the distilled wisdom of the ages. Schuon is concerned with the re-affirmation of traditional metaphysical and cosmological principles, with an explication of the inner dimensions of religion, with the penetration of religious forms, and with a critique of a modernist outlook that is indifferent or openly hostile to tradition.

Esoterism as Principle and as Way, like most of the author's books, comprises a collection of essays written over a period of years, each free-standing and not always in any obvious relationship to the others. Some of the subjects treated in this volume might appear to belong to the exoteric domain, which is to say the outer realm of religious forms. Nonetheless, as the author himself explains in his Introduction, these essays are all informed by an esoteric outlook and understanding; the title of the book signals its governing theme and method. A few introductory remarks about esoterism properly-understood and about the author's perspective may help some readers to find their bearings in approaching material that is not always easily accessible, especially to those not already familiar with the author's other works.

The distinction between the esoteric and exoteric domains within the religious traditions is integral in Schuon's work. In *Logic and Transcendence* he defined this distinction in the most lucid and unambiguous terms:

> Exoterism consists in identifying transcendent realities with the dogmatic forms—and if necessary with the historical facts—of a given Revelation, whereas esoterism refers in a more or less direct manner to these same realities.[3]

The distinction might also be couched in terms of "form" and "spirit". Religion, in its formal aspect, is made up of what Schuon calls "saving mirages" and "celestial stratagems"[4]—or, in Buddhist terms,

---

[3] Frithjof Schuon, *Logic and Transcendence* (Bloomington, IN: World Wisdom, 2009), p. 123.

[4] Frithjof Schuon, *Survey of Metaphysics and Esoterism* (Bloomington, IN: World Wisdom, 2000), p. 185, note 2.

upāya, "skillful means" that answer the necessities of the case. The limiting definitions of exoteric formalism are "comparable to descriptions of an object of which only the form and not the colors can be seen".[5] As the author states in the Introduction, "religious theses are certainly not errors, but they are cut to the measure of some mental and moral opportuneness" (p. xiv). Thus, partial truths that might be inadequate in a sapiential perspective may be altogether proper on the formal exoteric plane:

> The formal homogeneity of a religion requires not only truth but also errors—though these are only in the form—just as the world requires evil and just as Divinity implies the mystery of creation by virtue of its infinity.
>
> Absolute truth exists only in depth, not on the surface.
>
> Religions are "mythologies", which as such are based on real aspects of the Divine and on sacred facts—hence on realities but on aspects alone; this limitation is at once inevitable and completely effective.[6]

In other words religious dogmas represent certain accommodations that are necessary to bring various truths within the purview of the exoteric mentality. It is in the nature of things that only a small minority will be blessed with the contemplative intelligence necessary to penetrate the formal aspects of religion. For the normal believer the exoteric domain is the only domain. Nevertheless, we live in a time when religious exclusivism must either put itself in mortal peril or be transmuted by a revivifying esoterism:

> Exoterism is a precarious thing by reason of its limits or due to all that it excludes; but there comes a moment in history when a whole variety of experiences oblige it to modify its claims to exclusiveness, and it is then driven to a choice: either to escape from these limitations via the upward path, in esoterism, or via the downward path, in a worldly or suicidal liberalism (p. 8).

[5] Frithjof Schuon, *Understanding Islam* (Bloomington, IN: World Wisdom, 2011), p. 71.

[6] Frithjof Schuon, *Spiritual Perspectives and Human Facts* (Bloomington, IN: World Wisdom, 2007), p. 72.

Esoterism is concerned with the apprehension of Reality as such, not Reality as understood in such and such a perspective and "under the veil of different religious formulations" (p. 7). While exoterism sees "essence" or "universal truth" as a function of particular forms, esoterism sees the forms as a function of "essence". Or, as the author puts it, exoterism particularizes the universal, esoterism universalizes the particular:

> What characterizes esoterism to the very extent that it is absolute, is that upon contact with a dogmatic system it universalizes the symbol or religious concept on the one hand and interiorizes it on the other; the particular or the limited is recognized as the manifestation of the principial and the transcendent, and the transcendent in its turn reveals itself as immanent (p. 26).

Nevertheless, the two realms, exoteric and esoteric, are continually meeting and interpenetrating, not only because there is such a thing as a "relative esoterism" but because "the underlying truth is one, and also because man is one" (p. 4). Furthermore, even if esoterism transcends forms, it has need of "doctrinal, ritual, and moral supports" if it is to lead to realization (p. 18). And yet, from another point of view it must also be remembered that although "The presence of an esoteric nucleus in a civilization that is specifically exoteric in character guarantees to it a normal development and a maximum of stability", it is also the case that "this nucleus . . . is not in any sense a part, even an inner part, of the exoterism, but represents, on the contrary, a quasi-independent 'dimension' in relation to the latter".[7]

Esoterism is "situated" on the plane of mystical experience, intellection, and realization. The science of metaphysical principles can be called esoterism when pursued within the cadre of an integral religious tradition. If *gnosis* as such—"intellective knowledge of the Absolute"[8]—is under consideration then the question of religious orthodoxy cannot arise, this being a principle that is only operative on the formal plane:

---

[7] Frithjof Schuon, *The Transcendent Unity of Religions* (Wheaton, IL: Quest, 1984), pp. 9-10.

[8] Frithjof Schuon, *To Have a Center* (Bloomington, IN: World Wisdom, 2015), p. 54.

If the purest esoterism comprises total truth—and that is the reason for its existence—the question of "orthodoxy" in the religious sense quite obviously cannot arise; direct knowledge of the mysteries could not be "Muslim" or "Christian", just as the sight of a mountain is the sight of a mountain and not something else.[9]

Gnosis, precisely, is "knowledge of the mysteries", what Meister Eckhart calls "divine knowledge", the Hindus *jnāna;* as the author tersely remarks elsewhere, "*Gnosis* is not just anything"[10]; *gnosis* is divine wisdom; and esoterism, essentially, is *gnosis*.

"Understanding Esoterism", which opens the present volume, is one of the author's most extended and deliberate expositions of this subject. It elaborates the general principles which, in the rest of the book, inform the author's exploration of divergent forms and phenomena from the boundless world of Tradition.

These essays were first published by Dervy Livres in 1978 as *L'Ésotérisme comme Principe et comme Voie* and were translated into English by William Stoddart, a close associate of the author, appearing in 1981 as *Esoterism as Principle and as Way* (Pates Manor, Bedfont: Perennial Books). The translators and editor of this new, fully revised English translation take pleasure in acknowledging the earlier endeavors of Dr. Stoddart. The new edition takes its place within a series of fresh translations of Schuon's works, sponsored by World Wisdom. Like its companion volumes, it includes extensive editorial annotations, a full glossary of foreign words and phrases, and excerpts from the author's letters and other previously unpublished writings.

Harry Oldmeadow

[9] Frithjof Schuon, *Understanding Islam* (Bloomington, IN: World Wisdom, 2011), p. 139.

[10] The title of an essay in *To Have a Center*, p. 53.

INTRODUCTION

It is necessary, first of all, to be clear about the meaning of the word "esoterism": everyone knows that it designates *a priori* doctrines and methods that are more or less secret because they are considered as being out of reach for the limited capacities of average men. What calls for explanation is why this perspective is possible and even necessary, and how it applies to the various levels of human existence; all this presupposes that one is dealing with authentic esoterism and not its counterfeits or deviations, which can only compromise the word if not the thing itself, and which often merely serve to flatter a propensity for extravagance. Certainly, all esoterism appears to be tinged with heresy from the point of view of the corresponding exoterism, but this obviously does not disqualify it if it is intrinsically orthodox, hence conforming with truth as such and with the traditional symbolism to which it pertains; it is true that the most authentic esoterism can incidentally depart from this framework and refer to foreign symbolisms, but it cannot be syncretistic in its very substance. However, what concerns us here is not so much the historic esoterisms—such as Pythagoreanism, Shivaite *Vedānta*, Zen—but esoterism as such, which we would willingly term *sophia perennis* and which in itself is independent of particular forms since it is their essence.

It might be objected that it is contradictory to speak in public of things that are so precarious as regards their intelligibility; we would reply once again with the Kabbalists that it is better that wisdom be divulged than that it be forgotten, aside from the fact that our writings are addressed only to those who want to read and understand them. We live in an age of confusion and thirst in which the advantages of communication are greater than those of secrecy; moreover, only esoteric theses can satisfy the imperious needs for logical understanding that the philosophic and scientific positions of the modern world cause. To this it must be added that if the esoteric doctrines are not accepted as they deserve to be, it is not always from lack of goodwill; this lack may have inexcusable or excusable causes, and in the latter case—which is often a question of imagination—it is compensated by a spiritual attitude which, although no doubt limited, is nevertheless positive and efficacious. We do not seek to convert anyone who is at peace with God, if he truly is so, namely according to God's will itself and with a pure heart; and we would also stress that for our part the notion of esoterism evokes not so much intellectual superiority as the totality of truth and the imprescriptible rights of intelligence, always within the climate of a human and thus a living relationship with Heaven. In any case, the idea that non-esoterists by definition lack intelligence, or that esoterists are *de facto* necessarily endowed with it, does not even cross our mind.

As we have more than once remarked in our previous writings, it seems to become harder and harder to accept—from the point of view of the ideology of "our time"—not merely that a particular religion is the only true one, but also that there is such a thing as a true religion; in so far as the religions bear part of the responsibility for this situation—due to human limitations—this can be ascribed to the limitations of their cosmology and eschatology, and also to their exclusivism. Religious theses are certainly not errors, but they are cut to the measure of some mental and moral opportuneness; men come in the end to see through the adaptation as such, but they do so at the expense of the truth. Only esoterism can explain the particular adaptation and restore the lost truth by referring to the total truth; it alone can provide answers that are neither fragmentary nor compromised in advance by a denominational bias. Just as rationalism can remove faith, so esoterism can restore it.

We must now place ourselves at a much more general point of view. According to some, no "ideology" has ever saved the world; without dwelling on what the intentions behind this statement might be, we would reply that no spiritual system, no religion, has ever had this aim, for what matters is merely to provide men with the means of saving themselves, not of saving them in spite of themselves, and also to provide them with the means of creating a favorable framework, or the least unfavorable framework possible, for the realization of this end. It is only possible to save those who want to be saved: those who, firstly, realize that they are in the process of drowning and, secondly, who are willing to grasp the line that is thrown out to them; man, being free, is condemned to freedom. It is not the liberating truths and methods which have "failed", it is men on becoming so-called "adults", who have done so; the attenuating circumstances—the limits of the exoterisms when faced with certain experiences on the one hand and scientific discoveries on the other hand, in the absence of the capacity

to interpret them and integrate them—do not suffice to exonerate men from having become indifferent to innate proofs, which are always palpable, and from having shut themselves off from Mercy out of pride and puerility. Moreover, the history of a religion is always the history of a struggle between a divine gift and a refusal to accept it, which accounts in part for the compensatory exaggerations of the saints.

There are two ways of reading a book: either the reader starts at the beginning and proceeds patiently to the end, or else he freely chooses the chapters which arouse his immediate interest. It will readily be seen that this book is assembled in the same way as our earlier works, that is, it is composed of essays that are more or less independent from one another, and of varying importance, as is indicated moreover by the division of the book into several parts with very different contents.

Our frequent recourse to Sanskrit and Arabic terminology has the following significance: India, with the *Upanishads*, represents the most ancient metaphysical doctrine of humanity—we have in mind here metaphysics made explicit, and not pure symbolism, which is without origin and without localization—whereas Islam is the last Revelation of humanity, and thus closes the cycle of the great law-giving and salvational outpourings. These two traditional currents, the primordial Aryan and the final Semitic, met on the soil of India, a meeting which, far from being a chance occurrence—there is nothing fortuitous in phenomena on such a scale—is on the contrary a symbolic situation full of significance.

Although this book contains the necessary elements to permit one to situate esoterism in the most general sense of the term—the same could be said of our earlier works—it nevertheless is not a systematic treatise on this subject; it need not be so in fact to justify its title, given that esoterism resides not only in the choice of ideas, but also in the manner of envisaging things. In other words, one will find in this book subjects which in themselves are independent of the esoteric domain, but which nevertheless fit into it given our perspective, and thus play their part in communicating not so much doctrines that are historically classifiable, as a discipline of thought in conformity with these doctrines or rather with their essence.

Every doctrinal exposition immediately raises the question of the sources of certitude and consequently of the criteria of truth. Now, the truth comes to us either from the outside or from the inside, depending on whether it is indirect and formal or direct and essential: under normal circumstances we learn *a priori* about the reality of divine things through Revelation, which provides us with the symbols and the indispensable information, and we have access *a posteriori* to the truth of these things through Intellection, which reveals to us their essence lying beyond received formulations—but not against them— on condition that nothing either in our nature or will opposes them. Revelation is an Intellection in the macrocosm, whereas Intellection is a Revelation in the microcosm; the *Avatāra* is the outward Intellect, and the Intellect is the inward *Avatāra*.

It is well known that Revelation requires faith; it is less well known that Intellection also requires it in its fashion, and this may even seem paradoxical, since the Intellect entails certitude by defini- tion. But certitude has degrees from the point of view of assimilation or integration—or of sincerity, if one will; *credo ut intelligam*, but also: *intelligo ergo credo*. In the first case, faith consists in accepting truth obtained from the outside, and in accepting it in an instinctive, volitive, and sentimental manner; in the second case, faith consists, not in accepting what is evident, which would be redundant, but in causing it to penetrate our whole being, and this engages—as in the case of religious faith—both will and sentiment. Regarding sentiment, it is important to underline the fact that this faculty deserves blame only when it usurps intelligence and opposes truth, and not when it prolongs intelligence and serves truth, for this is its normal function; if sentiment were illegitimate, so too would be beauty, and there would be no reason to follow beauty and love back to their divine source.

And it is well to recall here the following axiomatic truth: that Intellection should make use of reasoning, which is humanly unavoid- able, does not mean that it is identified with the latter; nevertheless, correct reasoning, founded on adequate information, can be an occa- sional cause for a particular intellection, just as any symbol in nature or in art can be. Sufficiently adequate thought, even if tentative, can actualize a sudden awareness pertaining to a completely different dimension from the sequence of mental operations, for when compared to Intellection, it provides a symbolism and a point of reference; now, the function of every symbol is to break the shell of forgetfulness overlaying the knowledge immanent to the Intellect. Like a material symbol, intellectual dialectic is a transparent veil which, upon contact with the miracle of remembrance, is rent asunder and exposes a truth which, being universal, springs forth from our own being, which would not be so were it not That which is.

PART I

SOPHIA PERENNIS

Understanding Esoterism

The prerogative of the human state is objectivity, the essential content of which is the Absolute. There is no knowledge without objectivity of the intelligence; there is no freedom without objectivity of the will; and there is no nobility without objectivity of the soul. In each of these three domains, there is both horizontal and vertical objectivity; the subject, whether intellective, volitive, or affective, necessarily has in view both the contingent and the Absolute: the contingent, because the subject is itself contingent and to the extent that it is so, and the Absolute, because the subject partakes of the Absolute through its capacity for objectivity.

Esoterism, by means of its interpretations, its revelations, and its interiorizing and essentializing operations, tends to realize pure and direct objectivity; this is its reason for being. Objectivity takes account of both immanence and transcendence; it is both extinction and reintegration. It is not other than the Truth, in which subject and object coincide, and in which the essential takes precedence over the accidental—or in which the principle takes precedence over its manifestation—either by extinguishing it, or by reintegrating it, depending on the various aspects of relativity itself.[1]

To speak of objectivity is to speak of totality, and this on all levels: esoteric doctrines realize totality to the very extent that they realize objectivity; what distinguishes the doctrine of a Shankara from that of a Ramanuja is precisely totality. On the one hand, partial or indirect truth can save, and in this respect it is sufficient for us; on the other hand, if God has judged it good to give us an understanding that surpasses the necessary minimum, this is hardly our fault and we would be highly ungracious to complain about it. Man certainly is free to close his eyes to particular facts—and he may do so either from ignorance or as a matter of convenience—but the least that could be said is that nothing obliges him to do so.

---

[1] It follows that "objectivity" does not mean a knowledge that is limited to a purely empirical recording of information received from outside, but a perfect adequation of the knowing subject to the known object, which indeed is in keeping with the current meaning of the term. An intelligence or a knowledge is "objective" when it is capable of grasping the object as it is and not as it may be distorted by the subject.

All the same, the difference between the two perspectives in question lies not only in the manner of considering a particular object, but also in the objects considered; that is to say, one does not only speak differently about the same thing, one also speaks of different things—nothing could be more evident.

Nevertheless, if the world of *gnosis* and that of belief are distinct on the one hand, on the other and in another respect they meet and even interpenetrate. Perhaps we will be told that there is nothing specifically esoteric or gnostic about one or other of the points we make; we would readily agree and are the first to acknowledge this. That the two perspectives in question may or must coincide at many points, and at different levels, is only too obvious given that the underlying truth is one, and also because man is one.

—— .:. ——

In knowledge, it is necessary to make a distinction between the relationship of analogy and that of identity, for this is what fundamentally differentiates rational thought from intellectual inspiration, according to the proper and rigorous meaning of the term "intellectual". The relationship of analogy is that of discontinuity between center and periphery: created things, including thoughts—everything in fact that constitutes cosmic manifestation—are distinct from the Principle; the transcendent realities grasped by thought are distinct from the thinking subject. In other words, rational or mental knowledge is like a reflection separated from its luminous source, a reflection moreover that is exposed to all kinds of subjective perturbations.

The relationship of identity, however, is one of continuity between center and periphery, which is what distinguishes it from the relationship of analogy in the same manner as a star is distinct from concentric circles. Divine manifestation, around us and within us, prolongs and projects the Principle and is identified with it in its capacity, precisely, as the immanent divine quality; the sun is really the Principle perceived through existential veils; water is really universal Passivity perceived through these same veils. As far as knowledge is concerned, it is not enough to have a merely mental grasp of this relationship in order to confer on reasoning a character of divineness, and thus of truth and infallibility, although it is true that, objectively speaking, every thought manifests—in the metaphysical relationship of identity—the divine Thinker, if one may so put it; but this purely objective and existential or, if one prefers, ontological situation is completely general and therefore remains independent of qualitative differences, so that it has nothing to do with the subjective and cognitive realization specific to the relationship of identity. We have said that in rational or mental knowledge, the transcendent realities grasped by thought are separate from the thinking subject; however, in properly intellectual or cardiac knowledge, the principial realities grasped by the heart are themselves prolonged in intellection; cardiac knowledge is one with what it knows, it is like an uninterrupted ray of light.

Kantians will ask us to prove the existence of this way of knowing; and herein lies the first error, namely that only what can be proved *de facto* is knowledge; the second error, which follows in the wake of the first, is that a reality that one cannot prove—namely which one cannot render accessible to some artificial and ignorant mental demand—that this reality, owing to its seeming lack of proof, does not and cannot exist. Integral rationalism lacks intellectual objectivity as much as it does moral impartiality.[2]

But let us return to the distinction between indirect, rational, mental knowledge and direct, intellectual, cardiac knowledge; apart from these two modes there is a third one, and this is the knowledge of faith. Now, faith amounts to a cardiac knowledge that is objectified; namely, what the microcosmic heart does not tell us, the macrocosmic heart—the *Logos*—tells us in a symbolic and partial language, and this for two reasons: to inform us concerning those things our soul is in urgent need of, and to awaken in us as much as possible the remembrance of innate truths.

If there is an intrinsically direct knowledge, which nevertheless is extrinsically objectified as to its manner of communication, then there must be a corresponding knowledge which, albeit indirect in itself, must nonetheless be subjective as to its mode of operation, and this is the discernment of objective things from the starting point of their subjective equivalents, given that reality is one; for there is nothing in

---

[2] Kant terms "transcendental subreption" (*Erschleichung*) the "transformation" of the purely "regulative" idea of God into an objective reality, which proves once more that he is unable to conceive of any certitude outside of a reasoning founded on sense experience and operating beneath the reality that he pretends to judge and deny. In short, Kantian "criticism" consists in considering anyone who does not bend to its discipline a liar; agnostics do practically the same, by decreeing that no one can know anything since they themselves know nothing, or do not wish to know anything.

the macrocosm that is not derived from the metacosm and that cannot be found again in the microcosm.

Direct and inward knowledge, that of the Heart-Intellect, is what the Greeks called *gnosis;* the word "esoterism"—according to its etymology—designates *gnosis* inasmuch as it *de facto* underlies the religious, and thus dogmatic doctrines.

— ∴ —

On the exoterist side it is argued, against universalist esoterism, that Revelation says such and such a thing and consequently this must be accepted in an unconditional manner; on the esoterist side, it will be said that Revelation is intrinsically absolute and extrinsically relative and that this relativity results from a combination of two factors, namely Intellection and experience. To take an example: the fact that a form cannot be absolutely unique of its kind—any more than the sun, though intrinsically representing the unique center, cannot exclude the existence of other fixed stars—is an axiom of Intellection, albeit having only an *a priori* abstract import; this axiom becomes concrete, however, were we to be brought intimately into relationship with other solar systems of the religious cosmos; such an experience compels us precisely to distinguish, within Revelation, between an intrinsic or absolute sense and an extrinsic or relative sense. According to the first sense, Christ is unique, and he told us so; according to the second sense, he said this as *Logos*, and the *Logos*, which is unique, comprises in fact other possible manifestations.

It is true that experience alone, in the absence of pure Intellection, can give rise to completely opposite conclusions: one might well think that the plurality of the religions proved their falseness or at least their subjectiveness, since they differ. Most paradoxically, but fatally—civilizationism having prepared the ground—the official stratum of Catholic thought allowed itself to be carried away by the conclusions of profane experience by readily ignoring those of Intellection;[3] this leads

---

[3] Persistence in their errors is made easy for the modernists by the extreme, and largely arbitrary, positions of some traditionalists, who compromise tradition by making it responsible for a civilizationist and nationalist ideology, which is all too readily defamatory as regards *gnosis* or the East—to the delight of their adversaries and which has no connection with the Holy Spirit, to say the least.

these ideologues into accepting certain extrinsic postulates of esoterism—in particular that of the validity of the other religions—but at the cost of ruining their own religion and without understanding in depth that of the others.[4]

— ∴ —

The esoterist sees things, not as they appear according to a certain perspective, but as they are: he takes account of what is essential and hence invariable under the veil of different religious formulations, while necessarily adopting a given formulation as his own starting point. This, at least, is the position of principle and the justification for esoterism; but in fact it is far from always being consistent with itself, all the more as intermediary solutions are humanly unavoidable.

Everything that is universally true in metaphysics or in spirituality becomes "esoteric" to the extent that it does not agree, or does not seem to agree, with a given formalistic system, that is to say with a specific "exoterism", precisely; and yet every truth belongs by right in every religion since every religion is made of truth. This amounts to saying that esoterism is possible and even necessary; the whole question is to know at what level and in what context it is manifested, for relative and limited truth has its rights, as does total truth; relative truth has these rights in the specific context assigned to it by the nature of things, which is that of psychological and moral opportuneness and of traditional equilibrium.

The paradox of esoterism is that on the one hand "men do not light a candle and put it under a bushel", while on the other hand "give not that which is holy unto the dogs"; between these two images lies the "light that shineth in the darkness, but the darkness comprehended it not". There are fluctuations here that no one can prevent and which are the ransom of contingency.

---

[4] The modernists think they were the first to know how to combine extrinsic relativity with intrinsic absoluteness, but their choice of dividing line between the extrinsic and the intrinsic is totally false, precisely since from the outset they reduce the inward to the outward or the absolute to the relative. All question of civilizationism aside, it is necessary to state clearly here that modernism cannot derive from Catholicism in itself but on the contrary has taken possession of it and makes use of it like an occupying power. The law of gravity does the rest.

Exoterism is a precarious thing by reason of its limits or due to all that it excludes; but there comes a moment in history when a whole variety of experiences oblige it to modify its claims to exclusiveness, and it is then driven to a choice: either to escape from these limitations via the upward path, in esoterism, or via the downward path, in a worldly and suicidal liberalism. As one might have expected, the civilizationist exoterism of the West has chosen the downward path, while combining this incidentally with a few esoteric notions that remain inoperative in such conditions.

Fallen man, that is to say average man, is as it were poisoned by the passional element, whether grossly or subtly; this leads to an obscuring of the Intellect and the necessity of a Revelation coming to him from the outside. Remove the passional element from the soul and the intelligence—remove "the rust from the mirror" or from the "heart"—and the Intellect will be released; it will reveal from within what religion reveals from without.[5] And this brings us to an important point: in order to make itself understood by souls pervaded by passion, religion itself must adopt a so to speak passional language, whence dogmatism, which excludes, and moralism, which oversimplifies by schematizing; if the average man or collective man were not passional, Revelation would speak the language of the Intellect and there would be no more exoterism, nor for that matter any esoterism having to serve as an occult complement. There are three possibilities here: firstly, men can dominate the passional element and everyone lives spiritually through his inward Revelation; this is the golden age, in which everyone is born an initiate. Second possibility: men are affected by the passional element to the point of forgetting certain aspects of the Truth, whence the necessity—or the opportuneness—of Revelations that while being outward are metaphysical in spirit, such as the *Upanishads*.[6] Third possibility: the majority of men are dominated by passions, whence the formalistic, exclusive, and combative religions, which on the one hand provide these men the means of channeling the passional element in view of salvation, and on

[5] This release is strictly impossible—we must insist—without the assistance of a religion, an orthodoxy, a traditional esoterism with all that it implies.

[6] Such a Revelation has a function that is both conservative and preventive, it expresses the Truth in view of the risk of its being forgotten; consequently, it also has the aim of protecting the "pure" from contamination by the "impure", of recalling the Truth to those who run the risk of going astray out of heedlessness.

the other hand the means of overcoming it in view of the total Truth, thereby enabling them to transcend the religious formalism that veils this Truth while at the same time suggesting it in an indirect manner. Religious Revelation is both a veil of light and a light veiled.

— ⋮ —

For those who accept esoterism or, what amounts to the same, the *philosophia perennis*, while feeling that they are emotionally bound to a given religious climate, the temptation is great to mistake the sublime for the esoteric, believing that everything that they venerate pertains *ipso facto* to esoterism, starting with theology and sanctity. To escape all confusion of this kind, it is important to have a precise, not a vague, idea of what is in question; as a point of reference we shall choose the example of the non-personalistic and unitive non-dualism of Shankara and shall contrast it with the personalistic and separative monism of Ramanuja. While Ramanuja's perspective is substantially similar to the Semitic monotheisms, that of Shankara is one of the most adequate expressions possible of the *philosophia perennis* or sapiential esoterism.

According to Shankara, universal Reality comprises degrees, owing to an element of illusion that determines them in different ways. *Ātmā*, or *Brahma*, is alone absolutely real; it is the ineffable and supra-personal Self from which all relative consciousnesses derive and in which they participate; and it is veiled by *Māyā*, which creates the illusion of separativity and existence, and thus the world, creatures, objects, subjects. We will say, independently of Shankara, that this *Māyā*—which coincides with relativity and contingency—is an emanation of the Self by virtue of its infinity; that is to say, infinity requires universal radiation due to its as it were overflowing nature, whereas absoluteness on the contrary excludes by definition all duplication and diversification; but Shankara leaves unanswered this question of the metaphysical origin of *Māyā*, speaking of the latter only in a more or less practical fashion. For him, it is not possible to define the cause of *Māyā*, but the *jnānin* knows that it exists since he is immersed in it; he also knows that it is illusory since he can escape from it; he obtains this liberation through intellectual discrimination and profound and methodical concentration on his own essence, which in the final analysis is not other than the infinite Self.

Shankara has no intention of denying the relative value of the exoterisms, which by definition do not go beyond the consideration of a personal God. For them, God is the Absolute reflected in the limiting and diversifying mirror of *Māyā*; He is *Īshvara*, the creating, destroying, saving, and punishing Principle, and the "relatively absolute" prototype of all perfections. This personal and all-powerful God is perfectly real in Himself, and even more so in relation to the world and man; but He pertains nonetheless to *Māyā* when compared with the Absolute properly so called. For Shankara, personalistic monotheism is valid, and thus effective, within the framework of *Māyā*; but since the human spirit is identified in its essence—although difficult of access—with the supreme Self, it is possible for it to escape, with the aid of Grace, the grasp of universal Illusion and to reach its own immutable Reality. *Bhakti*, or love for the personal Divinity, is for the Shankarian Vedantin a necessary step towards Liberation—*moksha*—and even a quasi-indispensable and entirely natural concomitance of supreme knowledge, *jnāna*: on the one hand, worship founded on transcendence brings the spirit towards an awareness of immanence and consequently of identity, namely towards the transcending of duality and separativity; on the other hand, the awareness of transcendence and the *bhakti* that results from it are intimately connected with the very soul of man. To speak of "man" is to speak of a *bhakta*, whereas to speak of "spirit" is to speak of a *jnānin*; human nature is as it were woven of these two neighboring but incommensurable dimensions. There is certainly a *bhakti* without *jnāna*, but there is no *jnāna* without *bhakti*.

The Shankarian perspective coincides in substance with Platonism in the widest and deepest sense, with the sole proviso that the Platonists put more emphasis on cosmology, not to mention other obvious but non-essential differences.

If Shankara represents *jnāna*, Ramanuja is the great spokesman of *bhakti*;[7] this is not to say that he personifies and presents exoterism pure and simple, for there are in his perspective—as in Christian

---

[7] Shankara and Ramanuja were not contemporaries; the first lived in the ninth century, and the second in the eleventh century of our era. Ramanuja is not the only protagonist of bhaktic Vishnuism, but he is the greatest and his doctrine is in any case perfectly characteristic of this perspective.

exoterism—modes of relative esoterism,[8] but his overall perspective is in any case analogous to the direct and exoteric messages of the three monotheisms deriving from Abraham. For Ramanuja, the personal Divinity—God the creator and savior—is identified with the Absolute without any reservation; according to this way of seeing things, there is no reason to envisage an *Ātmā* or an Essence that would transcend a *Māyā*, nor therefore a *Māyā* which would bring about or determine the hypostatic limitation of an Essence. According to this doctrine, Vishnu creates the world, or the series of worlds, by emanation, and he reabsorbs them upon the completion of their respective cycles; but it is not this emanationism that concerns us here, since it is not a point of reference with regard to the monotheistic religions; the analogy is uniquely—or above all—in the personal character of the Divinity, then in salvation obtained exclusively through love of God, *bhakti*, or more commonly, trust in Him, *prapatti*,[9] and finally in eternal beatitude—for the elect invested with celestial bodies—in the Paradise of Vishnu. Just as in the Paradise of the Semitic monotheists, the elect participate intimately, in various degrees, in the nature of the Divinity, according to the principle "union without confusion"; this is the *unio mystica*, but the creature remains the creature. This, moreover, is also true for Shankarian non-dualism to the extent that it considers the strictly human modality, which cannot "become God"; that alone can "become God" which is so already, to the point that this expression, which is basically contradictory, reveals itself as being an ellipsis covering incommensurable realities.

Apart from secondary elements not relevant here, the three Semitic religions share their general perspective with the monism of Ramanuja and not with the non-dualism of Shankara, although this non-dualism does appear sporadically within these religions, that is, in their sapien-

[8] It should be noted that *bhakti* always pertains to the esoteric principle inasmuch as it transcends horizontal piety bound to prescriptions and actions, and inasmuch as it transforms man by interiorizing him.

[9] It is this difference between *bhakti* and *prapatti*, the vertical love of the hero and the horizontal love of the just man, which constitutes in monist Vedantism the polarity esoterism-exoterism.

tial esoterism. However, an error that must be avoided is the idea that the great theological authorities, even though they be Church Fathers, are by virtue of their importance promoters of total esoterism; such authorities as Thomas Aquinas, Ashari, and Maimonides incarnate the general religious perspective, admittedly with incidental openings to *gnosis*, but one cannot ask them to provide the integral equivalent of advaitic or Shankarian *Vedānta* simply because of the role of first magnitude they play in their respective religions.[10] Indeed, it is this role or this magnitude that prevents the explicit and public doctrine of the great theologians from transcending the point of view of Vishnuite monism, although—we repeat—elements can be found in their teaching which in fact transcend it; but neither these doctors nor their partisans draw the conclusions these elements imply.

It is necessary here to insist on two things. Firstly, that the witnesses of the Revelation themselves, whether apostles or companions, were not necessarily *jnānins*, and that the very form of the Message, or its direct intention, rules out that the majority of these venerable witnesses should have had this quality; those who possessed it were necessarily a minority. Secondly, that a consummate sage is always a saint, but that a saint is not always a sage; as for the polemical notion of a "wisdom of the saints", directed against sapiential esoterism, it is nothing but a misunderstanding and a misuse of language. The well-known *petitio principii* on the part of militant theology is familiar: Plato, Plotinus, Proclus, and others were not Christians, therefore they could not be saints; consequently their doctrines pertain to the "wisdom according to the flesh";[11] whereas the loftiness of their

---

[10] When Gregory Palamas misinterprets, underestimates, and slanders sages such as Socrates, Plato, and Plotinus, his attitude has the same significance as the hostility of Ramanuja towards Shankara; and there is absolutely no need to adduce considerations of "sanctity" or "mystery" to justify such banal polemics revolving around the meanings of words. It must not be forgotten that the theological perspective is characterized extrinsically by its concern with defending conceptual and moral interests, whereas pure metaphysics sets forth the nature of things, while being aware of aspects and points of view.

[11] Unless one contends they were Christian, as was done in the case of the "Dissertations" of Epictetus, or unless one concedes to so-called "natural" intelligence an honorable role, as was done for Aristotle; in this case, "flesh" becomes "nature", which is better than nothing, but is still less than the truth. If there is a "wisdom according to the flesh", it is certainly, and to the highest degree, this specifically modern thought in which the irrational is seen as being the supra-rational, while slaying the rational. According to the "Pastoral Constitution on the Church in the Modern World"—one

doctrines should have served as the basis for deducing their possible sanctity, all the more so since Christianity could not in fact do without them.[12] As for the profane and properly rationalistic philosophy of the Greeks, personified in particular by Protagoras and of which Aristotle is not completely immune, it represents a deviation of the perspective that normally gives rise to *gnosis* or *jñāna*: when this perspective is cut off from pure intellection, and thus from its reason for being, it becomes inevitably hostile to religion and open to all kinds of hazards; the sages of Greece did not need the Church Fathers to know this, and the Church Fathers could not prevent the Christian world from falling into this trap. Moreover, the Church, via the civilizationism that it claims as its own so as not to lose any claim to glory, paradoxically assumes responsibility for the modern world—described as "Christian civilization"—which really is nothing other than the outgrowth of that human wisdom stigmatized by the Fathers.

Since we are speaking here of intellectual deviation, we shall seize the opportunity to mention two conspicuous obscurations of the esoteric perspective, namely idolatry and pantheism, both deriving from the idea of immanence taken at the expense of transcendence, and both comprising legitimate prototypes, which moreover coexist with the deviations and which one must take care not to confuse with the latter.[13] There are nevertheless types of idolatry which have a purely magical and empirical origin, just as there are types of pantheism which have no other origin than the conjectures of philosophers.

---

of the masterpieces of the "Council"—"the human race has passed from a somewhat static concept of reality to a more dynamic and evolutionist concept"; now, a concept is either static or it is nothing. To say that a concept, or that the mind in general, has become dynamic after having been static for centuries or millennia, means concretely that normal thought, that of intelligent and disciplined men of all times, has been replaced by a pseudo-thought of boors and crude literalists. This observation is argument enough; to say more is merely euphemism.

[12] It should be noted that Meister Eckhart called Plato "the great priest", and that Jili had a vision of him "filling the whole of space with light"; also, that the disciples of Rumi see in Plato (Sayyidna Aflatun) a kind of prophet. Muslim authors in general see in him an eminent master of music, like Orpheus charming wild beasts with his lute in virgin nature whither he had withdrawn after a disagreement with Aristotle, an image full of meaning. It may be added that Plato, like Socrates and Pythagoras, was the providential spokesman of Orphism.

[13] Rumi and Ibn Arabi understood this well, which is all the more remarkable in that Islam is rigorously monotheistic and iconoclastic.

Be that as it may, there is a pertinent teaching to be found in the exoteric equation of intelligence with pride: whoever wishes to use his intelligence without the risk of going astray must possess the virtue of humility; he must be aware of his limitations, must know that intelligence does not come from himself, must be sufficiently prudent to make no judgments in the absence of adequate information. But this awareness, or this humility, is indeed a part of intelligence inasmuch as it implies objectivity by definition; if humility—not sentimental humilitarianism, which leads to absurd applications—constitutes a qualification *sine qua non* for *gnosis* or *jnāna*, this is because sapience is founded on intelligence which, being objective to the extent that it is integral, necessarily comprises the impartial awareness of that which is, including our possible limitations. The danger of pride occurs in rationalism, that is to say, due to the bias of relying on an intelligence that merely knows how to reason and doing so in defiance of indispensable information, the absence of which is not even suspected.

This being said, let us return to the question of esoterism as a traditional phenomenon. It would be completely false to believe that *gnosis* within a given religion presents itself as a foreign and superimposed doctrine; on the contrary, that which in each religion provides the key for total or non-dualist esoterism is not some secret concept heterogeneous in character, but no less than that religion's directive idea; and this is necessarily so, since religion, which presents itself with an absolute exigency—"outside the Church there is no salvation"—thereby vouches for the totality of the message and consequently cannot exclude any essential possibility of the human spirit. Christian *gnosis* doubtless finds supports in Thomas Aquinas as well as in Gregory Palamas, but these supports are in fact neutralized by the general bhaktism of Christianity, unless they can be isolated from this context, precisely; in any case they are not the basis of wisdom. Christian *gnosis* rests *a priori*, and of necessity, on the mysteries of Incarnation and Redemption, hence on the Christic Phenomenon as such, just as Muslim *gnosis* for its part rests above all on the mysteries of Transcendence and Immanence, and thus on the Koranic or Muhammadan Truth; furthermore, the *gnosis* of the two religions is founded on the mystery of divine Love, according to the accentuation characterizing each of them. Love of the theophany that is at once human and divine in Christianity, and love of the Principle that is at once transcendent and immanent in Islam.

— ∴ —

Regarding esoterism as such—which is nothing other than *gnosis*—we must recall two things, although we have already spoken of them on prior occasions. First, it is necessary to distinguish between absolute esoterism and relative esoterism; secondly, it is necessary to know that esoterism on the one hand prolongs exoterism—by deepening it harmoniously—because the form expresses the essence and because in this respect the two stand together, while on the other hand esoterism opposes exoterism—by transcending it abruptly—because the essence by virtue of its unlimitedness is of necessity not reducible to form; or, in other words, because form, inasmuch as it constitutes a limit, is opposed to whatever is totality and liberty. These two aspects are readily discernible in Sufism,[14] although, in truth, they are often so intertwined that it is not possible to say whether it is a case of pious unawareness, on the part of Sufi authors, or simply of their prudence or spiritual discretion; such a mixture, moreover, is entirely natural, as long as it does not give rise to dialectical absurdities.[15] The example of the Sufis in any case shows that it is possible to be a Muslim without being an Asharite; for the same reasons and with equal right, it is possible to be a Christian without being either a Scholastic or a Palamite, or let us say rather that it is possible to be a Thomist without accepting the sense-based Aristotelian outlook of Aquinas, just as it is possible to be a Palamite without sharing the errors of Palamas regarding the Greek philosophers and their doctrines. In other words, one can be a Christian and at the same time a Platonist since there is no competition between mystical voluntarism and metaphysical intellectuality, leaving aside the Semitic concept of the *creatio ex nihilo*.

[14] The first aspect can be seen, as is well known, in a Ghazali, who secured recognition for Sufism within the official religion, whereas the second—a Koranic trace of which appears in the story of Moses and the mysterious stranger (= Al-Khidr)—is found for example in a Niffari, who specifically stated that the exoteric revelation does not support the esoteric revelation, namely *gnosis*, and that the common religion sees things according to plurality and not according to unity as does the inward revelation. Likewise, Ibn Arabi: "God the Omnipotent is not limited by any belief for He has said (in the Koran): 'Wheresoever ye turn, there is the face of God'."

[15] Maruf al-Karkhi said "if God is favorable to his servant, He opens for him the doors of (spiritual) actions and shuts for him the doors of theological disputes", which is an indication among others of the independence of the Sufis with regard to theology, and which implies moreover much more than the literal meaning conveys to us.

This concept, or this symbolism, agrees moreover with the emanationism of the Greeks when emanationism is considered according to its own intention and not according to the creationist reasoning of the Semites, which is refractory to the mystery of immanence—namely to the relationship of continuity between Cause and effect—and is therefore prone to project divine activity into human time; creation becomes then a historical event and a "gratuitous" fact, that is to say, a fact cut off from the ontological necessities rooted in divine Nature. In integral metaphysics, this difficulty is resolved thus: on the one hand, the obvious relationship of discontinuity between God and the world does not exclude the no less obvious—but infinitely subtler—relationship of continuity; on the other hand, divine Freedom cannot exclude the perfection of Necessity, any more than Necessity can exclude Freedom, depending upon the relationships required by the nature of God.[16]

Finally, we must insist on the following point: the fact that transcendent truths should be inaccessible to the logic of a given individual or human group, cannot mean that they are intrinsically and *de jure* contrary to all logic; for the efficacy of logic always depends, on the one hand, on the intellectual scope of the thinker and, on the other, on the adequacy of the information or the knowledge of the indispensable facts. It is not that metaphysics is held to be true—by those who understand it—because it is expressed in a logical manner, but that it can be expressed in a logical manner because it is true, without—quite obviously—its truth ever being compromised by the possible flaws of human reason.

In their zeal to defend the rights of divine supra-rationality against the logic of the rationalists—*de facto* fragmentary—some go so far as to claim for the divine, or even the simply spiritual order, a right to irrationality, and thus to illogicality, as if there could be a right to

---

[16] Certainly we could have no objection to the "gratuitousness" of creation if it meant that God creates without being constrained to do so by a force other than Himself; but this "gratuitousness" cannot legitimately mean that God does not obey his own nature by creating the world, namely that, being God, He would be able not to create. The Hindu theory of cosmic cycles—*yuga, mahāyuga, kalpa, para*—provides an explicit account of the creative rhythm emerging from the divine nature itself, that is, of this radiating power—*Māyā*—required by the infinity of the Principle. And the following Augustinian idea is well-known: the good, by definition, tends to impart itself; now, God is the Sovereign Good.

intrinsic absurdity. To assert that Christ walked on the water is in no wise contrary to logic or reason—even if we do not know the basis of the miracle[17]—for the law of gravity is a conditional thing, and thus relative, whether we know this or not; and even without knowing it, we can at least guess what this is or consider it as being possible, given the level of the phenomenon. But to assert that Christ walked on water without walking on water, or that he did so by rising towards the sky, would assuredly be contrary to reason, since a phenomenon or a possibility cannot be in one and the same respect another phenomenon or possibility, or the absence of what they are; God may require acquiescence for a miracle or mystery, but he cannot require acquiescence for intrinsic absurdity, that is, for what is both logically and ontologically absurd.[18]

The closest and therefore the most striking example of what we term "relative esoterism" is provided by Christianity. Whereas in Judaism and Islam, the direct message is exoteric—esoterism constituting the indirect message because, being universal, it is supra-formal—Christianity's direct message is itself relatively esoteric. It is esoteric, not as regards a personalistic theism and an individualistic voluntarism—for this is its own general point of view—but with respect to the moralistic and ritualistic formalism of Judaism; this amounts to saying that it is esoteric within the framework of Jewish legalism in the same way that bhaktic Vishnuism is esoteric within the framework of formalistic and horizontal Hinduism. Christ's initial idea—if such a formulation is permissible—is in effect that the justification of a pious action resides in the piety of the intention, and that in the absence of piety, the action ceases to be pious; that it is better to realize inward piety

---

[17] By this we mean that miracles also have their mechanism, but in their case the causal link is "vertical" and not "horizontal": the ray of causal unfolding crosses through several existential planes instead of being operative on one plane alone.

[18] According to Saint Thomas Aquinas, the principles of logic reside in God, and it is according to them that we must think; which means that a contradiction between our intelligence and the truth founded in God is impossible. Certainly, extrinsic absurdities exist, but in their case there is contradiction only through our ignorance or dullness of mind. "Right reason is the temple of God", said Saint John of the Cross.

than to perform the outward manifestations or supports of this piety without love of God or of one's neighbor, or even with hypocrisy, because this piety's entire reason for being is the love of God.

The esoterism of *bhakti* transcends outward forms, namely pre-scriptions, just as the esoterism of *gnosis*, *jnāna*, transcends inward forms, namely anthropomorphist dogmas and the individualistic and sentimental attitudes corresponding to them; nevertheless, every esoterism needs doctrinal, ritual, and moral supports, not forgetting the aesthetic supports related to contemplativity. To speak of man is to speak of form; man is the bridge between form and essence, or between "flesh" and "spirit".

When one speaks of Christian esoterism, this can only mean three things: firstly, it can mean Christic *gnosis*, founded on the person, the teaching, and the gifts of Christ, and possibly benefiting from Platonic concepts, which in metaphysics is hardly illegitimate;[19] this *gnosis* was manifested in particular, although in a very uneven way, in writings such as those of Clement of Alexandria, Origen, Denis the Areopagite (or the Theologian or the Mystic, if one prefers), Scotus Erigena, Meister Eckhart, Nicholas of Cusa, Jakob Boehme, and Angelus Silesius.[20] Secondly, it can mean something completely different, namely the Greco-Latin—or Near Eastern—esoterism incorporated into Christianity: here we are thinking above all of Hermeticism and the craft initiations. In this case the esoterism is more or less limited or even fragmentary, residing more in the sapiential character of the method—now lost—than in the doctrine and in the goal; the doctrine was mainly cosmological, and conse-quently the goal did not transcend the "lesser mysteries" or hori-zontal perfection, or the "primordial" perfection if one is referring to the ideal conditions of the "Golden Age". Be that as it may, this Christianized cosmological or alchemical esoterism, and "humanist"

---

[19] Generally speaking, inter-traditional influences are always possible under certain conditions, but without any syncretism. Unquestionably Buddhism and Islam had an influence on Hinduism, not by adding new elements to it, of course, but by favoring or determining the development of pre-existing elements.

[20] In other words, one finds elements of esoterism in orthodox gnosticism—which finds an extension in the theosophy of Boehme and his successors—then in the Dio-nysian mysticism of the Rhinelanders, and of course in Hesychasm; without forgetting that partial element of methodic esoterism represented by the quietism of Molinos, traces of which can be found in Saint Francis of Sales.

in a still legitimate sense—since it was a question of restoring to the human microcosm the perfection of a macrocosm still in conformity with God—was essentially vocational, given that no science or art is mandatory for everyone; man chooses a science or an art for reasons of affinity and qualification, and not *a priori* to save his soul. Salvation being guaranteed by religion, man may *a posteriori*, and on this very basis, take advantage of his gifts and professional occupation, and it is even normal or necessary that he should do so when an occupation linked with an alchemical or craft esoterism becomes, for whatever motive, a matter of vocation.

Finally, and above all, and aside from any historical or literary considerations, "Christian esoterism" can and must be understood to mean the truth pure and simple—metaphysical and spiritual—insofar as it is expressed or manifests itself in the dogma, ritual, and other forms of Christianity. Conversely, this esoterism is the sum total of Christian symbols inasmuch as they express or manifest pure metaphysics and the one, universal spirituality. And this is independent of the question of knowing to what extent an Origen or a Clement of Alexandria may have been aware of what is involved—a superfluous question finally, since it is obvious that, for more or less extrinsic reasons, they could not be aware of all aspects of the problem, all the more as they were broadly bound to the *bhakti* that determines the specific perspective of Christianity. Be that as it may, it is important not to confuse esoterism as principle with esoterism as fact; or a virtual doctrine, holding all the rights of truth, with an effective doctrine that may not live up to the promise implied in its very point of view.

With respect to Jewish legalism, Christianity is esoteric owing to the fact that it is a message of inwardness: inward virtue takes precedence for Christianity over outward observance to the point of abolishing the latter. But since its point of view is voluntaristic, it can be transcended by a new inwardness, that of pure Intellection, which restores particular forms to their universal essences and replaces the point of view of penitence with that of purifying and liberating knowledge. *Gnosis* is of Christic nature in the sense that, on the one hand, it pertains to the *Logos*—the Intellect both transcendent and immanent—and because, on the other hand, it is a message of inwardness, and thus of interiorization.

——— .:. ———

We must reply here to the objection that the attitude of the esoterist entails a kind of duplicity towards religion, as something he pretends to practice while assigning a different meaning to things; such a suspicion takes account neither of the actual perspective of *gnosis* nor of its assimilation by the soul, in virtue of which the intelligence and the sensibility spontaneously combine different points of view without betraying either their particular reality or their own specific demands;[21] the concrete understanding of cosmic and spiritual levels excludes any secret lie. To speak to God while knowing that his necessarily anthropomorphic Personality is an effect of *Māyā*, is no less sincere than to speak to a man while knowing that he too, and with even greater reason, is only an effect of *Māyā*, as indeed we all are; likewise, it is not a lack of sincerity to ask a man a favor while knowing that the author of the gift is necessarily God. The divine Personality, as we have said, is anthropomorphic; apart from the fact that in reality it is man who resembles God and not inversely, God necessarily makes Himself man in his contacts with human nature.

Religious loyalty is nothing other than the sincerity of our human relations with God on the basis of the means which He has placed at our disposal; these means, being of the formal order, *ipso facto* exclude other forms, without for all that lacking anything whatsoever from the point of view of our relationship with Heaven; in this intrinsic sense, form is truly unique and irreplaceable, precisely because our relationship with God is so. Nevertheless, this uniqueness of the intrinsic support and the sincerity of our worship within the framework of this support do not authorize what might be termed "religious nationalism"; if we condemn this attitude—unavoidable for average man,

---

[21] As one knows, this sort of metaphysical flexibility is like a second nature for the Hindu contemplative and causes no difficulty; this means that the Hindu is particularly sensitive to what we have called on more than one occasion the "metaphysical transparency of phenomena". Doubtless, *bilinguis maledictus*: language with a double meaning is accursed; but, precisely, this is because it is situated on one and the same plane and not, as is esoterism, on two different planes; if this duo-dimensionality were illegitimate, it would be impossible to interpret the Song of Songs in a sense other than the literal, and a large part of patristic and mystical exegesis would have to be disavowed. Christ used both parables and metaphors.

but this is not the question—it is because it entails opinions contrary to the truth, and all the more contradictory when the believer lays claim to an esoteric wisdom and has access to facts enabling him to notice the limits of the religious formalism with which he sentimentally and incorrectly identifies himself.[22]

In order to gain a clear understanding of the normal relationship between common religion and wisdom, or between *bhakti and jnāna*, it is necessary to know that there is, in principle, a double subjectivity in man, that of the "soul" and that of the "spirit". Now, one of two things is possible: either the spirit is reduced to the acceptance of revealed dogmas, in which case the individual soul is the sole subject of the way towards God, or else the spirit is aware of its nature and tends towards the end for which it is conformed, in which case it is the spirit, and not the "I", that is the subject of the way, but without for all that abolishing the needs and rights of ordinary subjectivity, namely the subjectivity of the sensible and individual soul. The equilibrium between the two subjectivities, one affective and the other intellective—but which inevitably coincide at a certain point[23]—gives rises to the serenity whose perfume is transmitted to us by the Vedantic writings; an erroneous mixture of these subjectivities—in partial or poorly developed esoterisms—on the contrary produces the type of contradiction that could be termed, paradoxically, "metaphysical individualism": namely, a tormented mysticism replete with irritating expressions, yet nevertheless heroic and open to Mercy in the end; Sufism gives us examples of this.

The ego as such cannot logically lay claim to experience of what lies beyond egoity; man is man and the Self is the Self. One must beware of transferring the voluntaristic and sentimental individualism

---

[22] In the absence of these facts or this information, there is no reason to level the reproach of "religious nationalism"; on the one hand, the "Saracens" of the Middle Ages had no more than a symbolic reality in the eyes of Christians—no one knew what Islam was—and on the other, the Christians of that time did not dispose of any objective criterion or point of comparison that might allow them to notice the particularity and the limitations of their own universe. The attitude of medieval people is comparable to a natural patriotism that is innocent in itself, and not to a nationalism that is necessarily hypocritical due to the ingenuity of its prejudice and its lies.

[23] For the soul, though made of love, is intelligent, hence capable of objectivity and of transcending itself, while the spirit, though made of intelligence, is sensitive to beauty, goodness, and happiness, and recognizes itself in them.

of religious zeal onto the plane of transpersonal awareness;[24] one cannot desire *gnosis* with a will that is contrary to the nature of *gnosis*. It is not we who know God, it is God who knows Himself in us.

The question that arises here is to know what constitutes the basic nature of the soul: whether it is made of self-interested zeal or of disinterested contemplation; in other words, whether the soul finds its happiness and its fulfillment in a passion directed towards God, in a fervent desire for heavenly reward—which is certainly honorable, although it does not exhaust the whole of man's spiritual possibility— or whether the soul finds its happiness and fulfillment in a profound comprehension of the nature of things, and thus in a return to the Substance of which it is an accident. On the one hand, the two things are mutually exclusive, but on the other hand they are complementary; everything here is a question of relationships and proportions.

Metaphysical or esoteric doctrine is addressed to another subjectivity than is the general religious message: religion speaks to the will and to passional man, and esoterism speaks to the intelligence and to contemplative man; the intellectual aspect of exoterism is theology, whereas the emotional aspect of esoterism is the sense of beauty inasmuch as it possesses an interiorizing virtue; beauty of nature and of art and also, and even above all, beauty of soul, the distant projection of the Beauty of God.

This complex question of subjectivity merits, or indeed requires, that we should devote a few more remarks to it, at the risk of repeating ourselves on some point or other, but in the hope of providing explanations that are at least sufficient, if not exhaustive.

There is in man a subjectivity or a consciousness made for looking outwards and for perceiving the world, whether this world be earthly or heavenly; and there is also in man a consciousness that is made for

---

[24] When a certain Muslim mystic states that he would rather be in hell than in heaven, were this the will of God, he unjustifiably and paradoxically clothes intellectual detachment, or contemplative serenity, with the language of passional individualism; that is, he absurdly mixes two subjectivities, that of the transpersonal Intellect and that of the individual soul, for the latter, being ontologically directed towards happiness, cannot and could never wish to go to hell, whereas for the Intellect the question does not arise; wherever the Intellect is, there too is heaven.

looking inwards, in the direction of the Absolute or the Self, whether this vision be relatively separative or unitive. In other words there is in man a consciousness that is descending and obeys the creative intention of God, and another that is ascending and obeys the divine intention that saves or liberates; the two are incommensurable, even though there is a region between them where they overlap, giving rise to a single subjectivity as well as to an existential equilibrium between the two diverging modes of consciousness; this is why the spiritually realized man can see God in things, and also the principial prototypes of things in God. The psychic and mental consciousness perceives appearances; intellective or cardiac consciousness perceives the Essence; but the intermediary consciousness lives from both dimensions at once. In seeing phenomena, it sees God within them, and it sees them within God; it perceives that each thing is the manifestation of a divine possibility, whether in analogical or in privative mode, and at the same time, but in another respect, it sees things as though they were steeped in one and the same divine atmosphere; in the first case, objects allow divine Reality or its modes to shine through, whereas in the second case, the subjectivity participates in divine Consciousness both in an extinctive and in a unitive mode.

Be that as it may, human subjectivity is such an amazing miracle that it is enough to prove both God and the immortality of the soul: God, because this extraordinarily profound and all-encompassing subjectivity can be explained only by an Absolute that prefigures it substantially and projects it into the realm of accidentality; and immortality, because the incomparable quality of this subjectivity has no sufficient reason, or no motive proportionate to its excellence, within the narrow and ephemeral framework of an earthly life. If it were merely to live like ants, men would have no need whatsoever for their intellectual and moral possibilities, which amounts to saying that they would have no need to be men; the very existence of man would then be a luxury as inexplicable as it would be pointless. Not to understand this is the most monstrous as well as the most puzzling of blindnesses.

That man is saved who understands the purpose of human subjectivity: to be a mirror of the Absolute in relativity, while being at the same time a prolongation of divine Subjectivity. To manifest the Absolute in contingency, the Infinite in the finite, Perfection in imperfection.

Exoteric salvation is the fixation of the individual human subject, or soul, in the incorruptible aura of the divine Object, if one may so express it; esoteric salvation, for its part, is the reintegration of the intellective human subject into the divine Subjectivity; this second mode of salvation—the deliverance (*moksha*) of the Vedantists—implies the first mode, for man as such can never become God. Certainly, the immutable substance of man, which coincides with the supreme Self, can be liberated from the accident that is the ego; but it does not destroy it, any more than the reality of God prevents the existence of the world.

The human individual has one great concern that exceeds all others: to save his soul; to do this, he must adhere to a religion, and to be able to adhere to it, he must believe in it; but since one can, with the best will in the world, only believe what is credible, the man who is well enough acquainted with two or more religions, and who moreover is not lacking in imagination, may feel that he is prevented from adhering to one of them by the fact that it presents itself dogmatically as the sole legitimate religion and the sole one offering salvation; hence that this religion presents itself with an absolute exigency, and possibly without offering in its characteristic formulation some of the convincing and peace-bestowing elements that he may have found in other religions, and without having been able to persuade him that these elements and that these religions are not without value themselves. That the Psalms and the Gospel are sublime can be accepted without the least hesitation; but to believe that they contain in their very literalness or in their psychological climate everything offered by the *Upanishads* or the *Bhagavad Gītā*, is an altogether different matter. In fact, only sapiential esoterism, total and universal—not partial and formalistic—can satisfy every legitimate need for logical explanations, its domain being that of profound intentions and not of expressions fraught with prejudice; it alone can answer all the questions raised by religious divergences and limitations, which amounts to saying that in the objective and subjective conditions under consideration here, sapiential esoterism constitutes the only key enabling us to approach a religion, every question of esoteric realization notwithstanding. By the same token, integral esoterism can specify what in a given religion is truly fundamental, both from the metaphysical and mystical point of view—or operative or alchemical if one prefers—and consequently that which allows it to rejoin the *religio perennis*.

Given that religions must take account of psychological and social contingencies and confine themselves, in certain respects, not to what they include but to what they exclude, even while necessarily demanding absolute allegiance, they do not have the right to close themselves, as it were, to every argument that goes beyond their dogmatist perspective; and in fact Providence, which operates within the religions due to their divine origin, takes account of the situation resulting from the unusual circumstances of our time,[25] just as from time immemorial it has taken account, in one form or another, of certain exceptional situations.

Religions testify, from various points of view, to the divine Principle and eternal life; but they cannot give an account, as does esoterism, of the religious phenomenon as such, nor of the nature of the angles of vision. It would in fact be absurd to ask them to do so, for two reasons: firstly, for the obvious reason that by definition every religion has to present itself as the only one possible, since its point of view depends on the Truth and therefore must exclude any danger of relativism; and secondly, because in their intrinsic and essential content, which precisely transcends the relativity of formulation or symbolism, religions fully keep the promise implied by the total character of their requirements—fully, that is to say, by taking account of what is demanded by the most profound possibility of man.

What the Koranic denial of the Cross means is the rejection of the historical redemption as a condition *sine qua non* of salvation, given that for Christians the sole meaning of the Cross is this unique, exclusive, and historical redemption. The idea, within the framework of Christianity, that the redemption is *a priori* the timeless work of the principial *Logos*—non-human and non-historical; that the redemption can and must be manifested in different ways, at diverse times

---

[25] The fact that in our age everything is read and everything is known does not mean that religious people accept foreign spiritual traditions without question, but that a modified and often tolerant attitude is adopted towards them—except among those who confuse traditional orthodoxy with the right to calumny, thus harming the very cause they strive to defend. To reject Islam is one thing, but to allege that it excludes women from Paradise, or that Muslims have no virtue, is quite another.

and places; and that the historical Christ manifests this *Logos* in a given providential world, without its being either necessary or possible to set the limits of this world in an exact manner, is an idea that is esoteric with respect to Christian dogmatics, and to expect it from theology would be absurd.

The esoteric science of the relativity of religious forms is, quite obviously, of a more contingent order than the fundamental doctrine of each of these forms, not to mention their essence which, as we have just said, coincides with the very principle of esoterism.

We could say, simplifying a little, that exoterism puts the form—the credo—above the essence—universal Truth—and accepts the latter only on the basis of the former; the form, given its divine origin, is here the criterion of the essence. Esoterism, on the contrary, puts the essence above the form and therefore only accepts the form on the basis of the essence; for esoterism, and in accordance with the real hierarchy of values, the essence is the criterion of the form; the one and universal Truth controls the various religious forms of the Truth. If the relationship is inverse in exoterism, this is obviously not the result of a subversion, but because form, as a crystallization of the essence, is the guarantor of Truth; in other words, the Truth is deemed inaccessible apart from form—or more precisely: apart from a form that makes an absolute demand—and rightly so, as far as average men are concerned, otherwise the phenomenon of dogmatic Revelation would make no sense.

What characterizes esoterism to the very extent it is absolute, is that upon contact with a dogmatic system it universalizes the symbol or the religious concept on the one hand and interiorizes it on the other; the particular or the limited is recognized as the manifestation of the principial and the transcendent, and the transcendent in its turn reveals itself as immanent. Christianity universalizes the notion of "Israel" while interiorizing the divine Law; it replaces circumcision of the flesh with that of the heart, the "Chosen People" with a Church that includes men hailing from all origins, and outward prescriptions with virtues, all of this in view, not of obedience to the Law, but of the love of God and, in the last analysis, of mystical union. These principles or these transpositions could hardly have been unknown to the Essenes, and possibly to other Jewish initiates, but the originality of Christianity is that it made a religion of them and sacrificed Mosaic formalism to them.

According to a principle we have already referred to, absolute esoterism in Christianity can pertain only to the Christic message itself; it will be an indirect, not a direct, message, but its origin will be exclusively Christic, despite certain doctrinal convergences whose possibility and opportuneness have already been pointed out. The mainspring of Christianity is that "God became man that man might become God": this means, in Vedantic language—since our point of reference is Shankara—that "*Ātmā* became *Māyā* that *Māyā* might become *Ātmā*".[26] Union with Christ implies identity with him;[27] and to this we would add that union with the Virgin implies identification with the aspect of sweetness and infinitude of the *Logos*, for the *shakti* of the Absolute is the Infinite; all the qualities and prerogatives of Mary derive finally from the perfumes of divine Infinitude. Mary is a dimension of Jesus, a dimension that he expressed when he said: "My yoke is easy and my burden is light"; now, it is advantageous to address oneself to this dimension in particular in order to attain totality. In herself, the Virgin also personifies formless Wisdom, for she is the Woman "clothed with the sun" and mother of the Revelation: she is Wisdom in its aspect of radiance, and thus of Beauty and Mercy.[28]

Whereas in Shankarian and non-dualistic *Vedānta* it is the fundamental Intellect—the immanent divine Consciousness—that performs the reintegration into the Self, in Christianity this salvific Intellect is

---

[26] In Buddhist language: *Nirvāna* became *Samsāra* that *Samsāra* might become *Nirvāna*. *Nirvāna* become *Samsāra* is the Buddha; for Zen Buddhists, union with the Buddha takes place in the immanent Void; for Amida Buddhists, it takes place in the merciful Name of the Buddha.

[27] The rite of communion is the most obvious mark of this. To this rite undergone passively—albeit in a holy manner—an active complement must be added that is analogous in nature, namely the quasi-sacramental or eucharistic invocation of the Name of Jesus, which goes back to the very origins of Christianity.

[28] As Jesus had no human father, his body and his blood came to him from Mary, and this remains true also for the eucharistic species and reveals a new aspect of the quality of "Co-Redemptress".

objectivized and personified in Christ, and secondarily in the Virgin;[29] in Hinduism this role belongs either to the great *avatāra* or his *shakti*, or with the *guru*, depending on different points of view, which sometimes can be combined. The function of the historical Christ is to awaken and actualize the inward Christ; now, in the manner of the *Logos* that Jesus manifests humanly and historically, the inward Christ or the Heart-Intellect is universal, hence transpersonal.[30] It is "true man and true God", and therefore, speaking analogically, *Māyā* and *Ātmā*, *Samsāra* and *Nirvāna*: a play of veiling and unveiling and immutable Reality; cosmic drama and divine Peace.

It is a fundamental error to confuse the *jnānin* with the rationalist, even though rationalism is in fact a deviation of the intellective perspective; for the *jnānin*, or let us say one who is intellective by nature, neither desires nor claims *a priori* to know the root of things; he notices that he sees what he sees, that is, he knows what his "naturally supernatural" discernment reveals to him, whether he wishes it or not; he thus finds himself in the situation of a man who alone would see our solar system from a point in space and who thereby could know the causes for the seasons, the days and the nights, and the seeming motion of the stars, starting with the sun. The general, dogmatic, and formalistic religion shares—analogically speaking—the viewpoint of a given human subjectivity; esoterism, on the contrary, while accepting this system of appearances as a symbolism and at the level of a concomitant *bhakti*, is aware of the relativity of what we might paradoxically call "metaphysical phenomena". The rationalist, who lays claim to an

---

[29] According to the Blessed Father Kolbe, "Immaculate Conception is one of the Names of the Holy Spirit", and "it can be said that in espousing Mary, the Spirit was as if incarnated in her"; she is "united with the Holy Spirit to the point of being able to present herself in his Name"; and lastly "the Immaculate One personifies the Mercy of God".

[30] Saint Justin Martyr remarks, in his *First Apology*, that Christ is the "first born of God" and "the *Logos* in whom every human race participates", and he concludes: "Those who lived in accordance with the *Logos* (= the Intellect), which is in all men, are Christians—even though they be called godless—such as Socrates and Heraclitus and others amongst the Greeks. . . . Those who lived by the *Logos*, and those who now live thus, are Christians, without fear and without vexation."

intellection whose principle he no doubt conceives but which in fact he lacks, and who confuses reason with the Intellect, realizes a deviation comparable to the false inspirationism of heretical sects; but since "the corruption of the best is the worst", rationalism is much more harmful than false mysticism, which at least is not tempted to deny God and the life to come. It is appropriate to recall here something we have said on other occasions, namely that there are two sources of certitude, one outward and one inward, namely Revelation and Intellection: sentimentalism readily usurps the first, and rationalism the second; in fact Intellection must be combined with Revelation, just as Revelation must be illuminated by Intellection.[31]

Be that as it may, it is wrong to say, as do the fideists who adopt a sense-bound perspective out of expediency, that reason receives its contents from two sources only, namely from outside and from on high; the asymmetry of this schema is enough to indicate its inadequacy. In reality, reason can receive its contents from outside and from inside, from below and from above: from outside it obtains them either through the senses or through Revelation; from inside, it obtains them either through the soul or through Intellection. This means that the higher and the lower, or the supernatural and the natural, intervene both inwardly and outwardly; moreover, these various factors can be combined by virtue of the metaphysical transparency of things and in conformity with the Platonic principle of "remembrance".

Jnāna sets out from the idea that man is free from his destiny; for those who wish to be saved, there are the mysteries and the initiations; meanwhile, the mass of profane people go their own way. *Bhakti* become religion, on the contrary, distinguishes itself by the fact that it intends to force men to be saved, which has the advantage of transforming certain natures and the disadvantage of creating narrowness of mind and fanaticism, in the proper and not aberrant sense of these terms.

---

[31] The *daimonion* of Socrates is related to Intellection and with all the more reason to the immanent *Logos*, and so is the Delphic maxim: "Know thyself".

Two paradoxes need to be explained here, that of the craft initiations and that of the emperor. The craft initiations pertain to *jnāna*, but have been reduced to a cosmology and an alchemy, as was mentioned earlier: it is a question of bringing man back to the primordial norm, not by means of a sentimental heroism but simply on the basis of the nature of things and with the help of a symbolism derived from a craft;[32] now, it seems likely that, in the case of masonry, this perspective has surrendered the field to a humanistic universalism that is merely a caricature of the intellective point of view—the distant cause of this being the Renaissance, and the proximate cause the "Enlightenment". As for the case of the emperor, what is paradoxical is that the function of this monarch, on the one hand, concerns the world and not religion, and on the other hand, constitutes a continuation of the role of the *pontifex maximus* of the Roman religion, which was jnanic in type through its Aryan origin and in spite of the degeneration of its general and collective form; it is this pontifical and so to speak "gnostic" quality, or this direct investiture by Heaven—of which Dante and other Ghibellines seem to have been fully aware—that explains by what right, and without encountering any opposition, Constantine could convoke the Council of Nicaea; this same quality, however diminished it may have been in fact, explains the tolerance and realism of the emperors towards non-Christian minorities whom they sometimes were obliged to protect against the priests—one of the most striking examples of this being the understanding between Christians and Muslims in Sicily under the emperor Frederick II.

The difference between the exoteric and esoteric points of view appears clearly when their respective moral attitudes are compared: on the side of exoterism, the virtues readily lead to prejudices which, through excess of zeal, go against reality and therefore against intelligence; on the side of principial esoterism—namely one that is wholly faithful to its nature—"there is no right superior to that of truth", as

---

[32] It is doubtless right to say, *grosso modo*, that craft initiation is a "rational" and "operative" way, but at a modest level and in a possibly fragmentary manner, whereas religious exoterism amounts to an "emotional" and "penitential" way, but at a level which, humanly speaking, is exalted.

a Hindu maxim states, and every good must result from the nature of things and not from our sentiments inasmuch as they lose sight of this. From the esoteric or sapiential point of view, humility, for example, is not the desire to be lowly nor the autosuggestion of a lowliness that in reality one does not have, but the awareness of a lowliness that is first ontological and then personal—for every individual has limitations if not defects—and this objective and disinterested awareness dissolves ambition and vanity at their roots. This means that esoterism or wisdom operates not by means of a sentimental tendency responsible for inextricable complications but by means of discernment, and so independently of all distorting and moreover unavowed individualism; the contradiction of exoterism—although inevitable at its level—is the individualistic aspiration to transcend individual self-inflation; this is to seek to realize objectivity by means of subjectivity. Therefore, the man who is sentimentally humble, and thus humble out of zeal, finds himself obliged to flee flattering situations that for him are temptations to pride, whereas the man who is profoundly aware of the nature of things has nothing to flee, for errors cannot seduce him.

Be that as it may, this *distinguo* between two concrete perspectives—for this is not about philosophy—would doubtless remain too schematic were we not to add that man always remains human; in other words the most objective of attitudes is legitimately accompanied by a subjective element to the extent that this element does not compromise objectivity; and that, conversely, the most subjective attitude necessarily derives sustenance from an objective element, since humility in itself depends on a truth. One must also take into account combinations between the two perspectives in question, for it can happen that a subjectivism is aerated by an element of objectivity, and that, on the contrary, an objectivism is weighed down by an element of subjectivity; the Chinese *yin-yang*, apart from its other meanings, is a symbol of man.

What we have just said regarding humility applies likewise to charity and the other virtues, which moreover are all included in a certain fashion in humility. The fact that the excess of a good is an evil concerns, not the virtues in themselves, but our effort towards them, for this effort can be ill inspired; there could never be an excess of intrinsic virtue, just as there could never be an excess of objectivity, and thus of truth.

—— .·. ——

We would now like to make a comment or two about one of the modes of the esoteric dimension known as quietism. An association of ideas has been made between quietism and spiritualized sexuality, namely there is an assumption that these two positions can both be reduced to temptations of "ease"—as if the easy were synonymous with the false and the difficult with the true, and as if true quietism and spiritualized sexuality did not comprise aspects which, when not penitential, are at least exacting and full of gravity. In reality, quietism is founded on the ideas of existential substance and divine immanence and on the experience of the Presence of God: it consists of "reposing in one's own being" or, differently expressed, of resting in the divine Peace; this attitude essentially requires, first of all, a sufficient under-standing of sacred mystery, and then an attitude that is both active and operative, namely perpetual prayer—or the "prayer of the heart"—which entails a profound ascesis if it is to avoid turning into an altogether profane and ephemeral improvisation, more harmful than useful. In any case, the fact that there has been a sentimental quietism that has overlooked the rigorous and active aspects of holy quietude, does not authorize the anathematizing of quietism as such, any more than a sectarian and intrinsically heretical Gnosticism authorizes the condemnation of true *gnosis*; or any more than debauchery authorizes the calumniation of tantrism.

Besides the reproach of "ease", there is also that of "immorality"; a spirituality that recognizes the value of the sexual element seems compromised at the outset by its seeming quest for "pleasure", as if pleasure could deprive a symbol of its value, and as if the experience of the senses was not more than compensated by the concomitant contemplative and interiorizing experience; and finally, as if the dis-agreeable were a criterion of spiritual value. Quietism is also accused of being immoral owing to the fact that it allows for a state in which man is above sin, an idea referring to a type of sanctity—obviously misunderstood—in which the acts of man are golden because his substance is golden, and because everything that he touches turns to gold; this quite obviously excludes intrinsically bad actions, whether in regard to God or in regard to one's neighbor. In point of fact, quietism has often been ascetical, although by its nature it accepts without reticence the spiritual integration of sexuality, all the more as it is so to speak existentially connected with beauty, and so with love, or more precisely with the contemplative and peace-bestowing aspect of love. But this love is also a death (*amor* = *mors*) for otherwise it would not be spiritual; "I am black, but beautiful".[33]

—— ·⋮· ——

The man of *gnosis* is always aware of the ontological roots of things, or at least this is his predisposition and intention: for him the realm of the accidental is not just this or that particular thing, but above all the diversified and inexhaustible manifestation of Substance; now, to the extent that it is concrete and lived, such an intuition both requires and favors not only discernment and contemplativity, but also nobility of character, for knowledge of the All engages the whole man. Moreover, this nobility is in large part comprised within contemplativity itself, given that man is disposed to contemplate only what he already is himself in a certain fashion and to a certain degree.

---

[33] "Who loves not women, wine, and song, remains a fool his whole life long" (*Wer nicht liebt Wein, Weib und Gesang, der bleibt ein Narr sein Leben lang*): this old German saying may well have had an esoteric origin that would relate it to analogous expressions found in Omar Khayyam and others. "Wine" is in fact "love", according to the most varied traditions: on the one hand it is esoteric doctrine, inasmuch as it is liberating and essentializing even though ambiguous and dangerous, and on the other hand it is contemplative drunkenness, either transient (*ḥāl*) or permanent (*maqām*); "woman" is beauty, or the attractive and liberating vision of God in forms that manifest Him or that manifest His radiant Goodness; the "eternal feminine" also represents this Goodness in itself, inasmuch as it forgives, welcomes, and unifies, by freeing us from formal and other types of hardenings; and finally "song" is the quintessential prayer of the heart, the "praise" that makes the heart "melt" and reintegrates it into the Essence. It is very unlikely—be it said in passing—not that Luther uttered these words, as is believed, but that he would be their author, for they also exist in an Italian form whose origin is likewise apparently unknown (*Chi non ama il vino, la donna e il canto, un pazzo egli sarà e mai un santo*); in this form, the esoteric intention is in fact reinforced by the allusion to "sanctity": he will never be a saint—according to esoterism—who has not known these three things (*vino, donna*, and *canto*). Likewise, Omar ibn al-Farid in his *Khamriyah*: "He has not lived here below, who has lived without drunkenness, and he has no intelligence who has not died from his drunkenness"; the man "without intelligence" being precisely the "fool" (*Narr* or *pazzo*), that is to say, the profane or worldly man.

The accidental is the contingent subject and object; it is contingency, for only Substance is necessary Being. The accidental is the world that surrounds us and the life that sweeps us along; it is the aspect—or phase—of the object and the point of view—or presence—of the subject; it is our heredity, our character, our tendencies, our capacities, our destiny, as well as the fact of being born in a given form, in a given place, at a given moment, and of undergoing particular sensations, influences, and experiences. All this belongs to the realm of the accidental, and all this is nothing, for the accidental is not necessary Being; accidents are not only limited but also ephemeral. And in the final analysis, the content of all this is Bliss; this is what attracts us through a thousand reverberations and in a thousand guises; this is what we seek in all our inclinations, without knowing it. In accidentality, which is compressive and dispersing, we are not truly ourselves; we are so only in the sacramental and liberating extension of Substance, for the true being of every creature is in the last analysis the Self.[34]

If we compare the divine Substance with water, accidents may be likened to waves, drops, snow, or ice: phenomena of the world or phenomena of the soul. Substance is pure Power, pure Consciousness, pure Bliss; accidentality transcribes these dimensions in limitative or even privative mode; on the one hand, accidentality "is not", and on the other hand, it "is not other" than Substance. Esoterically speaking, there are only two relationships to take into consideration, that of transcendence and that of immanence: according to the first, the reality of Substance annihilates that of the accident; according to the second, the qualities of the accident—starting with their reality—cannot but be those of Substance. Exoterically speaking, the first point of view is absurd, since things exist; and the second is impious, a pantheism, since things cannot be God. That on the one hand things exist and that on the other hand they are not God is taken fully into

---

[34] Exoterically it will be said that we are unfaithful to ourselves in sin, which is true, but insufficient; we are also unfaithful in these dream asylums that seduce and imprison us, and which for most men constitute "real life"; it is these asylums that feed the poison-market that is worldly "culture". The earthly dream is an indirect sin: doubtless it does not prevent the practice of religion, but it does jeopardize the love of God, except when it is of such a kind as to insert itself transiently into this love, thanks to an opening heavenwards that transmits an otherworldly perfume beckoning us to rise above ourselves.

account by esoterism, but it adds a dimension of depth to these two initial observations that contradicts their superficial and as it were two-dimensional exclusivism. Whereas exoterism is enclosed in the world of accidentality, readily vaunting itself for this when it seeks to demonstrate its sense of reality vis-à-vis what strikes it as insubstantial clouds, esoterism is aware of the transparency of things and of underlying Substance, whose manifestations are Revelation, the Man-*Logos*, the doctrinal and sacramental Symbol, and also—in the human microcosm—Intellection, the Heart-Intellect, the lived Symbol. Now, to "manifest" is to "be"; the Name and the Named are mysteriously identical. The saint, and *a fortiori* the Man-*Logos*, is on the one hand: Manifestation of Substance in accidentality, and on the other hand: Reintegration of the accident into Substance.[35]

---

[35] In Islam, these are represented respectively by the "Night of Destiny" (*Laylat al-Qadr*) and the "Night of the Ascension" (*Laylat al-Mi'rāj*).

The Mystery of the Veil

The veil as such is a notion that evokes the idea of mystery, for it conceals from our view something either too sacred or too intimate; yet it also enfolds a mystery within its own nature when it becomes the symbol of universal veiling; in other words, the cosmic and meta-cosmic veil is a mystery because it pertains to the depths of divine Nature. According to the Vedantists, it is impossible to explain *Māyā* even though one cannot help noticing its presence; *Māyā*, like *Ātmā*, is without origin and without end.

The Hindu notion of "Illusion", *Māyā*, coincides in fact with the Islamic symbolism of the "Veil", *Hijāb*: universal Illusion is a power that on the one hand conceals and on the other hand reveals; it is the Veil before the Face of *Allāh*,[1] or according to an extension of the symbolism, the series of sixty-six thousand veils of light and darkness that screen either with clemency or with rigor the fulgurating Radiance of the Divinity.[2]

The Veil is a mystery because Relativity is a mystery. The Absolute, or the Unconditioned, is mysterious from sheer evidentness; but the Relative, or the Conditioned, is so out of unintelligibility. If it is impossible to understand the Absolute, this is because of its blinding luminosity; on the contrary, if it is impossible to understand the Relative, it is because its obscurity offers no point of reference. At least this is so when we consider Relativity in its seeming arbitrariness, for it becomes intelligible to the extent that it serves as the vehicle of the Absolute, or to the extent that it appears as an emanation of the Absolute. To be the vehicle of the Absolute, while veiling it, is the purpose of the Relative.

One must therefore seek to pierce the mystery of Relativity from the starting point of the Absolute or in terms of it, which compels us—or enables us—to discern the root of Relativity within

---

[1] In Sufic terminology derived from the Koran, the divine Essence (*Dhāt*) is called "Face" (*Wajh*), which at first sight seems paradoxical, but becomes comprehensible through the symbolism of veiling.

[2] Omar Khayyam: "Neither thou nor I shall solve the mystery of this world; neither thou nor I read this secret writing. We both would like to know what this veil hides; but when the veil falls there is neither thou nor I."

the Absolute itself: and this root is none other than Infinity, which is inseparable from the Real which, being absolute, is necessarily infinite. This Infinity implies Radiation, for the good tends to impart itself, as Saint Augustine observed; the Infinity of the Real is none other than its power of Love. And the mystery of Radiation explains everything: by radiating, the Real as it were projects itself "outside itself", and in moving away from itself, it becomes Relativity to the very extent of this distance. It is true that this "outside" is necessarily situated within the Real itself, but it nonetheless exists as outward-ness and in a symbolic fashion, which is to say that it is "thought" by the Infinite by virtue of its tendency to Radiation and hence to expansion in a void that in reality does not exist. This void has no reality except through the Rays that are projected into it; Relativity is only real through its contents which, for their part, are essentially of the Absolute. Thus space has no existence except through what it contains; an empty space would no longer be a space, it would be nothingness.

The principial prototype of the Veil, therefore, is the divine dimension of Infinity, which radiates so to speak from the Uncondi-tioned while remaining a rigorously intrinsic quality; in the Absolute, *Shiva* and *Shakti* are identical. Separative and playful *Māyā*, the *Māyā* that creates illusion, does not emerge inexplicably from nothingness, it proceeds from the very nature of *Ātmā*; for since the good has by definition a tendency to impart itself, the "Sovereign Good" cannot but radiate for itself and in its Essence, and then—and as a conse-quence—from itself and outside itself; being Truth, "God is Love".

This amounts to saying that there is in God a first Veil, namely the purely principial and essential tendency towards communication and thus towards contingency, a tendency that remains strictly within the divine Essence. The second Veil is as it were the extrinsic effect of the first: it is the ontological Principle, creative Being, which con-ceives the Ideas or the Possibilities of things. Being in turn gives rise to a third Veil, the creative *Logos* that produces the Universe, and this too, and to some extent *a fortiori*, is a Veil that both conceals and transmits the treasures of the Sovereign Good.

—— ·⁝· ——

Absolute, Infinity, Perfection; this third term designates the result of the Radiation produced by the Infinite by virtue of the Absolute, or rather: by the Infinitude pertaining of necessity to the Absolute. The first *Hypostasis* arising within Relativity, namely Being—the personal and creative Principle—is the first Perfection in the sense that it is All-Perfection; now, Perfection is essentially woven of Absoluteness and thus of Infinitude, but in relative and therefore differentiated mode, whence the profusion of divine Qualities.

In Being—the *Īshvara* of the Vedantists—the Absolute gives rise to the determinative and so to speak masculine or paternal pole of Being, *Purusha*, whereas the Infinite is reflected in the receptive and productive and so to speak maternal pole of Being, *Prakriti*. The new *Hypostasis*, which results from these, at the summit or at the very center of Existence, hence situated below Being and within creation, is the universal Intellect, *Buddhi*; this is the "Spirit", already created but nevertheless still divine; all told, it is the efficient extension of the creative and illuminative Intelligence of God, within creation itself.[3]

Perfection realizes the following paradox: to combine the Absolute, which is infinite, with Relativity, hence with a degree or a mode of limitation; now it is limitation, precisely, which enables a given potentiality of absoluteness or infinitude to be perceived, thus demonstrating that Relativity while on the one hand it veils by limiting, on the other hand it unveils by specifying.

— ∴ —

---

[3] Specifically theological thought, which is not well suited for grasping this simultaneity of the uncreated and the created, enshrouds it in the greatest mystery; this is the junction point between the transcendent and immutable Holy Spirit and the immanent and acting Holy Spirit, and also from another point of view, between the Holy Spirit and the immaculate soul of the Virgin. The Koran says of the "Spirit" (*Rūh*): "And they shall question thee concerning the Spirit. Tell them: the Spirit pertains to the Commandment (*amr*) of my Lord. And you have been given (on this subject) but little (divine) Knowledge. And if We (*Allāh*) wished, We could certainly take back from you what We have revealed to you . . ." (*Sūrah* "The Night Journey" [17]:85-86). The word "Commandment" indicates a direct emanation; moreover, the purpose of this whole passage is to enshroud in mystery the question of the "Spirit", and to protect this question from all profane, and virtually profaning, curiosity. In exoterism only what stimulates piety is true, not what threatens to trouble it.

Beyond-Being is the Absolute or Unconditioned, which by definition is infinite and thus unlimited; but one can also say that Beyond-Being is the Infinite, which by definition is absolute; in the first case, the accent is placed on the symbolism of virility; in the second case, it is placed on femininity; the Supreme Divinity is either Father or Mother.[4] Thus the notions of the Absolute and the Infinite do not in themselves indicate a polarity except when they are juxtaposed, in which case the juxtaposition already corresponds to a relative point of view. On the one hand, as we have said, the Absolute is the Infinite, and conversely; on the other hand, the Absolute suggests a mystery of unicity, exclusion, and contraction, whereas the Infinite suggests a mystery of totality, inclusion, and expansion.

As mentioned above, Relativity springs from the aspect of Limitlessness of the Unconditioned, and proceeds by successive veilings all the way to the outermost point of distance—a point never reached since it is illusory, or which is only reached symbolically; for our world, this outermost point is matter, but one can conceive of outermost points that are indefinitely more solidified, as well as, and *a fortiori*, much subtler. Now there is no cosmogenesis without theogenesis; this term is metaphysically plausible, but unfortunate in that it seems to attribute a becoming to the *Hypostases* when in fact it can only be a case of principial succession in the direction of the relative. The end-point of theogenesis is the most relative or the most outward *Hypostasis*, namely the "Spirit of God" which, while already being created, since it occupies the luminous center of creation, is nevertheless still divine; this is the *Logos*, which prefigures, on the one hand, the human species as the natural representative of God on earth, and on the other hand, the *Avatāra* as the supernatural representative of God amongst men.

The polarity "Unconditioned-Unlimited"—insofar as there is a polarity here resulting not from the meaning of these words but solely from their comparative juxtaposition, which, precisely, restricts their

---

[4] A well-known example of divine Femininity can be seen in Isis of the Egyptians, whom we mention here because of her connection with the Veil. Isis is *Māyā*, not as the opposite, but as an aspect or function of *Ātmā*, and thus as its *Shakti*, but less as the power of cosmic illusion than as that of initiatic dis-illusion. By removing the veils, which are the accidents and darkness, she reveals her Nudity, which is Substance and Light; being inviolable, she can blind or kill, but being generous, she regenerates and delivers.

meanings—is repeated in the very structure of the Veil, or of *Māyā*, or of Relativity, which brings us to the symbolism of weaving: the first term of the polarity becomes the warp, or the vertical or masculine dimension, while the second term becomes the woof, or the horizontal or feminine dimension; and each of these dimensions, at all levels, comprises elements of Existentiality, Consciousness, and Bliss, in accordance with the Vedantic ternary, and do so in either an active or a passive manner depending on whether the elements refer to the warp or the woof. The complementarity "Unconditioned-Unlimited", which comprises these three elements, thus produces the measureless stream of phenomena in an indefinite and iridescent display; the universe is thus a veil that on the one hand exteriorizes the Essence and on the other hand is situated within the Essence itself inasmuch as it is Infinitude.

In Islamic terms, the divine polarity, which we have just compared to the warp and the woof, is expressed by means of the letter *alif*, which is vertical, and the letter *bā*, which is horizontal; these are the first two letters of the Arabic alphabet, one symbolizing determinativity and activity, and the other receptivity or passivity.[5] The same functions are expressed by the Calamus (*Qalam*) and the Tablet (*Lawh*): in every phenomenon and at every level, there is an "Idea" that is incarnated in an existential receptacle; the Pen is the creative *Logos*, whereas the Ideas that it contains and projects refer to the ink (*Midād*). The same polarity is found in the human microcosm, man being both "vicar" (*khalīfah*), and "servant" (*'abd*),[6] or intellect and soul.

According to a famous *hadīth*, God was a hidden treasure who wished to be known and who for this reason created the world. He was hidden from men as yet inexistent; it is consequently the inexis-

---

[5] Nevertheless, the woof, represented by the shuttle, is active, which does not contradict feminine passivity, because woman is active in child-bearing, whereas man in this connection remains passive; this is why, in Hindu doctrine, creative activity is attributed to universal Substance, *Prakriti*, which in fact "produces" beings, whereas *Purusha* "conceives" them as ideas. This appearance of inversion provides an illustration of the Taoist doctrine of *Yin-Yang*, which finally is the theory of reciprocal compensation; without this compensation, the dualities would be absolute and insurmountable, which is an impossibility since Reality is one.

[6] This is why the Prophet is called both *Rasūl*, "Messenger", and *'Abd*, "Servant"; the latter is extinguished before God, while the former is a prolongation of Him.

tence of men that was the first veil; God thus created the world for men in order to be known by them and in order to project his own Bliss into innumerable relative consciousnesses. This is why it is said that God created the world out of love.

Wherever *Ātmā* is, there also is *Māyā*, intrinsic Life and extrinsic Power of unfolding. In Islamic terms, and leaving aside the notion of the *Hijāb*, it is said that wherever *Allāh* is, there also is *Rahmah*, the infinite Clemency and Mercy; this is what is expressed by the fundamental formula introducing the *Sūrah*s of the Koran and, in human life, everything written and everything undertaken: "In the Name of God, the most Clement, the most Merciful". The fact that these Names of infinite Goodness are added to the Name *Allāh* indicates that Goodness is in the very Essence of God and that, unlike most of the divine Qualities, it is not an element that appears only by refraction on the already relative plane of the attributes; this means that *Rahmah* belongs to *Dhāt*, the Essence, and not to the attributes, *Sifāt*.[7] *Rahmah* is *Māyā*, not in *Māyā*'s capacity as Relativity and Illusion, but in its capacity as Infinitude, Beauty, Generosity.[8]

In the *Vedānta*, *Ātmā* is robed in three great veils (or "envelopes" = *koshas*), which correspond analogically, via causal prefiguration, to the states of wakefulness, dreaming, and deep sleep: these veils or states are *Vaishvānara*, *Taijasa*, and *Prājna*; what they veil is unconditioned and ineffable Reality, *Turīya*, which in the human microcosm is the divine Presence in the depth of the heart. This reality, or this

---

[7] *Allāh* "was" good and loving "before" creation, and this is expressed by the Name *Rahmān*, "most Clement"; and He is good and loving "since" creation and towards it, and this is expressed by the Name *Rahīm*, "most Merciful". According to the Koran, *Ar-Rahmān* is synonymous with *Allāh*—which shows that this Name pertains to the *Dhāt* and not to the *Sifāt*—and it is *Ar-Rahmān* who created man, taught him speech (*bayān*, the capacity to express himself with intelligence, and thus to think), and revealed the Koran. It should be noted that the Name *Rahīm* pertains to the Attributes and not to the Essence, though it nevertheless prolongs the Name *Rahmān* into the created order.

[8] In other words, it is *Shakti* rather than *Māyā*; this amounts to saying that *Māyā*, insofar as it is inherent in *Ātmā*, has no ambiguity, and that it is thus properly the *Shakti*, the Power of divine Life and of cosmic Manifestation.

fourth "state" in an ascending sense, is Beyond-Being or *Ātmā* as such; it is said to be "neither manifested (*vyakta*) nor non-manifested (*avyakta*)", and this calls for an important point.

The idea of the non-manifested has two different meanings: there is the absolutely non-manifested, *Para-Brahma* or *Brahma nirguna* ("non-qualified"), and the relatively non-manifested, *Īshvara* or *Brahma saguna* ("qualified"); this relatively non-manifested, which is Being in its capacity as existentiating principle or matrix of the archetypes, may be called the "potentially manifested" in contra-distinction to the "effectively manifested", namely the world; for in the divine order itself, Being is the "manifestation" of Beyond-Being, without which manifestation properly so called, or Existence, would be neither possible nor conceivable. To say that the absolutely non-manifested is the principle both of the manifested—the world—and of the relatively non-manifested—Being—would be a tautology: Beyond-Being, as the principle of Being, is implicitly the principle of Existence. For the absolutely non-manifested, the distinction between the potentially manifested—which is the relatively non-manifested and creative—and the effectively manifested or the created, namely between Being and Existence, such a distinction has no reality; that is to say, it is neither a complementarity nor an alternative with respect to Beyond-Being.

Within the principial or divine order, it is important to take account first of the Absolute in itself, and secondly of the Absolute insofar as it unfolds in *Māyā*, or in the mode known as *Māyā*; in this second respect, "all things are *Ātmā*". In a similar manner, but within the context of *Māyā* itself, one can look at things firstly in themselves, that is to say as phenomena when seen from the standpoint of the separate existence that determines them, and secondly as archetypes when seen in Being. Every aspect of relativity—even principial—or of manifestation is *vyakta*, and every aspect of absoluteness—even the relative—or of non-manifestation is *avyakta*.

In order to realize Beyond-Being, which is the absolute Self, it is necessary, according to the *Katha Upanishad*, to pass "beyond obscurity"; now, this "beyond obscurity" is obviously the intrinsic luminosity of the Self, which reveals itself following the obscurity the non-manifested represents in relation to the illusory luminosity of the manifested. Since "extremes meet", the maximum of "inward" knowledge will have as its complement the maximum of "outward" knowledge, not of course in the sense of scientific knowledge, but in the sense that the man who sees God perfectly within or beyond phenomena will see Him perfectly in the outward or in phenomena;[9] thus the "ascent" of the spirit towards God entails subjectively a "descent" of God into things.[10] This "divine vision" of the world may well carry with it a "mandate from Heaven" or a spiritual mission, whatever be its degree of importance, but all the loftier as the inward knowledge is profound or total. Conversely, one could say that a particular predestined mandate coincides providentially with supreme knowledge; but one cannot in any event affirm that a degree of knowledge or realization *ipso facto* entails a law-giving prophetic mission, otherwise every perfect sage would be the founder of a religion.

Be that as it may, what needed to be emphasized here is that the lifting of the veil in the inward and intellective dimension is accompanied by an illumination or a transparency of the veils in which and through which we live; and of which we are made, owing to the very fact of our existence.

The Veil can be dense or transparent, unique or multiple; it veils or it unveils, violently or gently, suddenly or gradually; it includes or it excludes, constituting thus a division between two regions, one inward and the other outward. All these modes are manifested in the microcosm as well as in the macrocosm, or in the spiritual life as well as in the cosmic cycles.

The impenetrable Veil shields from sight something that is too sacred or too intimate; the veil of Isis suggests both relationships, since the body of the Goddess corresponds with the Holy-of-Holies. The "sacred" refers to the divine aspect of *Jalāl*, "Majesty"; the "intimate" for its part refers to *Jamāl*, "Beauty"; blinding Majesty and intoxicating Beauty. The transparent Veil, on the contrary, delivers both the sacred

---

[9] God, insofar as He manifests Himself through the cosmos, being called "the Outward" (*Az-Zāhir*) in the Koran.

[10] "It is not I who have left the world, it is the world that has left me", an Arab *faqīr* once told us; we would add that, by way of compensation, God makes Himself present in the world to the very extent that the world becomes absent for us.

and the intimate, like a sanctuary that opens its door, or a bride who gives herself, or a bridegroom who welcomes and takes possession.

When the Veil is dense, it hides the Divinity: it is made of the forms that constitute the world, but these are also the passions within the soul; the dense Veil is woven out of sensorial phenomena around us and passional phenomena within us; and it should be noted that an error is a passional element to the extent that it is serious and that man clings to it. The thickness of the Veil is both objective and subjective, in the world and in the soul: it is subjective in the world insofar as our mind fails to penetrate the essence of forms, and it is objective in the soul in the sense that passions and thoughts are phenomena.

When the Veil is transparent, it reveals the Divinity: it is made of forms insofar as these impart their spiritual contents, whether we understand them or not; in an analogous fashion, the virtues allow the divine Qualities to shine through, while the vices indicate their absence, or their opposites, which amounts to the same thing. The transparency of the Veil is at once objective and subjective, which can be understood without difficulty after what has just been said; for if on the one hand forms are transparent, not with respect to their existence but with respect to their messages, on the other hand it is our mind that renders them transparent by its penetration. If transcendence thickens the Veil, immanence for its part renders it transparent, whether in the objective world or within ourselves, through our awareness of the underlying Essence, although, from an entirely different standpoint, our understanding of transcendence is a phenomenon of transparency, whereas on the contrary the coarse enjoyment of what is offered to us by virtue of immanence, is obviously a phenomenon of thickening.[11]

The ambiguity of the Veil is expressed in Islam by means of the twin notions of "abstraction" (*tanzīh*) and "resemblance" (*tashbīh*). In the first perspective, visible light is nothing in regard to divine Light, which alone "is"; "nothing is like unto Him", says the Koran, thus proclaiming transcendence. From the second perspective, visible light "is" divine Light—or "is not other" than it—but manifested on a particular plane of existence, or through a particular existential veil;

---

[11] Mention should be made in this context, from the point of view of sacred art, of the use of the cloud in Taoist painting: this cloud sometimes expresses more than the landscape, which on the one hand it conceals and on the other hand enhances, thus creating an atmosphere both of secrecy and translucence.

"God is the Light of the Heavens and the earth", the Koran also says; thus visible light resembles Him, it "is He" in a certain respect, that of immanence. To metaphysical "abstraction" corresponds mystical "solitude", *khalwah*, the ritual expression of which is the spiritual retreat; "resemblance", for its part, gives rise to the grace of "radiance", *jalwah*,[12] of which the ritual expression is the invocation of God performed in common. Mystery of transcendence or "contraction" (*qabd*) on the one hand, and mystery of immanence or "dilation" (*bast*) on the other; *khalwah* withdraws us from the world, *jalwah* transforms it into a sanctuary.

According to a theory of Ibn Arabi, Adam and Muhammad correspond to each other in the sense that each of them manifests a synthesis—initial in the first case and terminal in the second—whereas Seth and Jesus correspond to each other in the sense that the first manifests the exteriorization of the divine gifts, and the second, their interiorization towards the end of the cycle; we are presenting here the meaning, not the literal words, of the doctrine in question. One might also say that Seth manifests *tashbīh*, "resemblance" or "analogy", thus symbolism, the participation of the human in the divine, and that, inversely, Jesus manifests "abstraction", thus the tendency towards a pure "beyond", for the kingdom of Christ is not of this world; in which case, Adam and Muhammad would manifest the equilibrium between *tashbīh* and *tanzīh*, Adam *a priori* and Muhammad *a posteriori*. Seth, the revealer of arts and crafts, illuminates the veil of earthly existence; Christ rends the dark veil;[13] Islam, like the primordial religion, combines the two attitudes.

Besides the word *hijāb*, "veil", there is also the word *sitr*, which can mean "curtain", "veil", "cover", and "modesty"; likewise *satīr*,

---

[12] A word derived from *jilwah*, "unveiling", when speaking of a bride; the meaning of "radiance" is contained in the root of the word itself. *Jalwah* is the concrete awareness of the divine Omnipresence, an awareness that makes it possible to understand the "language of the birds", metaphorically speaking, and to hear the universal praise that rises to God.

[13] It goes without saying that Christianity, in its general and characteristic form, sees in this sacrificial rending the only possible solution; it nevertheless comprises the inverse or complementary attitude to the extent that it is esoteric.

"chaste", and *mastūr,* "modest".[14] From the sexual point of view, one veils that which, in different respects, is earthly and heavenly, fallen and incorruptible, animal and divine, so as to be protected against the risk either of a humiliation or a profanation, according to the perspectives or circumstances. There are iridescent silks in which two opposite colors appear in an alternating pattern on the same surface, depending on the position of the material; this play of colors evokes cosmic ambiguity, namely the mixture of "closeness" (*qurb*) and "distance" (*bu'd*)—we might also say of greatness and smallness—characterizing the fabric of which the world is made and of which we ourselves are made. This brings us to the question of the subjective attitude of man before the objective ambiguity of the world: the noble man, and thus the spiritual man, sees in positive phenomena the substantial greatness and not the accidental smallness; yet he has no choice but to notice smallness when it is substantial and when, as a result, it determines the nature of a phenomenon. The base man, on the contrary, and sometimes the merely worldly man, sees the accidental before the essential and focuses on the aspects of smallness that are constituent parts of greatness, but without diminishing this greatness in the least, except in the eyes of the small-minded man.

The two iridescent colors, it goes without saying, can have an exclusively positive meaning: activity and passivity, rigor and gentleness, strength and beauty, and other similar complementarities. The universal Veil comprises a play of contrasts and shocks and also, and even more profoundly or in a far more real way, a play of harmony and love.

—— ∴ ——

The central tree is symbolically identical with the veil separating creation from the Creator.[15] The sin of the first human couple was to have lifted the veil, and the consequence was their exile behind a new veil,

---

[14] One should also note the invocation *yā Sātir,* "O Thou who coverest", to express a desire for protection.

[15] According to certain mythologies, and also on ancient Christian miniatures, the two trees, that of life and that of death, form one single tree, their opposition being recognizable in the difference of their branches or fruits. This symbolism evokes precisely that of the two sides of the veil, the one that includes and the other that excludes.

more outward than the first and separating them from intimacy with God. Proceeding from fall to fall, man created for himself new separative veils; hence each sin is for the individual a veil that separates him from a preceding grace. Conversely, every return to God brings about the dropping of a veil and the recovery of a lost Paradise.

Moreover, when Saint Augustine exclaims "O happy fault!" in speaking of the sin of Eve and Adam, he is in fact referring to the necessary character of the Fall: indeed, many cosmogonic doctrines present the loss of original beatitude as a neutral fact and as an unavoidable stage in the full realization of man, thus accentuating the compensatory effects, which is what Christianity does *a posteriori*. This can be seen in sexual union, the classic image of the Fall, at least from the perspective of Christian sensitivities; Islam and other religions stress instead the unfolding and perfecting virtue of sexuality, but without ever denying the possible merits of chastity, or of its necessity in certain cases. At all events, everything in the natural order is more or less relative, which means that it is possible for man to realize the sexual alchemy in a purely inward manner, just as the reverse is likewise possible; this is obvious and we have already said so, either explicitly or implicitly. Likewise, we are not stating anything new in recalling that man carries within himself the lost Paradise, which in reality always remains accessible—not easily, but on the basis of rigorous traditional and personal conditions; *intrate per angustam portam*. The angel with the flaming sword, or the dragon-guardian of the sanctuary,[16] will permit entry only to him who, having vanquished the Fall, has not been touched by sin; to him whose "descent into hell" was never but a "happy fault" from the very beginning; or to him who, knowing thus the "password", possesses the key to the heavenly Garden and to Deliverance.

---

[16] The serpent of Genesis is not unrelated to the dragon, but the figure of the dragon is positive, as is shown by the connection with the angel or the cherubim. Given that the perspective of the Bible is *a priori* moral and not initiatic—as is proved moreover by the way in which it presents the case of Solomon—the words of the serpent have a malefic character, whereas according to the sapiential perspective the dragon invites one, not to sin, but to initiatic trial and victory, while at the same time warning man of the danger he risks. Certainly, man has fallen into suffering and death, but this is the ransom of a higher possibility of perfection, without which there would be no reason to speak of a "happy fault". Buddhists would say that one cannot vanquish *samsāra* except by knowing it.

—— ·:· ——

One often speaks of a multitude of Veils, which indicates the complexity of the veiling process, or more precisely its ontological and existential degrees,[17] and also, from the human point of view, of the temporary and not irremediable character of the separation. The manifold nature of the Veil promises a progressively more welcoming movement or, on the contrary, provides reason to dread an inverse movement of successive exclusion.[18]

The Veil that opens gently betokens a welcoming invitation into some state of beatitude, whereas the Veil that opens abruptly—or the rending of the Veil—means on the contrary a sudden *fiat lux*, a dazzling enlightenment, a *satori* as the Zen Buddhists would say, unless its meaning is that—on the cosmic scale—of a *dies irae*: the unexpected irruption of a heavenly Light, at once avenging and saving, but ultimately stabilizing. As for the Veil that closes slowly, it does so charitably and without any intention of rigor; if on the contrary it closes abruptly, this indicates a disgrace.

We should like to mention here, by way of a traditional illustration of the mystery of unveiling, the *rāsa-līlā*, or dance of the *gopīs* in the company of Krishna; and also of the theft of the saris, by Krishna, while the *gopīs* were bathing. The loss of clothes signifies in each of these cases a return to the Essence, either in the ecstasy of perfect abandon to God as in the first example, or in the form of a spiritual trial as in the second; the theft of the saris symbolizes the loss of individuality in the love of God, then its restoration on a higher plane, that of detachment; but it may also symbolize, more generally, the divine requirement that the soul appear naked before the Creator. It should

[17] The first pertaining to the divine order, and the second to the cosmic order.

[18] Sufism makes an extensive use of the symbolism of multiple veils (*hujub*). For example, each virtue, to the extent that man attributes it to himself, is one of the veils that separate him from God; everything that is not God, or everything that is not envisaged in relation to God, or everything that is understood or accomplished imperfectly, is a veil. From the point of view of rigorous and sapiential esoterism, the common religion or exoterism is a veil, and some have gone as far as to say that by adhering to such and such a form of worship the adherents are worshipping themselves, their god being made in their image; a rather blunt way of putting it, but plausible with certain self-evident reservations.

be recalled that clothing is an image not only of individuality but also of exoteric formalism, the two shells having to be transcended in one way or another, then repossessed on a higher plane and with a new intention;[19] an intellectual transcending in the second case, in which the forms are relativized *a priori* and then universalized *a posteriori*, and a moral transcending in the first case, in which the ego is objectified and then reanimated with the perfume of holy childlikeness.

The symbolism of the Veil takes on a broader meaning when one envisages a new element superimposed upon it, namely embroidery, ornamental weaving, and decorative patterns: the veil thus enriched[20] suggests the play of *Māyā* in all its diversity and in all its iridescence, as does also the mysterious plumage of the peacock, but accentuating unfolding in this case, as does a painted fan, which on being opened displays its message and its splendor.[21] The peacock as well as the fan are emblems or attributes of Vishnu; and it is especially worthy of note that the fan, in the Far East and elsewhere, is a ritual instrument that, like universal *Māyā*, can both open and close, manifest and reabsorb, kindle and extinguish. The unfolding, whatever be its image, is the projection of Existence, which manifests all virtualities; the closing signifies reintegration in the Essence and a return to potential plenitude; the play of *Māyā* is a dance between Essence and Exis-

---

[19] Nonetheless, there is nothing exclusive about this symbolism, for one could with just as much justification speak of two forms of nudity, one lower and one higher: the nudity imposed by Krishna while the *gopīs* were bathing, and the nudity they freely assumed while dancing, the first referring to humility or sincerity, and the second to love and unitive ecstasy.

[20] The most famous example of which is the Kashmir shawl, without forgetting the decorated sari, which adds a communicative magic to the play of envelopment, as if by hiding the body it sought to reveal the soul; and this moreover applies especially to all princely and priestly vestments.

[21] The Japanese screen, which is often decorated with paintings inspired by Zen or Taoism, is not unconnected with the general symbolism discussed here; the same is true of the Islamic screen of perforated wood and of windows of the same kind. In these examples there is a partition that is either mobile, which distinguishes it from a fixed wall, or else rendered transparent, so that it may be reopened even when it has been shut; this ambiguity corresponds very well to the mobility or the transparency of the veil. The perforated screen allows one to see without being seen, and is thus a kind of veil that is transparent from one side and opaque from the other, which brings to mind the *hadīth* about "spiritual virtue" (*ihsān*): God must be worshipped "as if thou sawest Him, for if thou seest Him not, He nevertheless seeth thee".

tence—Existence being the Veil, and Essence Nudity. And the Essence is inaccessible to the existent as such, as the inscription on the statue of Isis at Sais declares: "I am all that has been, all that is, and all that will be; and no mortal has ever lifted my veil."

—— ·⦂· ——

Veils are divine or human, not to mention the veilings that other creatures represent or experience. The divine veils in our cosmos are the existential categories: space, time, form, number, matter; then the creatures with their faculties; and then also, but on a completely different plane, the revelations with their truths and their limits.[22] The human veils are, firstly, man himself, namely the ego in itself, then the passional and darksome ego, and finally passions, vices, sins, without forgetting—but on a normal and neutral plane—concepts and thoughts inasmuch as they clothe the truth.

One of the functions of the Veil is to separate; the Koran alludes to this in several respects, either when the curtain separates man from the truth that he rejects, or when it separates him from God who speaks to him, or when it separates men from women to whom they are not entitled, or finally when it separates the damned from the elect; but the most fundamental separation, the one that comes first and foremost to mind, is the one between the Creator and creation, or between the Principle and its manifestation. In rigorous or total metaphysics, one should add the separation between Beyond-Being and Being, the latter pertaining to *Māyā*, and so to Relativity; the dividing line between the two orders of reality, or the Veil precisely, is thus situated within the divine order itself.

If *Māyā* is understood as being its global cosmic manifestation, we may say that *Ātmā* is reflected in *Māyā* and assumes therein a central and prophetic function, *Buddhi*, and that *Māyā* in its turn is prefigured in *Ātmā* and anticipates or prepares therein the creative projection. In

---

[22] According to the Sufis, it is much more difficult to remove veils made of light than those made of darkness; for the veil made of light is the illuminating and saving symbol, the reflection of the sun in the water; but the water mirroring the sun is not the sun. Ramakrishna said that it was ultimately necessary to transpierce the image of Kali with the sword of *jnāna*. It is well known that Zen Buddhism readily presents iconoclastic propositions, the inward Revelation being supposed to burn its outward forms.

the same vein of thought, it is *Māyā* contained in *Ātmā*—hence the Creator *Īshvara*—that produces *Samsāra*, or the macrocosm, the hierarchy of worlds, and the sequence of cycles; and it is *Ātmā* contained in *Māyā*—in the sacramental *Mantra*—that dismantles *Samsāra* as microcosm. Mystery of prefiguration and mystery of reintegration: the first is that of Creation and also that of Revelation; the second is that of the *Apocatastasis* and also that of Salvation.

All of this evokes the Taoist symbolism of *Yin-Yang*: a white field and a black field, the first containing a black circle and the second a white circle; in the present context, this means that the relationship between the Face and the Veil is repeated on both sides of the Veil, first on the inside, *in divinis*, and then on the outside, within the universe. In Sanskrit terms: there is *Ātmā* and *Māyā*, but since Reality is one and since the nature of things could not imply a fundamental dualism, there is also *Māyā* in *Ātmā* and *Ātmā* in *Māyā*.[23]

In earthly use, that is to say as a material object and human symbol, the Veil hides the sacred pure and simple on the one hand, and the ambiguous or the perilous on the other hand. In the latter case, we may say that *Māyā* possesses an ambiguous character by virtue of the fact that it veils and unveils and also, from the point of view of its dynamism, by virtue of the fact that it takes things away from God because it creates, while at the same time bringing things close to God because it reabsorbs or liberates. Beauty in general and music in particular provide an eloquent image of the power of illusion, in the sense that they possess both an exteriorizing and interiorizing quality and act in one direction or the other depending on the nature and intention of each man: either a passional nature and an intention of pleasure, or a contemplative nature and an intention of "remembrance" in the Platonic sense of the word. Woman is veiled in Islam just as wine is forbidden, and she is unveiled—in certain rites or certain ritual

---

[23] A revealed Book, a Prophet, a rite, a sacred formula, a divine Name belong to the formal order, and are thus *Māyā*, but it is a *Māyā* that delivers since it is essentially the vehicle of *Ātmā*. It is "*Ātmā* in *Māyā*", whereas the creative Word, or the *Logos*, is "*Māyā* in *Ātmā*".

dances[24]—with the aim of producing a kind of magic by analogy; the unveiling of beauty with an erotic vibration works as a catalyst, evoking the revelation of the liberating and beatific Essence—of the *Haqīqah*, the "Truth-Reality", as the Sufis would say. It is by virtue of this analogy that the Sufis personify beatific and intoxicating Knowledge in the form of Layla, or sometimes Salma, a personification which moreover took on a concrete form, from the point of view of human reality in the Semitic world, in the Blessed Virgin, who combines in her person the substance of sanctity and concrete humanity: dazzling and inviolable sanctity and merciful beauty that conveys it with purity and sweetness. Like every heavenly being, Mary manifests the universal Veil in its function of transmission: she is Veil because she is a form, but she is Essence by her content and consequently by her message. She is at once closed and open, inviolable and generous;[25] she is "clothed with the sun" because she is clothed in Beauty, "the splendor of the True", and she is "black but beautiful" because the Veil is both closed and transparent, or because, after having been closed by virtue of inviolability, it opens by virtue of mercy. The Virgin is "clothed with the sun" because, as Veil, she is transparent: Light, which is at the same time Beauty, transmits itself with such a power that it seems to consume the Veil and abolish veiling, so that the Inward, which is the purpose of the form, seems as it were to envelop the form by transubstantiating it. "Whoever has seen me, has seen God": these words, or their equivalent, are found in the most diverse traditional worlds, and

[24] The "dance of the seven veils" has a malefic sense in the case of Salomé dancing before Herod, but a benefic sense in the case of the Queen of Sheba dancing before Solomon, which evokes precisely the dual function of beauty, woman, and of wine. In the case of the Blessed Virgin and according to the Koranic commentators, the seven veils become seven doors, which Zacharias had to open with a key each time he visited Mary in the Temple; Zacharias represents the privileged soul that penetrates the mystery thanks to a "key", which is yet another image of "unveiling". Similarly, the seventh day of creation marks the return to the Origin, or the "peace in the Void", as the Taoists would say, or the meeting with principial Reality, "naked" because non-manifested. There is an analogous meaning in the notion of the "seventh Heaven", which coincides with the "Garden of the Essence".

[25] The Russian Church celebrates a "feast of the Veil" in remembrance of an apparition of Mary at Constantinople, in the course of which the Virgin lifted her luminous veil and held it, in a miraculous fashion, above those present. The Russian word *pokrov* means both "veil" and "intercession": the *Māyā* that conceals the Essence is at the same time the *Māyā* that transmits graces.

they apply notably also to the "divine Mary", "clothed with the sun" because reabsorbed in it and as it were contained therein.[26] To see God in beholding man as theophany, is in some fashion to see the Essence before the form: it is to experience the imprint of the divine Content together with that of the human container, and to do so "before" the human by reason of the pre-eminence of the divine. The Veil has become Light, there is no longer any Veil.

— ⋰ —

There is nothing but Light; the veils necessarily originate in Light itself, and are prefigured in it. They do not come from its luminosity but from its radiation; not from its clarity but from its expansion. The Light shines for itself, then it radiates to impart itself, and by radiating, it produces the Veil and the veils; by radiating and diffusing itself it gives rise to distance, veils, gradations. The intrinsic tendency to radiation is the first Veil, which later becomes specified as creative Being, and then manifests itself as cosmos. Esoterism or *gnosis*, being the science of Light, is thereby the science of veilings and unveilings, and necessarily so since on the one hand discursive thought and the language that expresses it constitute a veil, while on the other hand the purpose of this veil is the Light.

God and the world do not mix; there is but one sole Light, seen through innumerable veils; the saint who speaks in the name of God does not speak by virtue of a divine inherence, for Substance cannot be inherent in the accidental: it is God who speaks; the saint is only a veil whose function is to manifest God, "as a light cloud makes the sun visible", according to a comparison used by the Muslims. Every accident is a veil that makes Substance-Light more or less indirectly visible.

---

[26] The *Avatāra*s are "contained" in the heavenly *Logos*, which they represent on earth or of which they manifest a function, as they are likewise contained pre-existentially in the divine Names, which diversify the undifferentiated mysteries of the Essence and whose aspects are innumerable. In Sufism, the Blessed Virgin personifies the pre-existential and existentiating *Sophia*: the *Logos* inasmuch as it "conceives" creatures, then "engenders" them, and finally "forms" or "embellishes" them; if Mary thus represents the non-manifested and silent *Logos*—*nigra sum sed formosa*—Jesus will be the manifested and law-giving *Logos*.

In the *Avatāra* there is quite obviously a separation between the human and the divine—or between accident and Substance—then there is a mixing, not between human accident and divine Substance, but between the human and the direct reflection of Substance in cosmic accidentality; this reflection may be called divine with respect to the human, but only on condition that the Cause is not in any way reduced to the effect. For some, the *Avatāra* is God "descended"; for others, he is an "opening" that allows God immutably "on high" to be seen.[27]

Universal radiation is the unfolding of the accidental, starting from initial Relativity; necessary Being, radiating by virtue of its infinitude, gives rise to Contingency. And the Heart that has become transparent conveys the one Light, thus reintegrating Contingency into the Absolute; this means that we are truly ourselves only through our awareness of Substance and through our conformity to this awareness, but not that we must depart from all relativity— supposing we were able to—for God, in creating us, wishes us to exist.

To summarize: the possibilities are the veils that on the one hand restrict the absolute Real and on the other hand manifest it; Possibility as such, in the singular and in the absolute sense, is the supreme Veil, shrouding the mystery of Unicity and at the same time unfolding it, while remaining immutable and without depriving itself of anything; Possibility is nothing other than the Infinitude of the Real. To speak of Infinitude is to speak of Potentiality: and to affirm that Possibility as such, or Potentiality, both veils and unveils the Absolute, is simply a way of expressing the duo-dimensional nature—in itself undifferentiated—that we can discern analytically in the absolutely Real. Likewise, we can discern in the Real a tri-dimensional nature, it too intrinsically undifferentiated but heralding a possible unfolding: these dimensions are "Being", "Consciousness", "Bliss". It is by virtue of the third element—immutable in itself— that Divine Possibility overflows "out

---

[27] What becomes "incarnate" in the *Avatāra* is an aspect of *Buddhi*, such as Vishnu or Shiva; it is not *Ātmā* as such. It should be recalled in this connection that the purpose of Christianity is to emphasize the "divine Phenomenon", whereas that of Islam, on the contrary, is to reduce the phenomenon to the Principle or the effect to the Cause.

of love" and gives rise to that mystery of exteriorization that is the universal Veil, whose warp is made of the worlds, and whose woof is made of beings.

Hypostatic and Cosmic Numbers

The symbolism of numbers and geometrical figures provides a relatively simple way of describing the modes and degrees of veiling and unveiling; not that symbols will facilitate our understanding as such of these things, but they at least provide keys and clarifying elements.

Absolute Reality—or the Essence, or Beyond-Being—can be represented by the geometrical point; it would doubtless be less inadequate to represent it by the void, but the void is not a figure properly speaking, and if we give the Essence a name, we can with the same justification, and with the same risk, represent it by a sign; the simplest and hence most essential sign is the point.

Now, to speak of Reality is to speak of Power or Potentiality, or of *Shakti* if one prefers; there is thus in the Real a principle of polarization, wholly undifferentiated in the Absolute, yet capable of being discerned and the cause of every subsequent unfolding. This principial polarity can be represented by an axis, either horizontal or vertical: if horizontal, it signifies that Potentiality, or supreme *Māyā*, remains within the Supreme Principle, *Paramātmā*, as an intrinsic dimension or as latent potency; if vertical, the axis signifies that Potentiality becomes Virtuality, that it radiates and imparts itself, and that consequently it gives rise to the first *hypostasis*, Being, the creative principle.[1] It is in this first bipolarity, or in this principial duality, that all possible complementarities and oppositions are prefigured or pre-realized: subject and object, activity and passivity, static and dynamic, unicity and totality, the exclusive and the inclusive, rigor and gentleness. These couples are horizontal when the second term is the qualitative and thus the harmonious complement of the first, in other words, if it constitutes its *Shakti*; they are vertical when the second term tends in an efficient manner towards a more relative level or when it is already at such a level. We need not mention here pure and simple oppositions, in which the second term has only a privative

---

[1] The combination of point, horizontal line, and vertical line is transcribed by the circle, which expresses the union between the Divinity and its radiating Power, or between the *Deva* and his *Shakti*; it is, so to speak, divine "Totality", whereas the point represents "Unicity".

character, and which cannot have any divine archetype except in a purely logical and symbolic manner.

In the human microcosm, duality is manifested by the twofold function of the heart, which is at once Intellect and Love, the latter referring to the Infinite and the former to the Absolute; but, from another standpoint, which reflects the descending hypostatic projection, the Intellect corresponds to Beyond-Being, and the mental element to Being.

—— ·:· ——

The divine archetype of all positive ternaries is the Vedantic trinity *Sat, Chit, Ānanda*: God, from the starting point of his supra-ontological Essence, is pure "Being", pure "Consciousness", pure "Bliss".[2]

Like the binary, the ternary presents two different aspects depending on the position of the triangle, geometrically speaking. In the upright triangle, the duality of the base is contemplative in the sense that it indicates, through the apex, an infolding towards unity; the ternary in this case represents relativity intent on conforming to absoluteness and refusing to move away from it; it brings to an end all movement towards the multiple. In the inverted triangle, the duality is operative in the sense that it tends, through the inverted summit, towards extrinsic radiation or production.

This amounts to saying that the element *Ānanda* either constitutes the internal and intrinsic radiation of *Ātmā*, which desires nothing other—if one may so put it—than the enjoyment of its own infinite Possibility, or on the contrary tends towards the manifestation—and countless refractions—of this now overflowing Possibility. Thus it is that in sexual love the end or the result can be outward and quasi-social, namely the child; but it can also be inward and contemplative, namely realization—by means precisely of the living experience of this symbolism—of the one Essence in which the two partners fuse, which is a birth in an upward direction and a reabsorption into

---

[2] "Being", in this context, is not solely the ontological and creative Principle, but is Reality as such. Regarding the distinction between creative Being and Beyond-Being, we may observe that the terms *esse* and *posse*, in their juxtaposition and correlation, provide a clear indication of the relationship between the two aspects in question.

Substance.[3] In this case the result is essentiality, whereas in the preceding case it is perfection; this amounts to saying that the dimensions of absoluteness and infinity pertain on the one hand, to the Essence, which unites them, and on the other hand produce perfection, which manifests them.

But there is still another type of ternary, the most immediate example of which is the hierarchy of the constituent elements of the microcosm, *corpus, anima, spiritus,* or *soma, psyche, pneuma;* the Vedantic ternary of the cosmic qualities, *tamas, rajas, sattva,* is of the same order. This ternary is founded, not on the union of two complementary poles with a view to a third element, either higher or lower, or inward or outward, but on the qualitative aspects of space measured from the starting point of a consciousness that is situated within it: ascending dimension or lightness, descending dimension or heaviness, horizontal dimension open to both influences.

The ternary previously considered—that of *Sat-Chit-Ānanda*—also has a spatial foundation, but in this case it is purely objective, namely the three dimensions of space: height, breadth, and depth; the first corresponds to the masculine principle, the second to the feminine principle, and the third to the fruit, which is either intrinsic or extrinsic; this last distinction is expressed precisely by the position of the triangle. Now, the new ternary just mentioned—body, soul, spirit, or darkness, warmth, light—is also to be found in the triangle, and in two ways that are highly instructive: in the first instance, the spirit is situated either at the apex, in which case the image expresses the transcendence of the Intellect with regard to the sentient soul and the body, which are then placed on the same plane, with the difference however that the soul is situated on the right, the positive or active side; or else, the body is situated at the inverted apex, in which case the image expresses the superiority of both the soul and of the spirit with regard to the body.

And this indicates two aspects of the corresponding divine ternary: in one sense, the world is the "Body" of God, while Being, as the matrix of the archetypes, is His "Soul", and the Essence His "Spirit"; in another sense—and here we rejoin the Vedantic rigor—the Essence,

---

[3] The two points of view can be combined, and must even necessarily be so, when a social vocation coincides with a contemplative vocation, a concurrence that the Islamic perspective facilitates, especially by the example of the Prophet.

or Beyond-Being, is the "Spirit" of God, whereas the subordination of *Māyā* or Relativity is expressed by the juxtaposition, on the base of the triangle, of Being and Existence, and so of "Soul" and "Body".

But let us return to the ternary *Sat-Chit-Ānanda* represented by the triangle, wherein the apex indicates *Sat*, and the two lower angles indicate respectively *Chit* and *Ānanda*: by inverting the triangle, the apex, which is Being and radiating Power in the upright triangle, becomes separating and coagulating power, and thus ultimately subversive power, in the inverted triangle; this is the image of the fall of Lucifer, in which the highest point becomes the lowest, an image that explains the mysterious and paradoxical relationship between powerful, but immutable, Being and the manifesting power that departs from Being until it finally rises up against it.[4] The positive and innocent cosmogonic power ends at the terminal point that is matter, whereas the subversive centrifugal power ends in evil; these are two aspects that must not be confused.

There is a particularly concrete image of the Vedantic ternary, which is that of the sun: the solar star, like all fixed stars, is matter, form, and radiation. Matter, or mass-energy, manifests *Sat*, which is Being-Power; form is equated with *Chit*, which is Consciousness or Intelligence;[5] radiation corresponds to *Ānanda*, which is Beatitude or Goodness. Now, radiation comprises both warmth and light, just as *Ānanda* participates in both *Sat* and *Chit*, warmth referring to Goodness and light to Beauty; light spreads the image of the sun far and wide, just as Beauty transmits Truth; "Beauty is the splendor of the True". According to a somewhat different and no less plausible symbolism, the sun presents itself to human experience as form, light, and warmth: *Sat, Chit, Ānanda*; in this case, substance is one with form,

---

[4] The devil being the humanized personification—upon contact with man—of the subversive aspect of the centrifugal existential power, but not the personification of this power insofar as its mission is to manifest divine Possibility in a positive way.

[5] In every kind of creature—human, animal, vegetable, or mineral—form expresses *Chit*; matter, *Sat*; and extension or growth, *Ānanda*. Even so, it is impossible to isolate any one of these dimensions from the other, for they always "operate" together: if the form that distinguishes one flower from another manifests the element "Knowledge", *Chit*, it nonetheless expresses, within the very framework of this element, the dimension "Joy", *Ānanda*, whence the beauty of the flower. It should be specified that in the case of conscious beings, a psychological application of the ternary is obviously superimposed on the physico-vegetative application that we have just outlined.

which indicates fundamental Power, whereas light manifests Intelligence, and warmth Goodness.[6]

As for the reflection of the hypostatic ternary in the human being, we would say that the Intellect, which is the "eye of the heart" or the organ of direct knowledge, is projected into the individual soul by limiting and polarizing itself; it is then manifested under a triple aspect or, if one prefers, it is divided into three modes, namely intelligence, will, and sentiment. This means that the Intellect itself is at once cognitive, volitive, and affective in the sense that it comprises three dimensions, which refer respectively to the "Consciousness" (*Chit*), the "Being" (*Sat*), and the "Beatitude" (*Ānanda*) of the Principle (*Ātmā*).

The intelligence enables the understanding of God, the world, and man; the knowing subject is entirely determined by the object known or to be known; God appears *a priori* in the relationship of transcendence. The will in its turn enables, spiritually speaking, the movement towards God, hence above all contemplative concentration—on the basis of the conditions required, it goes without saying; here, it is the subject that predominates since, of necessity, God is in practice envisaged from the standpoint of immanence. In the third domain, that of the soul, man is reduced neither to the known object nor to the realizing subject, for this is the plane in which he and God are brought face to face; it is therefore the plane of devotion and faith, and of the humanly divine—or divinely human—dialogue between the person and his Creator.

It is worth pointing out here that, in knowledge, the subject is extinguished before the object: if this object is positive, it absorbs the subject, as it were, while extinguishing it, but if it is negative the extinction of the subject indicates simply the exactness of the perception. On the other hand, in contemplative and realizational concentration—which pertains to the will as regards the immediate operation—the human subject is unitively absorbed by the divine

---

[6] It is curious to note that in liturgical images of the sun, such as the monstrance or the framing of the monogram of Jesus, straight rays alternate with flames; this expresses the distinction between the "light" and the "warmth" of the divine Being.

Subject and at the same time this quite obviously entails an extinction before the latter.

The natural symbol of the trinity is provided by the three dimensions of space: when interpreted in connection with the human microcosm, height evokes intelligence, breadth sentiment, and depth will. For intelligence tends upwards, towards the essential and the transcendent; when it is perverted by error, it falls by contradicting its own nature. Sentiment, for its part, is ourselves in our existential totality, *hic et nunc*, and this is expressed by breadth, with a qualitative difference between the right and the left; in other words, sentiment, in the complete and profound meaning of the word we have in view here, represents the human person and the choice that he can make of his destiny. As for the will, it moves ahead as do our steps when walking; it penetrates into the future as our steps penetrate into the space before us, unless it moves backwards by opposing its own spiritual and eschatological vocation; in either case, there is a reference to the dimension of depth.

— ∴ —

When one wishes to explain metacosmic Reality by means of numeral *Hypostases*, one could stop without arbitrariness at the number three, because this number constitutes a limit that is all the more plausible in that it marks a withdrawal as it were into Unity; indeed, it expresses Unity in the language of plurality and seems to halt its unfolding. But one can with no less reason proceed further, as various traditional perspectives in fact do.

When considered from the principle of quaternity, the Essence comprises four qualities or functions, which are reflected on earth by North, South, East, and West. With the help of this analogical correspondence, it will be all the more easy to discern, in the Essence itself and consequently in a latent and undifferentiated state—where "all is in all"—but quite obviously as a potentiality of *Māyā*, the following four principles: firstly, Purity or Emptiness, Exclusivity; secondly, as the complementary opposite—symbolically the North-South axis—Goodness, Beauty, Life, or Intensity, Attraction; thirdly, Strength or Activity, Manifestation; and fourthly—this is the East-West axis—Peace, Equilibrium, or Passivity, Inclusivity, Receptivity. These principles are referred to in the Koran by the Names *Dhu'l-Jalāl, Dhu'l-Ikrām,*[7] *Al-Hayy, Al-Qayyūm*: the Possessor of Majesty, the Possessor of Generosity, the Living, the Immutable;[8] these Names could also be expressed by the following notions: inviolable Purity, overflowing Love, invincible Power, unalterable Serenity; or Truth, which is Rigor and Purity, Life, which is Gentleness and Love, Strength, which is active Perfection, and Peace, which is passive Perfection.

The image of quaternity is the square, and also the cross; the latter is dynamic, the former static.[9] Quaternity signifies stability or stabilization; when represented by the square, quaternity is a solidly established world, and a space that encloses; when represented by the cross, it is the stabilizing Law that proclaims itself to the four directions, thereby indicating its character of totality. The static quaternity is the Sanctuary, which offers security; the dynamic quaternity is the radiation of organizing Grace, which is both Law and Benediction.[10] All of this is prefigured in God: in an undifferentiated manner in the Essence and in a differentiated manner in Being.

When static, the Quaternity is intrinsic and in a certain fashion turned in on itself, and this is *Māyā* radiating as Infinitude within *Ātmā*; when dynamic, the Quaternity radiates, and this is *Māyā* in its

---

[7] Reunited in a single Name: *Dhu'l-Jalāli wa'l-Ikrām*, "Possessor of Majesty and Generosity" (*Sūrah* "The All-Merciful" [55]:78). The *Sunnah* records the two equivalent Names of *Jalīl*, "Majestic", and *Jamīl*, "Beautiful", whence these two fundamental divine aspects: *Jalāl*, "Majesty", and *Jamāl*, "Beauty", that is to say: Rigor and Gentleness.

[8] Or more precisely: He who subsists by Himself. In this context, "Passivity" means pure "Substantiality" and implies the ideas of Harmony and Peace; God is "passive" in the sense that He is infinitely in conformity with Himself, or with the Essence when it is Being that is in question.

[9] Logically, there might be a certain advantage in representing the dynamic quaternity by a square standing on one of its corners rather than by a cross since the central intersection of the cross already constitutes a fifth element; this would replace the sides of the square with corners, which would effectively indicate radiation as opposed to a contemplative turning inwards.

[10] This brings to mind, on the one hand, the Kaaba, the interior of which is a sanctuary protected by its walls, and thus enclosed and not open, and on the other hand, the call to prayer on the minarets, which is made towards the four directions of space. Moreover, whoever prays inside the Kaaba is no longer able to turn towards the center since he is there himself, and must therefore prostrate himself towards the four directions; this combines the static symbolism of the square with the dynamic symbolism of the cross.

function of conveying *Ātmā* and unfolding its potentialities; in this case, it establishes the cosmos according to the principles of totality and stability—this is the meaning of quaternity as such—and infuses into it the four qualities that it needs to subsist and to live;[11] and this is the meaning of the four Archangels who, emanating from the divine Spirit (*Rūh*) whose functions they represent, sustain and govern the world.

The Quaternity is but a development of the Duality *Ātmā-Māyā*, *Deva* and *Shakti*: the Divinity and its Power, both of internal Life and theophanic Radiation.

But the quaternity does not refer only to equilibrium, it also determines unfolding, and so time, or the cycles: there are the four seasons, the four parts of the day, the four ages of creatures and worlds. This unfolding cannot apply to the Principle, which is immutable; what it entails is a successive projection, in the cosmos, of the principial and consequently extra-temporal quaternity. The temporal quaternity has above all a cosmogonic meaning, and remains moreover in a crystallized state in the four great degrees of universal unfolding: the material world corresponding to winter, the vital world to autumn, the animic world to summer, and the spiritual world—angelic or paradisal—to spring; and this applies in the microcosm as well as in the macrocosm.[12]

The passage from trinity to quaternity is accomplished, if one may so put it, by the bipolarization of the summit of the triangle, which comprises virtually a duality due to its double origin; it is the passage from the triangle to the square. The trinity is, to take an example, the father, the mother, and the child; but the child cannot be neutral; it must necessarily be either male or female; whichever it is, logically it calls for the presence of the other. Analogously, the complementary opposition between North and South calls for an intermediate region which, by polarizing in its turn into two, gives rise to East and West, the latter in a certain manner participating in the North, the former in the South.

---

[11] The Heavenly Jerusalem corresponds to the square, being a city and a sanctuary; the earthly Paradise, with its four rivers, corresponds to the cross. The Islamic Paradise—the "Garden" (*Jannah*)—combines the two images: on the one hand it is a world and a sanctuary, and on the other hand four rivers spring from its center. Beatitude of security in the first case, and of radiation in the second.

[12] This hierarchy is that of the earthly kingdoms: mineral, vegetable, animal, human—the human species standing out from the animal kingdom by the Intellect.

This principial process of progression is repeated in the case of the quaternity, as it is repeated for the other numbers, *mutatis mutandis*: every quaternity is a virtual quinary and owes its character only to the fact that the center is so to speak projected into the four extremities: the quaternity is the center envisaged in its quaternary aspect. But it is enough to accentuate the center apart from its extension in order to obtain the quinquenary: thus, when one speaks of the four ages, the individual that undergoes them, is comprised in each age; and in the four seasons, the earth that undergoes them is also implied, otherwise the seasons, like the ages, would be abstractions.

— ⁘ —

The divine Quaternity is reflected in each of the three modes of the human microcosm: intelligence, will, sentiment; or consciousness that is intellective, volitive, and affective; or again, understanding, concentration, and conformity or virtue. In the place of sentiment, one could say simply "soul", for the reference here is to the human person as such, who by definition is loving; or more precisely, who is capable of including or excluding from his fundamental love the things that present themselves to his experience.

We have discerned in the divine nature the following four "cardinal points": Purity, Strength, Life, Peace; or Emptiness, which excludes, Activity, which manifests, Attraction, which reintegrates, and Equilibrium, which includes. Now, intelligence illuminated by truth—in keeping with its reason for being—comprises these poles given the fact that it is capable of abstraction, of discrimination, of assimilation or certitude, and of contemplation or serenity.

In connection still with intelligence, we must take account of yet another quaternity, whose constituent elements are to the four qualities just described what the intermediary regions are to the cardinal points: these elements are reason and intuition on the one hand, and imagination and memory on the other, corresponding respectively to the North-South and East-West axes. The reason enables, not intellection but cohesion, interpretation, ordering, and conclusion; intuition, its complementary opposite, enables immediate perception—albeit veiled and mostly approximate, on the plane of external and internal phenomena, because what is in question here is the mind and not the pure Intellect. As for imagination and memory, the first is prospective and enables invention, creation, and production to one degree or another; the second on the other hand is retrospective and enables conservation, rooting, empirical continuity. It might be added here that the quality associated with reason is justice, which is objective; that associated with imagination is vigilance, which is prospective; that associated with intuition is generosity, which is subjective; and that associated with memory is gratitude, which is retrospective.

Analogous things could be said concerning the two other planes of the microcosm, namely the will and sentiment, or the volitive soul and the affective soul if one prefers, but it is not our intention to push this analysis further, having presented it only by way of application and illustration.

— ·:· —

As for the Divinity seen from the aspect of the number five, it presents the characteristics of the Quaternity with the difference that the four functions are essentially considered in their connection with the center or the summit, in a sense that is either static and centripetal, or dynamic and centrifugal. If we take the example of the elements— earth, fire, air, water—they will be envisaged here, not in themselves, but as modalities of the central element, ether; or again, taking the example of the mental faculties—reason, intuition, imagination, memory—they will be considered either as tending contemplatively towards the Intellect, or as emanating operatively from it. As for the four directions of space, they also depend on a center, namely consciousness, which establishes the spatial relationships. These examples reflect a hypostatic situation that we shall not examine in detail given all that has been said previously.[13]

---

[13] In the mystical cosmology of the majority of the Indians of North America, the quinquenary results from the fact that man is situated at the center of the four cardinal points; on the one hand he observes them around him, he is their measure in a certain fashion, and on the other hand he contains them in himself, they are part of his substance. Speaking very schematically, the perspective of these Indians may be reduced to a vertical line divided into three superimposed planes of varying meaning, each plane comprising in its turn four poles, which correspond to the cardinal points, these being conceived either in a static or a dynamic manner; in the latter case one will picture a circular movement—sometimes centripetal—namely the "four winds", which fundamentally are the essential cosmic determinations.

The image corresponding to this number is the pentagram, with the apex above when it is a question of the static aspect turned towards the Essence, and with the apex below when, on the contrary, it is a question of the dynamic aspect and of the tendency towards manifestation. The image representing the number five can also be the cross, as mentioned earlier; the difference is that in the image of the cross, the center is even more implicit than in the pentagram, where it is exteriorized in a certain fashion, and from being center becomes apex; it is as though the heart had become brain. Furthermore, if the cross combines verticality and horizontality, the pentagram accentuates the distinction between highness and lowness: verticality in the cross becomes superiority in the pentagram, in such a manner that in the latter, the North-South axis is represented by the two upper corners, and the East-West axis by the two lower corners, the apex of the pentagram being equivalent to the center of the cross.

This indicates that the pentagram is indeed an image of man, but also, and *a priori*, an image of the divine Prototype. In this Prototype, the "right Hand" ("South": Gentleness) is open; the "left Hand" ("North": Rigor) is closed; the "right Foot" ("East": Activity) is approaching; the "left Foot" ("West": Passivity) is moving away. In man, the right hand—still in symbolic terms—accomplishes the good; the left hand avoids or prevents evil; the right foot approaches God; the left foot moves away from the world. More fundamentally, and giving the two passive perfections the positive meaning that they contain first and foremost—for "My Mercy taketh precedence over My Wrath"—we can say that the left Hand of God refers to Purity, and thus also to the purification of man, whereas his left Foot refers to Motionlessness—and the man who prays stands upright before God— and thus to Peace and also to patience and gratitude.

If the pentagram applies either to God or to man, it applies likewise, but in a new way, to the meeting of the human and the divine in the *Avatāra*; Islamic symbolism provides us with an explicit example of this, when it describes the mystery of the Prophet by means of the following five terms: the "Praised" (*Muhammad*); the "Servant" (*'Abd*); the "Messenger" (*Rasūl*); "Blessing" (*Salāt*); "Peace" (*Salām*). The qualities of "Servant" and "Messenger" pertain to the human nature of Muhammad: the "avataric" man is in perfect submission to God and thereby serves as the instrument of God; the Revelation of the divine presupposes the extinction of the human. On these two qualities or functions are superimposed two divine gifts, one that confers on the "Servant" the equilibrating, harmonious, and appeasing graces, and another that confers on the "Messenger" the lightning-like, illuminating, and vivifying graces—these two kinds of graces being, precisely, "Peace" and "Blessing".[14] The apex of the pentagram is the name Muhammad, which esoterically designates the *Logos* as "Muhammadan Light" (*Nūr muhammadī*); when the pentagram is inverted, the apex then being below, the same name designates the human and historical personality of the Prophet.[15] The synthesis of these five elements is crystallized in the appellation "Friend" (*Habīb*), which in fact implies the whole mystery of the *Avatāra*.

As for the number six, its image is either the seal of Solomon or the three-dimensional cross: North, South, East, West, Zenith, Nadir. In the seal of Solomon, the interpretation varies according to whether the accent is placed on the upper apex or the lower apex; in the latter case, it is the tendency towards manifestation that predominates.[16]

[14] These four notions constitute the fundamental landmarks of what might be called Muhammadan theology; every Muslim must bear witness that the Prophet is "Servant" (*'Abd*) and "Messenger" (*Rasūl*), and add to the name Muhammad, every time that it is pronounced, the wishes of "Blessing" and "Peace".

[15] In Shiism, the "five persons", namely the "family" (*āl*) of the Prophet, sum up the avataric quality and consequently manifest the divine Nature according to the number five: these are Muhammad, his daughter Fatima, his son-in-law Ali, and their sons Hasan and Husayn. Muhammad is at the apex of the pentagram; Fatima—who according to a *hadīth* had the perfume of Paradise between her breasts—is situated above on the left, for she incarnates passive Perfection; Ali, who incarnates active Perfection, is above on the right. In the lower part of the pentagram, Hasan is situated on the left, for he personifies holy patience; Husayn, who personifies holy combativeness, is below on the right. These "five persons" are sometimes compared to the five sense faculties and the five elements.

[16] The seal of Solomon obviously also symbolizes Duality from the particular standpoint of interpenetration, each of the two poles being in its own manner *Sat*, *Chit*, and *Ānanda*. Certain tantric *yantras* are based on this image, developing it in a variety of ways. It has been maintained, on the basis of a biblical symbolism—the seventh day of creation being that of the Creator—that the number six is that of imperfection; on the one hand, however, the number of the directions of space from the starting point of the center cannot be imperfect, and on the other hand, none of the simple or fundamental numbers can be reduced to a negative significance. The number six, being that of creation, is that of manifestation, completion, cosmic totality, and thus of productive *Māyā*.

The number six is that of total unfolding—whence the six days of creation—and by the same token it is the number of the *hypostases*.

As for the number seven, the corresponding image is once again the seal of Solomon, but including the central point; it is also the star of the six directions of space with, in addition, the consciousness that measures them; what the number five is to the number four, the number seven is to the number six. The difference is that, in the even numbers, the Essence is hypostatized in the poles involved, whereas in the odd numbers, it appears first and foremost as their principle, or as the center that determines them either by enjoying them from within, or by making them radiate outwards. In the first case, that of internal enjoyment, it is the element *Ātmā* or *Shiva* that predominates; in the second case, that of radiation, it is the element *Māyā* or *Shakti*.

We can conclude with this number seven, which is that of divine radiation, both centrifugal and centripetal, and thus of the projection of the Principle as well as of the return to it following unfolding;[17] the "seven Spirits of God", or the "Angels of the Face", on the one hand "stand ever ready to enter the presence of the Glory of the Lord", according to the Book of Tobit, but on the other hand are "sent forth into all the earth", according to the Apocalypse.[18] This denotes the divine *Māyā* that emerges from God and returns to Him, the return explaining the holiness of the seventh day.[19] The same thing is also expressed, to speak with Zacharias, by the "seven eyes of Jehovah", which look upon the world and which, we would add, close again upon the Essence.[20]

---

[17] According to a Hindu doctrine, a total cosmic cycle—a *kalpa*—comprises seven "descending" and seven "ascending" *manvantaras*; the manifesting phase is followed by a reintegrating phase.

[18] The "book sealed with seven seals" pertains to the same symbolism, with its double sense of occultation and revelation. In a completely different symbolic category as to the form, the "dance of the seven veils" also combines the number seven with the two phases of veiling and unveiling, which indicates its fundamental connection with the mystery of *Māyā*; each of the two phases being capable of having a positive or negative meaning, either in themselves or according to the points of view.

[19] The number seven being that of *Māyā*, there is nothing surprising in its having been taken to signify maternity. The seven joys and the seven sorrows of Mary express the maternal aspect as well as the ambiguity of *Māyā* or the *Shakti*; the ambiguity residing precisely in the opposition between the sorrows and the joys.

[20] The candlestick with seven branches in the Temple of Jerusalem is one of the most expressive liturgical representations of the Angels who abide before the Face of God; or before the Real Presence, the *Shekhinah*.

Each of the divine or hypostatic numbers is a veil that on the one hand hides Unity and on the other hand renders it explicit. Now, these veils, as we have said, cannot be counted, *Māyā* being indefinite by virtue of the Infinity that animates her, and which she manifests by a diversifying and inexhaustible unfolding.

— ⋰ —

This having been said, let us return to the number six insofar as it applies to the diversity—or unfolding—of the "dimensions" comprised in the divine nature. The following presentation of the aspects of the supreme Reality coincides in fact with the seal of Solomon: on the one hand, the Absolute, the Infinite, Perfection; on the other hand, Transcendence, Immanence, Manifestation. The Absolute may be likened to the geometrical point; the Infinite, its *Shakti*—or "Energy" if the Absolute is envisaged as "Substance"—may be likened to the line that extends the point, or to the cross or the star, since space is multi-dimensional;[21] Perfection, for its part, is like the circle, which on the one hand expands the point and on the other hand limits the cross. The series of concentric circles symbolizes the succession—at first ontological and later cosmological—of the planes of refraction of universal radiation; these are the receptacles—in some cases the worlds—into which the Absolute, prolonged by the Infinite, projects itself and in which in a certain fashion it is incarnated. The first of the circles marks the degree of the divine Qualities: God is perfect in His Qualities, whereas His Essence transcends this first polarization or this first relativity.

Then comes the second ternary, constituted by Transcendence, Immanence, and Manifestation: these *hypostases* are distinguished from those previously mentioned by the fact that they presuppose the world. Indeed, divine Reality can only be transcendent and immanent in relation to the world that it surpasses and at the same time penetrates; with all the more reason, it can only manifest itself in a world which, by definition, is already manifested. This last element, divine Manifestation or Theophany, is the direct reflection of the Principle in the cosmos—in the form of the various appearances of the *Logos*—and brings to a close the unfolding of the divine aspects or the *Hypostases*.

---

[21] The seal of Solomon represents the *hypostases* in a simply "topographical" and non-descriptive manner.

The Primordial Tree

Esoterically, the tree-symbol is the universal center offering the fruits of diverse possibilities; by its trunk, which is vertical, it suggests ascension and thereby also descent; by its branches, it serves as a ladder. The tree also provides shelter from the heat of the sun: it gives shade and thereby, through this aspect, it suggests the hearth, safety, rest, freshness; shade is one of the gifts enjoyed by the blessed in the Muslim Paradise.[1] But the most important aspects of the symbolism of the tree are without doubt its axial position and its fruits.

We are told in Genesis that at the center of the earthly Paradise grew the tree of Life, and it mentions another tree, that of the knowledge of Good and Evil, the fruit of which was forbidden to man. The central tree is that of synthetic or unitive knowledge, which consists in seeing accidents, or contingencies, in Substance or in relation to Substance. The forbidden tree is that of separative knowledge, which consists in seeing accidents apart from Substance and in forgetting Substance, as though accidents were autonomous substances, which amounts in practice to denying the one and only Substance; this was the sin of the first human couple. Now, for a voluntaristic and penitential perspective, which sees evil above all in the passions of the flesh, it is very tempting to see the Fall in the sexual act; in reality, the cause of the Fall cannot reside in a positive law of nature, but resides exclusively in the fact of detaching natural goods from their divine Source, of experiencing them outside God, and of attributing to oneself their glory and their enjoyment. The sin of Adam and Eve was finally not so much a specific outward action as the act of placing themselves outside the divine Center: of isolating—in the act of knowing or of willing—both subject and object, and thus in practice of cutting them

---

[1] For birds and squirrels, the tree is a nourishing abode as well as a sort of paradise; the latter symbolism results especially from the tiers formed by the branches, and from the crown opening onto the infinite. The origin of the Christmas tree is unknown—of Germanic origin, it would seem that it does not go back beyond the seventeenth century—but it is in any case inspired by various prototypes—from Indo-European Antiquity—whose function was to inaugurate the seasons, and thus the phases of a cycle. The evergreen nature of the fir-tree indicates moreover a victory over winter, and thereby immortality.

off, albeit illusorily so, from God, who in the last analysis is the sole Subject and the sole Object; in so doing, the first human couple necessarily committed a principial act of disobedience.[2]

The theological interpretations of the forbidden tree are not always conclusive: thus, to recognize that the first man necessarily possessed moral discernment, and then to assert that original sin was a usurpation of the faculty—reserved for God—of deciding what is good or evil, is contradictory to say the least. For if Adam had moral discernment, he thereby had the faculty of applying it; and the formulation "deciding for himself what is good or evil" does not make sense, unless it indicates the wish to go against discernment; in which case there is violation of a human faculty and not usurpation of a divine privilege. Moreover, to say that by deciding what is good or evil man puts himself in the place of God is to insinuate that good and evil result from a divine decision, namely from a verdict whose causes may elude our understanding, and not from objective qualities or circumstances; this is an opinion reminiscent of some of the excesses of Asharite theology. Clearly, moral evaluation, whether its scope is extrinsic or intrinsic, circumstantial or essential,[3] has nothing arbitrary about it: evil is whatever is opposed to God,[4] whether by its nature or on the plane of its manifestation, or it is whatever *de facto* is harmful to man, the higher interest always taking precedence over the lower. Let us recall in this connection, although the point is self-evident, that an objective good may be subjectively an evil for a particular individual or a certain category of men, and inversely; for reasons of expediency, codified and simplifying morality finds it easier to accept

---

[2] According to the *Theologia Germanica*, "sin is none other than this: that the creature turns itself away from the immutable Good and turns itself towards the changing good"; Adam fell "because he claimed something for himself. . . . If he had eaten seven apples, without having ever claimed something for himself, he would not have fallen." The apple was forbidden precisely because it coincided for Adam with the desire for a good "for myself"; this amounts to saying that the cosmic "sin" is the *principium individuationis*.

[3] It is particularly important to distinguish between rules of conduct and virtues.

[4] Nothing can be opposed to God absolutely since nothing existent escapes from divine Possibility; consequently, apparent opposition is only symbolic and transitory, though nonetheless real on the plane of its relativity, which is yet another example of what we have more than once termed—paradoxically but unavoidably—the "relative absolute".

the second point of view than the first, in the sense that it readily calls "evil" every good that is morally or socially inopportune.

— ⋅⋮⋅ —

What then is the meaning in Genesis of the idea that the knowledge of Good and Evil is the privilege of God? It means that God alone can will all that He desires, because God alone is the Sovereign Good and for this reason He can only will the good;[5] only the absolute Good has the right to absolute Freedom, and only the absolute Good possesses it, which amounts to saying that it possesses Freedom by definition. In what sense was the sin of the first human couple a usurpation of a divine privilege? In the sense that, by eating the forbidden fruit, this couple acted as if it were the Sovereign Good, to which every possibility is ontologically allowed; in other words, Adam and Eve attributed to the relative the rights of the Absolute. Positively, the tree of the knowledge of Good and Evil is All-Possibility considered as divine Freedom; negatively or restrictively, it is this Possibility which, in unfolding itself in Existence—thus as it were in a downward direction—necessarily moves away from the divine Source.

In this latter respect, the tree of the distinction between Good and Evil denotes "impure" *Māyā*, that which descends and disperses and at the same time gives rise to density and heaviness; this is cosmic Possibility, but in its inferior and centrifugal aspect. Therefore it is not without reason that this tree should be the abode of the serpent as instigator of the Fall: indeed, the serpent represents, in its negative symbolism, the Luciferian and tenebrous mode of the demiurgic tendency; thus it had to be present in the primordial Paradise as the virtuality of evil, given that Eden is in fact situated on the path of cosmogonic expansion. The heavenly Garden, on the other hand, is situated on the path of return and prefigures in its fashion the *Apocatastasis*; in it, consequently, the centrifugal tendency is neutralized, being static and not dynamic; it determines the existential limitations within Beatitude, but it cannot break the framework of the latter. The earthly Paradise

---

[5] Ashari understood this very well, but expressed it rather poorly—and pushed it to the point of absurdity—by maintaining that an injustice on the part of God, were it possible, would be justice.

was situated in the corruptible dimension; the heavenly Paradise, on the contrary, is beyond this dimension, being relative without being unstable; it lives by the incorruptible Light stemming from the nearness of God. The descending Paradise hinges as it were on human freedom, whereas the ascending Paradise is founded on divine Grace alone.

— ⋮ —

When God seems to do what would be evil were it done by man, He compensates for this by a greater good, much as the cure compensates for the bitterness of the medicine; this necessarily results from the fact that God is the absolute Good and therefore contains in His nature a compensatory quality that excludes evil as such. But man, not being necessary Being, is by definition contingent, and being contingent, he does not benefit from the compensatory nature that results from Absoluity or Infinity; the evil that man does is not a virtuality of good, it is an evil pure and simple, because the human agent is a fragment and not a totality, an accident and not a substance.

We might also say that the Creator—given His unique and inimitable nature—essentially has the right to a separative and descending vision of possibilities, because this vision does not go outside the divine Subject; for God is Unity and Totality, everything subsists in Him, and He cannot therefore sin by stepping outside Himself as does man, whose existence is limited to an individuality and whose act affects existences other than his own. Man, who must contemplate God in his heart, cannot *a priori* have the right to a separative, descending, and creative vision, for this vision takes him outside himself and separates him from God; but once this separative vision has been acquired—through a paradoxical Providence—man must subordinate his works to divine inspiration.

Man can only be free in God and through God, for, unlike God, he does not have his center within himself, except in a relative sense and by indirect participation, otherwise he would not be man. There is thus a point within man where he must freely renounce his freedom; being made in the image of God, he must at the same time recognize that he is not God, and he must do so on the very basis of his deiformity, that is, by virtue of this total intelligence which, being total, is capable of objectivity.

—— ·÷· ——

Exoterically speaking, God "allows" evil in view of a greater good, and this is incontestable though not in itself sufficient, for an "omnipotent" God could *a priori* do away with the necessity to allow evil simply by abolishing evil, no less. The esoteric solution is of an altogether different order: that is to say, from the point of view of divine Subjectivity the Will that wills evil is not the same as the one that wills good; from the point of view of the cosmic object, God does not will evil as evil, He wills it as a constituent element of a good, hence as a good. Moreover, evil is never such by its existential substance, by definition willed by God; it is such only through the cosmic accident of being a privation of a good, a privation willed by God as an indirect element of a greater good. If the reproach is made that we are introducing a duality into God, we admit it without hesitation—but not as a reproach—just as we admit all the various differentiations within the Divinity, whether it be a question of hypostatic degrees or qualities or energies; the very existence of polytheism is justification enough for this, if one disregards the aspect of deviation or paganization that it may sometimes assume.[6]

At all events, it is important to distinguish between the divine Will with regard to existence, and the divine Will with regard to man who is intelligence and will: in the first case, everything that exists or happens is willed by God; in the second case, only the truth and the good are divinely willed.

Concerning Omnipotence, it is worth specifying once again that it extends to everything that is situated in the order of contingencies as such, but not to those things pertaining to the play of principles rooted in the divine nature, whether directly or by way of consequence; God could never have the power of being other than He is, nor of making possible what is ontologically absurd.[7]

[6] Original polytheism envisages the Divinity both as *Ātmā* and through *Māyā*; it is pagan only from the moment that it forgets *Ātmā* and attributes absoluty to diversity, and thus to relativity.

[7] To bring the dead to life or to create the appearance of a sun that comes towards us and whirls round is not ontologically absurd, as would be the possibility of being God without "creating the world", or of creating the world without "allowing evil". To speak of the Absolute is to speak of radiation, and thus of relativity, and to speak of relativity is to speak of a movement away from the Absolute, and hence the possibility of evil.

— ⁙ —

In loving each other, Adam and Eve loved God; they could neither love nor know outside of God. After the Fall, they loved each other outside of God and for themselves, and they knew each other as separate phenomena and not as theophanies; this new kind of love was concupiscence, and this new kind of knowledge was profanity. On the one hand, man henceforth looked on things in their isolated and plain phenomenality, and on the other hand, he had become insatiable; he had become *homo faber*, a maker and producer; nevertheless he still worked under divine inspiration—there are no primordial inventions—for he had been reconciled with God; invention properly so-called was reserved for later phases of the Fall.[8] The danger of promethean or titanic productivity explains, moreover, the prohibition of images among the monotheistic Semites, nomadic in origin, who tend to keep man in a kind of unproductiveness bordering on primordial simplicity; the biblical symbols of the "sin of creating" are the Tower of Babel and the golden calf.[9]

"And they saw that they were naked": their intelligence and their will, and likewise their way of feeling, had become exteriorized, and their love had thereby become detached from the divine essence of things and transmuted into concupiscence; as reflections of the divine Sun on the water of Existence, they had taken themselves for the Sun itself, forgetting that they were but reflections, and they were ashamed of the humiliating consequences of this error. If in the Biblical and Koranic symbolism the sexual parts evoke shame and humiliation, it is because they remind man of blind and God-fleeing passion that is unworthy of man because it robs him of his intelligence and his will; but it goes without saying that this moral perspective does not represent the whole truth and that the positive symbolism of *nuditas sacra* is much more profound: on the one hand, it evokes the semidivinity of primordial man, and on the other hand, it seeks to draw

[8] Such as so-called classical Antiquity, the Renaissance, and the nineteenth century.

[9] From the point of view of peoples who traditionally practice the plastic arts, the Divine *Artifex* places itself in the human subject, so that it is God who acts through man and who creates or produces the work; the product resulting from this will thus have an interiorizing virtue, not an exteriorizing one as it does in specifically "idolatrous" or profane art.

us away from accidentality, which is diverse and outward, towards substantiality, which is simple and inward. Moreover, the Bible does not reproach Adam and Eve for their nakedness; it records that they looked upon it with shame, but this refers to the Fall and not to nudity as such.[10]

The tree of the knowledge of Good and Evil represents the manifesting or cosmogonic, and thus exteriorizing, Power, along with the isolating and contrasting knowledge required by exteriorization. The tree of Life, on the contrary, represents the reintegrating, and thus interiorizing, Power, along with the participative or unitive knowledge required by interiorization.

This is why the first men, if they could have eaten the fruit of the tree of Life after eating the fruit of the tree of Good and Evil, would have risen to the summit of the angelic hierarchy, by usurpation and not by right; but this is a mere figure of speech, for such a usurpation was in fact impossible, something Genesis expresses by placing cherubim armed with swords at the gateway of Paradise.[11]

The tree of Life and the tree of the knowledge of Good and Evil could well be the same tree —as their central position would indicate—but viewed from opposite sides; this interpretation would bring us to the symbolism of Janus and also to the Islamic idea of the *barzakh*, the "intermediary region" separating the ontological and cosmic degrees.[12] The Hindu idea of *Māyā* is analogous in the sense that Rela-

---

[10] According to Islam, clothing is a divine revelation, and this accords with the biblical story; but the Koran adds: "and the clothing of the fear of God is better" (*Sūrah* "The Heights" [7]:26), meaning that awareness of the Divine is a better protection than clothing against deifugal concupiscence, an idea that evokes the principle of sacred nudity, of which all religions, moreover, provide at least some examples.

[11] These cherubim, we carry them within ourselves, in the depth of our heart and at the gateway of the immanent Paradise, and this is why profane pseudo-spiritual experimentation cannot yield the slightest real result, but on the contrary can only intensify darkness and illusion.

[12] "... Then there will separate them a wall (*sūr* = *barzakh*) wherein is a gate, the inner side whereof containeth Mercy, while the outer side thereof is toward the Doom" (*Sūrah* "Iron" [57]:13).

tivity, which *a priori* is one, comprises two dimensions, one higher and one lower, and comprises in addition a power that is descending and productive and another that is ascending and liberating.[13]

The Fall can be interpreted at different levels: thus, it is not illegitimate to believe that it can symbolize the entry into matter, namely the cosmogonic passage from the animic state to the material state; one may equally well believe—always with obvious reservations—that the creation of Eve symbolizes this passage,[14] or again, that the Fall represents a later and negative stage of this passage. But this is not the original intention of Genesis, which begins indeed with the creation of the material world, and which then—in the second chapter[15]—tells of man's degeneration, which was to cause the deterioration of matter and of all the living species found in this state.

Plato has been reproached for having had too negative a conception of matter; but, regarding this, we overlook that there are two movements in his thinking:[16] the first refers to fallen matter, and the second to matter in itself and in its capacity as a support for the spirit. For matter, like the animic substance that precedes it, is a reflection of *Māyā*: consequently it comprises a theomorphic and ascending aspect and a deifugal and descending aspect; and just as there was the fall of Lucifer—without which there would not have been a serpent in the

---

[13] Plotinus divides *Māyā* into *Nous*, Intellect, and *Psyche*, Soul; the latter, he says, "escapes like a disobedient child" and plunges into the adventure of matter. In other words, the process of moving away produces *ipso facto* a phenomenon of separation (Lucifer) and, in the last analysis, of inversion (Satan), and this, in biblical symbolism, is the serpent in Paradise, which marks the final phase of the cosmogonic trajectory.

[14] In this case, Adam is the primordial androgyne, who in fact is conceivable only in the animic state.

[15] In the Bible, there are not two divergent "layers", one "Elohist" and the other "Jehovist"; there is only diversity of point of view or accent, as in all sacred Scripture.

[16] By "thinking" we do not mean an artificial elaboration but rather the mental crystallization of real knowledge. This may not be to the liking of anti-Platonic theologians, but Platonism is not true because it is logical, it is logical because it is true; as for the possible or apparent illogicalities of the various theologies, these can be explained not by an alleged right of the mysteries to absurdity, but by the fragmentary character of particular dogmatic positions and also by the insufficiency of the means of thought and expression. We may recall in this connection the alternativism and the sublimism typical of the Semitic mentality, as well as the absence of the crucial notion of *Māyā*—at least at the ordinary theological level, meaning by this reservation that the boundaries of theology are not strictly delimited.

earthly Paradise—so also there was the fall of man. For Plato, matter—or the sensible world—is bad insofar as it is opposed to spirit, and in this respect only; and it does in fact oppose the spirit—or the world of Ideas—by its hardened and compressive nature, which is ponderous as well as dividing, without forgetting its corruptibility as regards life. But matter is good with respect to the inherence in it of the world of Ideas: the cosmos, including its material limit, is the manifestation of the Sovereign Good, and matter demonstrates this by its quality of stability, by the purity and nobility of certain of its modes, and by its symbolist plasticity, in short by its inviolable capacity to serve as a receptacle for influences from Heaven. As a distant reflection of universal *Māyā*, matter is thereby like a prolongation of the Throne of God, a truth that a "spirituality" obsessed by the cursing of the earth has too readily lost sight of, at the price of a prodigious impoverishment and a dangerous disequilibrium; and yet this same spirituality was aware of the principial and virtual sanctity of the body, which *a priori* is "image of God" and *a posteriori* an element of "glory". But the fullest refutation of all Manicheism is provided by the body of the *Avatāra*, which is capable in principle of ascending to Heaven—by "transfiguration"—without having to pass through that effect of the "forbidden fruit" which is death, and which shows by its sacred character that matter is fundamentally a projection of the Spirit.[17] Like every contingent substance, matter is a mode of radiation of the divine Substance; no doubt a partially corruptible mode, as regards the existential level, but inviolable in its essence.[18]

Just as the virtuality of evil was present in the soul of the first man, so material corruption existed virtually in his paradisal and incorruptible body; this body could not become corrupt in its normal state, but the actualization of evil in the soul caused the four sensible elements to emerge from their ethereal homogeneity, which was that of the Edenic body; this is what the Kabbalah teaches. The soul having abandoned, in its deifugal movement, the contemplation of the One, the four bodily elements in their turn, and by repercussion, departed

---

[17] The "Night Journey" (*isrā'*, *mi'rāj*) of the Prophet has the same significance.

[18] Moreover, the biblical narrative regarding the creation of the material world implies symbolically the description of the whole cosmogony, hence that of all the worlds, and even that of the eternal archetypes of the cosmos; traditional exegesis, notably that of the Kabbalists, bears witness to this.

from their primordial unity, the *quinta essentia* or Ether: they became dissociated and opposed to one another, while reuniting in the end on a lower level in order to compose the corruptible body of fallen man, who henceforth contained his incorruptible body as a pure virtuality. Thus the Edenic body has not completely disappeared, but is like a "kernel of immortality" deeply hidden under its corruptible shell; our actual body is corruptible because it is composed of four elements and because every composed thing is, by definition, fated to decompose.

Bodies in the celestial state are also composite, but being immortal, they "decompose", not at death, but at the *apocatastasis*; moreover, the verb used here, in keeping with this analogy, is inappropriate, for it is a question of a positive and glorious reabsorption into the divine Substance, and not a destruction. This Substance alone is absolutely simple, and thus eternal in an absolute sense; the relative eternity—if it may be so expressed—of the paradisal worlds opens, without destruction and by reintegration, onto divine Eternity.

The most serious consequence of the Fall is not the degeneration of primordial matter, and consequently both its contradictory and corruptible character, but the closing of the "eye of the Heart" or the loss of inward Revelation, and so of the integrity of the Intellect, whence also the loss of the "state of grace" and the corruption of the soul. The inward and permanent Revelation is always there, for it coincides with our kernel of immortality, but it is buried under a layer of ice, which requires the intervention of outward Revelations; but these cannot have the perfection of what could be termed the "innate Religion" or the immanent *Philosophia Perennis*. Esoterism, by definition, takes this situation into account; although heretics and profane philosophers are often conscious of it in their fragmentary fashion, they are obviously unwilling to understand that religions in fact furnish the indispensable keys for the pure and universal Truth. This may seem a paradoxical thing for us to say, but each religious world not only renews in its fashion the lost Paradise, but also bears in one way or another the marks of the Fall, from which only the supra-formal Truth is unscathed; and this inward Truth, we must repeat, is inaccessible *de facto* without the assistance of its outward, objective, and prophetic manifestations.

The layer of ice that isolates individual consciousness from immanent sanctity not only covers the flood of light that is Intellection, but thereby also covers the flood of Love or Beatitude, which also is inseparable from our immortal substance. Depending on the nature of the obstacles, this ice must either be broken by violence, or melted by gentleness: it is broken by means of Fear and melted by means of Love; but it also yields, and even *a fortiori*, from the effect of Knowledge, which dispels illusion by means of an acute awareness of the nature of things, namely through the effect of pure objectivity.

The loss of the inward Revelation, or of the eye of the Heart, indicates that Eden was lost as the result of a sin of outwardness or exteriorization, as we have already mentioned; for the loss of Inwardness and its Peace is proof of an illegitimate movement towards outwardness and a fall into passion. Eve and Adam yielded to the temptation of "cosmic curiosity", that is to say they wanted to know and to taste, outside God and independently of the inward Light, the things of the outward world; instead of being content with the simple, synthetic, and symbolist vision of things, they sank into a perception of things that was both explorative and concupiscent, thus engaging in a path without end and with no way out, which moreover is like the inverted reflection of inward Infinity. This is the path of exile, suffering, and death; all errors and all sins retrace the first transgression and lead to this same path, which is incessantly renewed. The sin of the spirit or the will always reflects the first fault, whereas Religion or Wisdom on the contrary reflects and renews the lost Paradise within that very world of dissonances that issued forth from the forbidden fruit.

Yet the passage from primordial innocence to the "knowledge of good and evil" and to the experience of centrifugal possibilities is not always presented as a first sin and a fall; according to various mythologies, man was in fact destined *a priori* to this full development of his personality represented by the entry into the world of oppositional and moving contingency; it was necessary that he be the witness, in the name of God, of the vicissitudes of cosmic outwardness.[19]

---

[19] What in the Bible is presented as a fall, appears elsewhere as a simple change of state: for the Omaha Indians, "Men, at the origin, were in the water; they opened their eyes but saw nothing. . . . Coming out of the water they saw the day. . . . They were naked without being ashamed. But after many days they desired to cover themselves. . ." (Fletcher and La Flesche, *The Omaha Tribe*, Lincoln, 1972). Water here indicates a subtler state, as well as a state of blissful ignorance as regards the outward and centrifugal unfolding of the possibilities of *Māyā*.

From this point of view, the *felix culpa* of Saint Augustine can be explained and justified, not by the lone salvific advent of Christ, but by the necessity of the full development of the human being; Christ and the Virgin—new Adam and new Eve—appear then, less as an unforeseen compensation than as a proof of this paradoxical necessity of human possibility: the necessity to fall in order to be able to carry the consciousness of God to the outermost limits of what is humanly possible.

PART II

SPIRITUAL & MORAL LIFE

The Triple Nature of Man

Human intelligence is essentially objective, hence total: it is capable of disinterested judgment, reasoning, assimilating and deifying meditation, with the help of grace. This attribute of objectivity also belongs to the will—it is this attribute that makes it human—and this is why our will is free, in other words capable of self-transcendence, sacrifice, and ascesis; our willing is not inspired by our desires alone, fundamentally it is inspired by the truth, which is separate from our immediate interests. Likewise for our soul, our sensibility, and our capacity for loving: this capacity, being human, is by definition objective and thus disinterested in its essence or in its primordial and innocent perfection; it is capable of goodness, generosity, compassion. This means that it is capable of finding its happiness in the happiness of others, and to the detriment of its own satisfactions; likewise, it is capable of finding its happiness above itself, in its celestial personality, which is not yet completely its own. It is from this specific nature, made of totality and objectivity, that the vocation of man derives, together with his rights and his duties.

To say that the prerogative of the human state is the capacity to be objective, amounts to recognizing that the quintessential content and the ultimate purpose of this capacity is the Absolute: for the intelligence is objective to the extent that it records not only that which is, but also all that is. An intelligence that refuses to admit the Absolute does not take into account the total Reality to which it is proportioned; it is no longer human, yet not capable of being animal since in fact it is the intelligence of man, it has no other choice than to be satanic. As for the will, it is objective insofar as it aims for not only a realizable and useful end or a real good, but also and even above all for the Sovereign Good, and inasmuch as it aims for things in their connection, near or distant, with this Good. And the soul is objective insofar as it loves that which is worthy of being loved, the transcendent essence of which is the divine Beauty and the divine Love.

The human subject necessarily seeks the contingent because it is itself contingent, and to the extent that it is so; and it seeks the Absolute because it derives from the Absolute precisely by its capacity for objectivity, and because this capacity reveals to it that every positive reality belongs to the Absolute, and thus everything that we term a good.

Clearly, objectivity is nothing else than the truth, in which subject and object coincide as far as is possible, and in which the essential takes precedence over the accidental—or the necessary over the contingent—either by extinguishing it in some fashion, or, on the contrary, by reintegrating it, according to the various ontological aspects of relativity itself.

It has been said that man is a rational animal, an expression which, though inadequate and ill-sounding, nevertheless suggests in an elliptical fashion an undeniable truth: indeed, the rational faculty indicates the transcendence of man with respect to animals. Man is rational because he possesses the Intellect, which by definition is capable of the absolute and consequently of the sense of the relative as such; and he possesses the Intellect because he is made "in the image of God", which he shows moreover—it is hardly necessary to be reminded of this—by his physical form, by the gift of speech, and by his capacity to produce and construct. Man is a theophany, by his form as well as by his faculties; to deny this is an indirect way of denying God. Without an opening towards transcendence, human intelligence would be a luxury as inexplicable as it would be useless.

The soul loves beauty, and it is thereby constrained to virtue, which is the beauty and happiness of the soul; beauty, and the love of beauty, give the soul the happiness to which it aspires by its nature. The soul loves beauty, desires happiness, and practices goodness; to say that the soul is fundamentally happy only through beauty, amounts to saying that it is happy only in virtue.

Sensible beauties are situated outside the soul, and their encounter with it is more or less accidental; if the soul wishes to be happy in an unconditional and permanent fashion, it must carry the beautiful within itself. Now, this inward beauty is nothing else than the consciousness of the Source of all harmony; it is the sense of the sacred and also faith, the "yes" of the soul in meeting God. From this inward source spring the virtues, which convey the beauty of the soul and, more fundamentally, that of the Sovereign Good.

Virtue is this message of beauty that is goodness. Outwardly, however, goodness takes on different modes depending on the situation: sometimes it must become adamantine, and sometimes, on the contrary, lightning-swift upon contact with whatever opposes it; but it is always goodness that is clothed in these veils. Good combats evil, not by ceasing to be the good, but because it is good.

Virtue consists in allowing free passage, in the soul, to the Beauty of God.

———— ·:· ————

Sat, Chit, Ānanda: Being, Consciousness, Bliss. Being, and therefore Power; Consciousness, and therefore Wisdom; Bliss, and therefore Beauty. To this divine ternary corresponds, in the human microcosm, the ternary will, intelligence, sentiment; or activity, knowledge, love.

This doctrine of the three human dimensions could be expressed in a quite simple and immediately plausible way as follows: the good that man is capable of knowing he must also will insofar as this good can be the object of the will; in addition, he must love this good, and at the same time love the knowledge of it as well as the will towards it; just as he must will and love the earthly and contingent reflections of this good according to what is required or allowed by their nature. One cannot devote oneself to knowledge without loving it and willing it, any more than one can will something without knowing it and without loving its realization; and one cannot love without knowing an object or without wishing to love it. This interdependence shows that the immortal soul is one and that its modes have one and the same significance, that of manifesting God while realizing Him.

There can be no knowledge of God without a knowledge of the eschatological truths; there is no willing God without willing the good things that bring us close to God and rejecting the evils that separate us from Him; and there can be no love of God without love for one's neighbor, and without love of whatever bears witness to God and brings us close to Him, within ourselves as well as around us.

———— ·:· ————

Man can know, will, and love; and to will is to act. We know God by distinguishing Him from whatever is not Him and by recognizing Him in whatever bears witness to Him; we will God by accomplishing whatever leads us to Him and by abstaining from whatever removes us from Him; and we love God by loving to know and to will Him, and by loving whatever bears witness to Him, around us as well as within us.

To these three elements correspond respectively understanding, which is intellective, concentration, which is volitive, and conformity, which is affective; now, what distinguishes affective conformity is that, on the one hand, it binds itself both to will and to intelligence by as it were amplifying them,[1] and, on the other hand, when taken alone, it is inspired by those two sister-faculties. The result of this situation is that the third element, whether we call it conformity, love, or sentiment, comprises two poles: faith, which refers to intelligence and knowledge, and virtue, which refers to will and practice; nevertheless, neither of these two elements can be reduced either to the intelligence or the will, given precisely that both of them—virtue as well as faith—have as their substance our living soul, and not some particular faculty.

In a certain sense, man's virtue responds to the divine quality that enables him to live and showers him with blessings, and man's faith responds to the divine quality that saves and liberates him.

But let us return to the intelligence and the will: symbolically speaking the first pertains to the brain, and the second to the heart; this complementarity has its basis in the fact that the mind opens itself to the object that presents itself to discernment, whereas the heart is identified with the subject that enables volition; however the mind is merely the organ of recording and formulation, and also of rational fumbling and searching, but not of intellection, whose seat is the subtle center of which the heart is the vital manifestation. This center—the Intellect—is the source at one and the same time of discernment, will, and love.[2]

In Islamic terms, the divine roots of the spiritual dimensions of man are the *hypostases* of "Power" (*Qudrah*), "Wisdom" (*Hikmah*), and "Clemency" (*Rahmah*), the last being bipolarized into the two

---

[1] Thus, the sentiments of certitude and serenity, for example, amplify intellectual operations, just as the sentiment of decision and that of satisfaction or appeasement amplify the operations of the will.

[2] Pure intellection is independent of will and sentiment; and likewise, pure volition and pure sentiment are sufficient unto themselves. Nevertheless, it is impossible to think without willing to do so and without finding some satisfaction in it, just as it is impossible to will something without thinking—unless it be a question of a sudden intuition or a reflex—and so on.

divine Names: "the infinitely Good in Himself" (*Rahmān*) and the "infinitely Merciful" (*Rahīm*). We can interpret these Names by saying that "Beauty", which is intrinsic, and "Goodness", which is extrinsic, constitute "Beatitude" (*Rahmah*, the equivalent of the Vedantic *Ānanda*).[3]

— ⁖ —

The third dimension of man, as we have said, is love, or conformity of soul; or what amounts to the same thing, faith and virtue. We could also add to these elements another discipline, although it is secondary, namely that of our surroundings: by this we mean the frequenting of men of ascending tendency—this is the Hindu *satsanga*—and also, in a wider sense, the search for a congenial setting, and this brings us to the field of liturgy, sacred art, traditional craftsmanship, and the role of nature, in short to the problem—if problem there be—of the function of appearances that are directly or indirectly theophanic. To repeat, all this pertains to the principle of *satsanga*, namely "associating with saints", and also to that of *darshan*, "contemplation", either of a saint or of the sacred in all its forms; the sense of the sacred being the sap of both virtue and faith.

Leaving aside now this more or less extrinsic dimension—even accidental when compared with the conditions *sine qua non* of spirituality—the spiritual functions could be summed up in the following terms: discernment, union, faith, virtue. Discernment covers the range from metaphysical principles to earthly things: the "discernment of spirits" is incumbent on all men; and even on the most contingent of planes, both our intelligence and the nature of things make discrimination unavoidable whether in the intuitive and direct form proper to intellection, or in the discursive and indirect form proper to reasoning, as the case may be.

The application of the will to the spiritual way culminates in contemplative concentration, or in the practice that supports this, namely

---

[3] In analogical terms, the invincible substance of the sun is *Qudrah*, "Power"; its perfect form is *Hikmah*, "Wisdom"; its radiance is *Rahmah*, "Beatitude". And within this radiance, light is *Rahmān*, "Beauty", whereas heat is *Rahīm*, "Goodness". This interpretation of the terms *Rahmah*, *Rahmān*, and *Rahīm* conveys the intention of the hypostatic constellation.

prayer in all its forms or meditation, in short the "remembrance of God"; this is why this supreme function of the will may be termed "union", although it is not a question of a union of grace, such as ecstasy or the station of unity. Whereas the summit of contemplative concentration is identified with the intrinsic will—in the sense that the will, in this application, is united to its immanent source—at a lower level, namely outside of its central function, the will of necessity applies itself to a thousand things that contribute to advancing us towards our end, be it only by contributing to equilibrium without which it is impossible to take wing.

If a man seeks to realize that which transcends him immensely in fact, he must *a priori* be in conformity with this end or this model, otherwise he will fail either simply by collapsing, or else by being broken; and this conformity, which is like an anticipation of realization *hic et nunc*, is faith combined with virtue, the one being inseparable from the other. Faith is a "yes" from our entire soul to the Divinity and to divine things, and if this "yes" is sincere, it will produce, develop, or stabilize virtue; "be ye therefore perfect, even as your Father in Heaven is perfect". We could also say that the soul is made of love and that this substance coincides with faith, for love in itself is the love of God; and as the good tends to impart itself—quasi-ontologically—the radiation of faith is the totality of the attitudes that manifest beauty of soul and which culminate in generosity.

The function of the intelligence, whether we call it knowledge, understanding, or something else, comprises a passive mode, which is contemplative, and an active mode, which is discriminative. The intelligence cannot but be passive with respect to the divine Object that determines it, but it is active when it discerns the relative from the Absolute and proceeds to all the other distinctions that result from this initial distinction; without forgetting that this activity is that of the divine Intellect within us; our certitude is the trace of this immanence.

Will or activity, considered in relation to its loftiest object, is synonymous with spiritual concentration, which in the last analysis refers to the mystery of identity; now, this concentration is either efficient, in the present, or latent, in duration. In other words, this realizing and unitive concentration must in itself be perfect or total—it must be everything that its nature requires— but it must also be persevering, for perfection in the moment would be inoperative without its fixation in time, hence without the reduction of duration to the instant of God.

Sentiment or love, or the conformity of our person and thus of our sensibility to the divine Reality that both determines us and attracts us, is either inward or outward, devotional or generous; it is faith, devotion, or piety with regard to God, and virtue, moral beauty, generosity with regard to other creatures. In faith, resignation is combined with fervor; and in virtue, patience is combined with generosity.

One could also say that to know God is to see Him "here" and "everywhere": to see Him in Himself and in His manifestations. In an analogous manner, one could say that to will God, that is, to act in accordance with Him and for Him, is to will God "now" and "always": in the act, which coincides with the present, and in the disposition, which guarantees duration and enables us to reduce it to the present. And likewise in the case of the sensible soul: to love God is to love Him "solely" and "totally", to love Him more than creatures, but at the same time to love creatures in Him.

— ·:· —

In seeking particularly adequate or suggestive terms to designate the spiritual dimensions of man, we could propose the following quaternity: objectivity, inwardness, faith, and virtue.

Objectivity is the perfect adaptation of the intelligence to objective reality; and inwardness is the persevering concentration of the will on that "Inward" which, according to Christ, coincides with the heart, whose door it is fitting to lock upon having entered, and which opens onto the "Kingdom of God", which in fact is "within you".

And this on a foundation of faith and virtue, of intensity and radiance, without which man, in the eyes of God, would not be man.

— ·:· —

Given that the divine Principle is tri-polarized into Being-Power, Consciousness-Wisdom, and Beatitude-Mercy, one might ask what the hierarchical relationship is between these three *hypostases*. Without falling into an unrealistic schematization, we would say that there are sufficient grounds for stating that Being-Power and Consciousness-Wisdom are two undifferentiated aspects of the Absolute—undifferentiated but differentiable on the already relative plane of creative Being—whereas Beatitude-Mercy coincides with the Infinitude of the Principle. Beatitude—*Ānanda*—also possesses two aspects, namely, projecting *Māyā*, which refers to Being-Power, and reabsorbing *Māyā*, which refers to Consciousness-Wisdom.

The question as to whether it is Power or Consciousness that comes first is subjectively insoluble because objectively it cannot be posed. When it is said that *Sat*, Pure Being, is the Root-Principle, it is presupposed that Being comes before Knowing; when on the contrary one speaks of *Ātmā*, the Self, as being the supreme Reality, one takes as one's starting point the truth that the divine Principle is essentially Light, Spirit, Consciousness, and that Power and Goodness are its first aspects or functions.[4] Unquestionably, this truth or this reality is manifested in man, of whom it can be said that he is an intelligence that prolongs itself in—or by—the will and the sentiments; voluntarists, nevertheless, put all the emphasis on the will and seem to be saying that the will, by choosing God, determines both sensibility and intelligence. This last way of seeing things appears in any case in the axiom "God is Love", and this gives rise to a perspective that even diverges from voluntarism, in the sense that it puts sentiment and not will at the summit of the triangle; this is the point of view of *bhakti*, which subordinates both will and intelligence, not indeed to sentiment pure and simple, but to that love which coincides with the whole soul and which, upon meeting divine Love, becomes imbued with a supernatural and liberating Presence.

Since the Intellect contains the three elements and prefigures them in its unity, it is always possible to subsume one or other of these elements, as they appear in man, to the Intellect and to subordinate to it the two remaining elements: in other words, it is always possible to subordinate the will and love to the Intellect-Intelligence; intelligence and love to the Intellect-Will; and intelligence and will to the Intellect-Love.

---

[4] In Sufism, as elsewhere, there have been many controversies regarding the priority of the objective and the subjective *in divinis*.

The Virtues in the Way

Man, "made in the image of God", has an intelligence capable of discernment and contemplation; a will capable of freedom and strength; a soul, or a character, capable of love and virtue.

Intelligence discerns horizontally between the essential and the secondary, between good and evil, and vertically between the real and the illusory, the absolute and the relative, substance and accident, the permanent and the impermanent. And it contemplates the real or the absolute either from the standpoint of its transcendence or that of its immanence: it conceives the divine reality either beyond things, or on the contrary within things inasmuch as they manifest it.

Free will chooses horizontally between the useful and the useless, between good and evil, and vertically between the real and the illusory, salvation and perdition. And it realizes the real either by abstaining from things insofar as they are illusory, or on the contrary by accepting them as messengers of the real, according to both subjective and objective conditions.

The soul, or character, loves horizontally that which manifests the real, its goodness, its beauty, and vertically the real itself, or its goodness or its beauty. And the soul assimilates the nature or the qualities of the Beloved by participating in them through virtue, or the virtues; in relation to things, the virtues are either exclusive or inclusive: thus the virtue of detachment excludes, whereas the virtue of generosity includes.

All of this has been explained previously, but we need to mention it again so as to prepare the ground for an analysis of the qualities of the soul. Likewise, let us mention again the following points: what distinguishes man from animals is totality, and this implies transcendence. Man possesses an intelligence, a will, and a power for love; now, each of these three dimensions is characterized by objectivity. Man is essentially capable not only of an objective and transcendent knowledge and will, but he also realizes these qualities by his capacity to love; which amounts to saying that he is capable of compassion towards his fellow human beings, be they strangers or even enemies, because he is capable of loving God. It is indeed compassion and love of God, to whatever degree, that characterize the man worthy of the name, or man as such if we overlook his decadences and perversions; there is no people that does not practice a certain charity and that does not possess a sort of religion. This observation cannot be invalidated by the entirely recent phenomenon of the philosophical and artificial dehumanization of man, which proves, not that man is something other than he is, but simply that he is capable, precisely because he is man, of denying the human without however really being able to succeed in this aim. He can deny himself because he is man, yet it is for the same reason that he fails finally in so doing.

Knowledge, the function of intelligence, cannot be false: it either is or is not; but volition, the function of the will, can be false by its object, though not of course by its power. In an analogous manner, happiness can be false by its object or by its level; in the latter case, the object can be good, but happiness can be wrong if it separates it from its divine context, this constituting the sin of idolatry. Intelligence can also be mistaken by the falseness of its content, but then it is mistaken as thought and not as knowledge; to speak of a false knowledge would be as absurd as to speak of a blind vision or a dark light. Error is an ignorance, and thus a privation of knowledge, although there is always in error an underlying element of knowledge or of truth, without which it would not even exist; but the will towards evil always remains a volition, and thus a use of our freedom, just as an illusory happiness always remains an experience of well-being, and thus an ontological and distant participation—even should it be perverse—in the only Happiness there is. Or again: to will or to love evil is evil; but to know evil is not evil, it is even good, since this enables us to situate evil and vanquish it.

In other words, knowledge in itself is as infallible and incorruptible as the instinct of plants that turn towards the sun without ever erring, whereas the two extensions of the intelligence—the will and love—are fallible; but they are so only through having separated themselves from knowledge in order to unite with passion or inertia; when reintegrated in knowledge, they once more become, like it, infallible and incorruptible. And this shows that man is essentially identified with integral or total intelligence; this totality *ipso facto* confers freedom on that mode of intelligence that is the will, just as it confers generosity on that other mode of intelligence that is the soul or character. Human intelligence entails, by its very nature, these two prolongations or functions along with their perfections; it is only by unfolding itself in the will and in the soul, or in love, that intelligence is in a position to engage operatively—and with impunity—in the vertical dimension that leads from earthly accidents to celestial Substance.

Man cannot exercise self-domination, still less transcend himself, without the assistance of the intelligence, the will, and the character, the last named being love in its permanently underlying primordial reality; in order to make the best use of these three faculties, it is necessary to direct them to the end to which they are proportioned, and which constitutes *a priori* their supernatural and transpersonal substance, hence also their prototype and their *raison d'être*.

Man is a whole whose parts are interdependent; to know or love God is to know or to love Him with all that one has, and consequently with all that one is, as the very totality of the divine Nature demands.

Man has the right to be happy, but he must be so nobly and, what amounts to the same thing, within the framework of the Truth and the Way. Nobility is that which corresponds to the real hierarchy of values: the higher takes precedence over the lower, and this applies on the plane of sentiments as well as on that of thoughts and volitions. It has been said that nobility of character consists in putting honor and moral dignity above self-interest, which means in the last analysis that we must put the invisible real above the visible illusory, morally as well as intellectually.

Nobility is made of detachment and generosity; without such nobility, the gifts of intelligence and the efforts of the will can never suffice for the Way, for man consists of more than these two faculties, he also possesses a soul capable of love and destined for happiness; and happiness cannot be realized—except in a wholly illusory fashion—without virtue or nobility. We could also say that the Way is made of discernment, concentration, and goodness: of discernment for the intelligence, of concentration for the will, of goodness for the soul; the fundamental goodness of the soul is also its beauty, just as every outward beauty reveals an underlying cosmic goodness.

Detachment entails objectivity with regard to oneself; generosity entails equally the capacity to put oneself in the place of others, and thus to be "oneself" in others. These attitudes, which *a priori* are intellectual, become nobility on the plane of the soul;[1] now nobility is a mode of objectivity as well as of transcendence.

Within duration, detachment leads to patience and generosity to fidelity; patience and fidelity prolong and perfect as it were the virtues by anchoring them in time, so that it could be said that patience proves the sincerity of detachment, whereas fidelity proves the sincerity of generosity;[2] every quality, to be complete, requires perseverance.

What we owe to God, we owe, in appropriate fashion, to our neighbor; and if we believe that we owe something *a priori* to our neighbor, this is because we owe it fundamentally to God. Let us take the example of extinction in God: there is also a sort of extinction with regard to one's neighbor, and this—apart from the union of love in which the extinction is positive in an immediate way—is perfect objectivity with regard to an ego other than our own. To be perfectly objective is to die a little: it is to cease to be oneself in order to put oneself perfectly in the place of another, but which could never mean that we ought to adopt his errors or his vices, any more than objectivity in regard to oneself implies any sort of complacency with regard to defects or sins. At all events, our death in God, or our "extinction", is only sincere if we realize concurrently a kind of death or extinction towards our neighbor, depending on what the situation may demand; in other words, to do justice to a quality that is foreign to us and which our own character does not enable us to recognize immediately, we must "cease being what we are" in the particular relationship involved; and the capacity to do this must become for us a second nature, which is nothing other than humility. In many cases it is nobility that brings out intelligence, which proves that nobility itself, like every virtue moreover, is a mode of intellection; each virtue is an eye that sees God.

Strictly speaking, it is not we who realize virtue, it is God alone who possesses it and imparts it to us; this is obvious, and universally

---

[1] It is significant that a chivalric perspective such as *Bushidō* places generosity and compassion at the summit of the virtues; thus it is hardly surprising that the samurai were able to combine, on a similar basis, a spirituality such as Zen with their profession of arms.

[2] In Islam, sincerity (*sidq*) is the mother of all virtues: to believe sincerely in God is to be humble and charitable, detached and generous, patient and faithful; everything derives from faith. In other words, faith is hypocritical to the extent that the virtues are missing from it, subjectively speaking—for objectively the worth of faith lies in its content.

recognized, in the world of the Spirit at least. What we believe to be the realization of a virtue, is in reality but our heart's gaze towards God, or God's gaze towards our heart. The accident of human virtue cannot be a production of the creature, and this is precisely why the qualities or talents of a man are called "gifts". Pride is to believe we are making a gift of our virtues to God.

— ·:· —

The divine model of generosity is Mercy, or more precisely the element Goodness-Beauty-Beatitude; the Mercy of God calls for trust on the part of man—a virtue that opposes doubt, bitterness, and despair—whereas human generosity necessarily partakes of divine Mercy. As for detachment, its divine model is Purity, namely the divine quality of adamantine impenetrability or inviolability: nothing created can enter God, who being Plenitude has no need of anything and cannot desire anything; the Purity of God calls for submission on the part of man, or resignation or contentment—qualities that oppose curiosity, dissipation, and revolt—whereas human detachment partakes of Divine Purity.

Virtue, we have said, is made of detachment and generosity; now, each of these qualities is to be applied in a horizontal mode and in a vertical mode, which means it is either an element of nobility or an element of piety. The noble man is naturally detached from petty things, sometimes counter to his own interests; and he is naturally generous out of greatness of soul. The pious man, for his part, detaches himself from the things of this world—either within the framework of a legitimate equilibrium, or else by breaking this framework—because these things do not lead to Heaven, or to the extent that they do not contribute to this end; and he is generous out of his love of God, because this love allows him to "see God everywhere", and because "God is Love". That the two dimensions—the horizontal and the vertical—are linked in depth, results from the nature of things: each conditions the other and each proceeds from the other, and they are destined to coincide, if they do not do so from the outset.

Objective intelligence, free will, virtuous soul: these are the three prerogatives that constitute man. Virtuous soul: this means that only the human soul, not the animal soul, is capable of transcending itself in the direction of the Absolute and also in the direction of its neighbor, whose dignity, personality, need for happiness, and capacity for suffering it perceives. Virtue, a human prerogative like intellectual objectivity and volitive liberty, is made of piety and goodness; what is required of man in the first place, is that he should be pious and good. The moral substance of man is love of God and generosity towards his neighbor.

—⁖—

Detachment, generosity, vigilance, gratitude: these virtues derive from four principles that could be characterized by the following terms: purity, goodness, strength, beauty; or cold, warmth, activity, rest; or death, life, combat, peace; or again, applying them to spiritual alchemy: abstention, trust, accomplishment, contentment. Purity and beauty are static; strength and goodness are dynamic; from another point of view, purity and strength derive from rigor, beauty and goodness from gentleness. This amounts to saying that virtue in itself, or conformity of soul, possesses two complementary modes, one static and one dynamic; and in another respect, a rigorous mode and a gentle mode; and that the four principles or the four virtues derive from these modes or these poles.

This quaternity of the spiritual or moral principles—and these are above all metaphysical and cosmological—has obviously nothing arbitrary about it; it corresponds to the four cardinal points: North, South, East, West; sapiential discernment is manifested by the Zenith, and unitive concentration by the Nadir, whereas the four virtues are situated on the intermediary plane, the Horizon, which here is the domain of the soul, of conformity, and of piety.[3]

Through discernment, we grasp the Absolute and *ipso facto* its relationships with relativity; through concentration, our spiritual consciousness is so to speak reabsorbed into its immanent divine source; in the first case, everything is reduced to the absolute Object; in the second case, everything is reduced to the pure Subject. Piety, which coincides with virtue, is the encounter of the human subject with the divine Object: man is harmoniously placed before God; the holy

---

[3] We have indicated these correspondences in the chapter on the hypostatic numbers, but see no harm in repeating them in the present context.

receptivity of the soul is combined with the sanctifying Presence of God. In other words, the soul perceives or realizes the divine Presence *hic et nunc*, in its very existential relativity, whereas the intelligence and the will tend to pierce the screen of existence and to open onto the Principle, whether transcendent or immanent.

This having been said, let us now examine each of the key-virtues: detachment, generosity, vigilance, gratitude.

Detachment: first it should be noted that attachment is in the very nature of man; and yet he is asked to be detached. The criterion of the legitimacy of an attachment is that its object should be worthy of love, namely that it should transmit to us something of God, and, even more importantly, should not take us away from Him; if a thing or a creature is worthy of love and does not take us away from God—in which case it indirectly brings us towards its divine model —it may be said that we love it "in God" and "towards God", hence in keeping with Platonic "recollection" and without idolatry and centrifugal passion. To be detached means not loving anything outside of God or *a fortiori* against God; it is thus to love God *ex toto corde*. But there is also another perspective to be found in every religious climate, namely that of penitential asceticism: instead of taking as starting-point the idea that every excess is an evil and that the good is situated between two excesses, which is the view of Aristotle and also what Islam in general teaches, this kind of asceticism sees good in an excess of detachment; and this attitude also has its justification depending on the point of view, the temperament, the vocation, and the social setting. According to this perspective there is no excess, there are only sincerity and totality; the fact remains nonetheless that this attitude cannot or will not take account of all human or, more exactly, of all spiritual reality.

Detachment is the opposite of concupiscence and avidity; it is the greatness of soul that, inspired by a consciousness of absolute values and thus also of the imperfection and impermanence of relative values, allows the soul to keep its inward freedom and its distance with regard to things. On the one hand, consciousness of God annuls, in a certain fashion, both forms and qualities while, on the other hand, conferring on them a value that transcends them; detachment means that the soul is as it were imbued with death, but it also means, by compensation, that it is aware of the indestructibility of earthly beauties; for beauty cannot be destroyed, it withdraws into its archetypes and into its essence, where it is reborn, immortal, in the blessed nearness of God.

— ·:· —

Generosity: how could the sanctified man not be generous, since he trusts in the divine Mercy, and since he does not do so blindly? For it is not enough to expect from Mercy the benefits that it promises, it is necessary in addition, and even above all, to open oneself to it and to love it for itself; now, to love Mercy is to understand its nature and its beauty and to wish to be united to it by participating in its function. To love is to some degree to wish to be what one loves, or to become what one loves; hence it is to imitate what one loves.

Generosity is the opposite of egoism, avarice, and pettiness; nevertheless it should be specified that it is evil which is opposed to good and not inversely. Generosity is the greatness of soul that loves to give and also to forgive, because it allows man to put himself spontaneously in the place of others; which therefore grants one's adversary all the chances that he humanly may deserve, however minimal, and without harming justice or the greater good. Nobility comprises *a priori* a benevolent attitude and a certain gift of self, without affectation and without violation of the nature of things; the noble man tries to help, to meet the other, before condemning and carrying out harsh measures, while being implacable and swiftly decisive when the reality of the situation demands it. Goodness out of weakness or wishful thinking is not a virtue; generosity is beautiful to the extent that man is strong and lucid. There is always, in the noble soul, a certain instinct of the gift of self, for God Himself is the first to overflow with charity, and above all with beauty; the noble man is only happy in giving of himself, and he gives himself above all to God, as God gives Himself to him, and wishes to give Himself to him.

— ·:· —

Vigilance: the sanctified man is also, and necessarily so, a disciplined man; to be disciplined is, intrinsically, to exercise self-domination and, extrinsically, to do things correctly; to do nothing by halves or against the logic of things, in short to be neither negligent nor disordered, nor moreover extravagant. In nature, each thing is entirely what it must be, and each thing is in its rightful place according to the laws of hierarchy, equilibrium, proportions, rhythms; freedom of form and movement is combined with an underlying coordination; thus perfection of soul requires that the outward be in conformity with the inward. Musicality must be combined with geometry, for the consciousness of the absolute must penetrate the joy of infinitude, and this is a fundamental condition of art; discipline of character and of demeanor is a mark as much of humility as of discernment, the one cannot go without the other. Although it may indeed happen that a saint is negligent regarding the things of the world, this is because he is steeped in contemplation; outside of contemplation, he would be perfectly conscious and mindful; and the least that can be said is that it is not enough to be negligent in order to be a contemplative or a saint. The sanctified man avoids all ostentatious singularity, unless he have a particular vocation; this is why outward discipline, which seeks the norm and not originality, is one of the very first stages towards the extinction of the autocratic and untamed soul.

Vigilance is the affirmative and combative virtue that prevents us from forgetting or betraying the "one thing needful": it is the presence of mind that ceaselessly reminds us of the remembrance of God, thereby keeping us alert to anything that takes us away from it. This virtue excludes all negligence and all carelessness—in small as well as in big things—since it is based on awareness of the present moment, of this ceaselessly renewed instant that belongs to God and not to the world, to Reality and not to dreaming. It is in this context, we repeat, that one must place the quality of discipline, self-domination, and rectitude in all things.

— ∴ —

Gratitude: the grateful man is one who maintains himself in holy poverty or, in other words, in a sort of holy monotony in the midst of inevitable distractions and complex occupations; he also maintains himself in a state of holy childlikeness, keeping blessedly apart from every unhealthy curiosity, from every temptation that both imprisons and harasses us. The pious man knows that he lives in exile—but without bitterness and without ingratitude—and he lives both on certitude and hope; that man alone will go to Paradise who is already there here-below through his resignation to the will of God, and through the graces resulting from this.

Gratitude is a virtue that allows us, not only to be content with small things—this is holy childlikeness—but also to appreciate or respect small things or great things because they come from God, beginning with the beauties and the gifts of nature; one must be sensitive to the innocence and mystery of the divine works. Worship of the divine Substance involves respect for the accidents that manifest it; to worship God "in spirit and in truth" is also to respect Him through the veil that is man, which amounts in practice to saying that one must respect the potential sanctity that is in every man, insofar as it is reasonably possible for us to do so; in a word, to accept, if not to understand, the transcendence of the Creator is to recognize His immanence in creatures. We owe it to others to show them, as far as is possible, that we do not remain fixed on their earthly accidentality, but that on the contrary we show a willingness to be aware of their heavenly substance, and this excludes all triviality in our social comportment. Politeness is a distant manner of helping our neighbor to sanctify himself, or to remember that, being made of sanctity as an image of God, he is thereby made for sanctity.[4] To speak of respect for one's neighbor is to speak of respect for oneself, for what is true for others is also true for us; man is always a virtual saint. Dignity is incumbent upon us owing to our deiformity, to our sense of the sacred, to our knowledge, and to our worship of God; integral nobility is part of faith.

The noble man always maintains himself at the center, he never loses sight of the symbol, the spiritual gift of things, the sign of God, a gratitude both ascending and radiating.

---

[4] It is this truth that explains the reason for the traditional importance of the rules of conduct, whether it be a question of common civility, or a particular etiquette. In Shinto as in Islam—to mention only these two examples— politeness is part of the religion, which proves the profundity of its motivation.

Now, out of scruple's sake, we would like to add a word about the limits of the principle of pious courtesy, although doing so is to state the obvious. Man is very far from his own substance, and being in fact an accident, he is exposed to holy wrath to the extent that he disavows his human dignity; he deserves rigor from those who may have the function of manifesting it, namely prophets and spiritual masters, then from every legitimate authority, and even from any upright man, depending on the circumstances. This severity is charitable and not vindictive when it is exercised towards those who may profit from it; in this case its intention is not to stigmatize an irremediable perversion—this refers to another possibility—but to free by means of a salutary shock, a virtue hidden under a layer of ice or darkness, thus helping theomorphic man to "become what he is", and what, in his pure substance, he has never ceased to be.

The most outward form of discipline is traditional etiquette, which regulates social contacts, within elites especially; and the most inward form of discipline or rectitude is moral dignity, which sums up everything that makes a man worthy of trust, for example truthfulness in his promises and faithfulness to his given word. To speak of one's "word of honor" is already redundant, for every word engages the honor of him who utters it; every word should be guaranteed by the honor of its author, moral dignity being a "categorical imperative" of the human condition. One must nevertheless be careful not to isolate this dignity of man from its divine context, for everything that is humanly worthy is so by virtue of this context or this foundation; the best honor is the one that has its roots, not in our self-esteem, but in our sincerity towards God. Or again, and fundamentally this amounts to the same thing: the only irreproachable honor is the one that on earth prolongs the honor of Heaven.

If we were asked—despite the obviousness of the thing—what virtue has to do with questions of spiritual realization, namely with matters of strict and extra-individual technique, we would answer as follows, placing ourselves at the same purely practical point of view: spiritual realization imposes on the soul an immense disproportion owing to the fact that it introduces the presence of the sacred into the darkness of human imperfection; now this inevitably provokes disequilibrium-producing reactions that in principle carry with them the risk of an irremediable fall, reactions that moral beauty, together with the graces that it attracts by its very nature, can largely prevent or attenuate. It is precisely this beauty that ambitious dilettantes without imagination think they can disdain, for they see in it only a sentimentalism foreign to what they believe to be the technique of realization; and yet, when the soul finds itself as it were suspended between two worlds, one already lost and the other not yet attained, only inherent virtue together with grace can save it from vertigo, and only this virtue renders it immune from the outset to temptations and deviations.

On this level of spiritual alchemy, it is important not to confuse a purely extrinsic morality with intrinsic virtue—the latter sometimes appearing amoral in certain cases—nor a natural virtue of modest scope with a virtue deeply rooted in the heart and involving the whole soul. Above all it is important to understand the following principle: the intrinsically moral is that which, while comprising a benefit in some degree or another, harms no one; the intrinsically immoral is that which, without profiting anyone, harms others or ourselves; always bearing in mind the hierarchy of values.

On the one hand, virtues favor or even condition contemplative attitudes, and on the other they result from them, to the extent that these attitudes are sincere. A virtue is profound inasmuch as it coincides with the transcending of oneself, this being synonymous with objectivity, fundamental impartiality, and a serenity that is already celestial. For the virtuous man is such because his intelligence and sensibility perceive the very being of things.

Sapiential discernment and unitive concentration: the first is objective in the sense that mental knowledge implies the encounter of a subject with an object, whereas the second is subjective in the sense that subjectivity taken in isolation and deepened to the level of its very essence, represents a knowledge—cardiac, not mental—that transcends the scission between a subject and an object. Wisdom, as the science of universal principles, is the objective pole of knowledge;

sanctity, as the experience of being and not of thought, is its subjective pole.[5]

To sapiential discernment—determined by the Absolute—is joined the virtue of truthfulness; to unitive concentration—in view of the Absolute—is joined the virtue of sincerity. Sincerity is subjective and volitive truthfulness, just as truthfulness is objective and intellective sincerity.

The principle of truthfulness is formulated in the best possible way in the maxim of the maharajahs of Benares: "There is no right superior to that of truth"; similarly, the principle of sincerity is best expressed in the juridical formula: "The truth, the whole truth, and nothing but the truth", but applied in moral mode and therefore paraphrased: "The good, the whole good, and nothing but the good": namely the movement of approach to God.

This virtue of sincerity raises the question of the boundary line between what is obligatory and what is not. This is where the distinction comes into play between the absolute truth and relative truths, on the one hand, and between the absolute good and relative good in all of its possible forms, on the other; now, one must not mistake a relative truth for error, nor a relative good for evil; with even greater reason there can never be any question of taking error or sin for a relative good. What must be understood is that the sincere man or the truthful man has the right to be human: he has by definition the right to the intellectual and moral relativities that he needs in order to live, provided that they are in accordance with what he can and must grasp of the Absolute, intellectually and morally. On the one hand, nothing resembles the transcendent Principle, and if this were the only aspect of total truth, man would have to renounce everything; however, his very existence proves that truth comprises another aspect, that of participation, which allows us to add: on the other hand, everything manifests the Principle—which is immanent while remaining tran-

---

[5] But the objective pole also has its superiority, in the sense that the object is not only that which is known by a subject, but above all a reality in itself, and it is moreover only in this capacity that it is of interest to us; conversely, the subjective pole has an aspect of inferiority, precisely because the subject is the locus of the illusory limitation of the object. The interpretation of the pure subject—or of pure subjectivity—as the door towards the transcending of the subject-object division, is based on the notion of the divine "Self", the objectivation of which is *Māyā*, *Īshvara*, *Buddhi*, *Samsāra*, and thus the Universe, from stage to stage.

scendent—otherwise nothing would exist. Consequently, if on the one hand things present an aspect of opacity, which obliges us to seek God beyond them, on the other hand they also present an aspect of transparency, which allows us to accept them while seeking God; to accept them precisely to the extent that they are objectively or subjectively transparent and not otherwise. This amounts to saying that the man who loves God with sincerity nevertheless has the right to love a creature "in God", not against Him; to be human and to live in relativity is not to betray the sincerity that we owe to the Absolute.[6]

Humility, as one knows or ought to know, has its source in our total dependence on God; normally this awareness leads to an ever alert sense of proportion, which prevents us from overestimating ourselves as well as underestimating others. Nevertheless, we need to curb, not this virtue of course, but its possible excess; and it is curbed by the complementary virtue, truthfulness, which reminds us that no virtue has the right to go against truth, and which prompts us moreover not to overestimate anyone or to underestimate ourselves when the contrast between respective merits is obvious. A schoolmaster must notice the fact that a particular child is more gifted than himself, but he is not entitled to believe that he, the master and the adult, is more ignorant and has less experience than the child.

An analogous observation applies to sincerity, which consists in being what one expresses and expressing what one is; here too there is a virtue that keeps in check misinterpretation and excess, and this is prudence. For sincerity does not oblige us to confide to others what is beyond their understanding or does not concern them; or what is of no use to them, or might even harm them; in short, whatever they do not desire to know if they are upright men. We are well aware that in referring again to the role of truth in the economy of the virtues we are repeating ourselves, but no matter; there is little need to excuse

---

[6] Islamic doctrine distinguishes between "abstraction" (*tanzīh*) and "analogy" (*tashbīh*): this is what allows, by way of consequence, the realization of the human equilibrium that Islam advocates. One *Avatāra* or one religion manifests renunciation and, of necessity, equilibrium in renunciation; another *Avatāra* or another religion manifests equilibrium and, with the same necessity, renunciation in equilibrium.

ourselves since in the religion of "our time" it is constantly being reiterated that the Kingdom of Heaven is outside us and that we should accept this out of humility or even charity.

If elliptical expressions were easily understood, we would willingly say that the greatest of the virtues is truth: truth insofar as it is lived, and not merely thought, and becoming within us the sense of the sacred and worship.

— ·:· —

Virtue in itself is the worship that attaches us to God and attracts us to Him, while radiating around us; the primordial and quasi-existential worship that declares itself above all by the sense of the sacred, as we have just said. The sacred is the perfume of Divinity, it is the divine made present; to love the sacred is to imbue ourselves with the perfume of pure Being and its serenity. The soul of the Blessed Virgin, prototype of every sanctified soul, is made of innate worship, and this actualizes the real Presence as a mirror reflects light; the virginal soul is consubstantial with this Presence just as space coincides with the ether that it contains.

The one and only virtue, or substantial devotion, is repose in Being, which is at once transcendent and immanent while being sacramentally present, *hic et nunc*. And every virtue, through participation in its own essence, is a mode of worship, and hence of beatitude.

God has put into our substance all the virtues; they derive from the nature of our substance, and this nature is primordial worship. This is why, and we repeat it, a virtue is never an acquisition or a property, it always belongs to God, and through Him to the *Logos*; our concern must be to eliminate whatever is opposed to the virtues, not to gain the virtues for ourselves; we must give free passage to the qualities of the Sovereign Good. And in transmitting this message we must become it, by a sort of active extinction or extinctive activity; we must become it because we are it, within the depths of ourselves and, above all, within the creative intention of God.

The Nature and Role of Sentiment

The question of the virtues, like that of aesthetics, rightly or wrongly brings to mind the question of sentiment: rightly if sentiment is understood as playing a legitimate role in morality and art, but wrongly if sentiment connotes a pejorative nuance, as if there were a question of an excess or a weakness. In reality, sentiment is a state of awareness that is not mental, objective, and mathematical, no doubt, but vital, subjective, and so to speak musical: it is the emotional color taken on by the whole ego upon coming into contact with any phenomenon whatsoever, including thoughts and mental images on the one hand, and spiritual intuitions on the other. The quality of the sentiment depends on that of the ego as well as on that of the phenomenon; if one distinguishes between noble, virtuous, and contemplative men, on the one hand, and men who are vulgar, vicious, and superficial, on the other, then one will also distinguish between phenomena relating to different levels, from the physical to the spiritual, and finally between different types of phenomena, such as those of an aesthetic order and those of a moral order. Phenomena elicit in the ego a variety of colorations, susceptible of an indefinite series of gradations as regards quality and intensity, and these colorations indicate directly or indirectly what we are; sentiment is either an image or a modality of the person, depending on his degree of profundity.

Like intelligence and will, sentiment is a faculty both of discrimination and of assimilation; if we loathe, this is because the object prevents us from loving, that is to say, from experiencing feelings that are in conformity with our nature and, because of this fact, allow us to be on the surface what we are in depth. And if in spirituality it is important to know That which knows, and to will That which wills, it is no less important to love That which loves.

Sentiment can be diverse in its accidentality, but in its substance it is love. Love responds intuitively and vitally to beauty, goodness, and to the good; it derives its nourishment from them, so to speak, and transforms and assimilates the soul by awakening in its depths immanent Beauty, the one and only Beauty, since it is the Beauty of God. Outward beauty is, precisely, the reflection of this immanent Beauty: by loving sensible beauty intelligently and piously—and thus in a contemplative manner—the soul remembers its own immortal essence; by loving, it seeks to become the other, so as to be able to re-become itself.

Sentiment, envisaged in all its aspects, enables on the one hand a sort of vital discrimination between what is noble, lovable, and useful and what is not and, on the other, an assimilation of what is worthy of being assimilated and thereby realized; in other words, love is premised on the worth of the object. If love takes precedence over hatred to the point that there is no common measure between them, this is because absolute Reality is absolutely lovable; love is substance, hatred is accident, except in the case of perverse creatures. There are two kinds of hatred, one legitimate and one illegitimate: the first derives from a love that is the victim of an injustice, such as the love of God clamoring for vengeance, and this is the very foundation of all holy anger; the second kind is unjust hatred, or hatred that is not limited inwardly by the underlying love that is its purpose and that justifies it; this second type of hatred appears as an end in itself, it is subjective and not objective, it seeks to destroy rather than to repair.

Both the Koran and the Bible accept that there is a divine Anger;[1] and thus also a human "holy anger" and a "holy war"; man can "hate in God", according to an Islamic expression. Indeed, objective privation permits or demands a privative reaction on the part of the subject, and the main thing is to know whether in a particular case our pity for a given human substance should prevail over our horror for the accident that makes the individual hateful. For it is true that, from a certain point of view, one must hate the sin and not the sinner; but this point of view is relative, and does not prevent one from being sometimes obliged, as a matter of proportion, to despise the sinner inasmuch as he identifies himself with his sin. We once heard it said that whoever is incapable of contempt is likewise incapable of veneration; this is perfectly true, on condition that the evaluation is correct and that the contempt does not exceed the limits of its sufficient reason, subjectively as well as objectively.[2] Rightful contempt is both a weapon and a means of protection; there is also such a thing as indifference, certainly, but this is an attitude befitting a hermit that is not necessarily practicable or good to have in human society, for it runs

---

[1] If, according to Islam, God's Mercy takes precedence over His Wrath, this means that the first is in the essence, whereas the second asserts itself in view of the accident.

[2] According to Mencius, to be angry over a paltry insult is unworthy of a superior man, but indignation for a great cause is a just anger.

the risk of being misinterpreted. Moreover, and this is important, a just contempt is necessarily combined with a measure of indifference, otherwise one would lack detachment and also that fund of generosity without which anger cannot be holy. Seeing an evil must not cause us to overlook its contingency; a fragment may or must bother us, but we must not lose sight of the fact that it is a fragment and not totality; now, awareness of totality, which is innocent and divine, in principle takes priority over everything else. We say "in principle", for contingencies retain all their rights; this amounts to saying that serene anger is a possibility, and even a necessity, because in hating an evil, we do not cease loving God.

—— ·:· ——

It is important not to confuse the notions of sentiment, sentimentality, and sentimentalism, as is too often done owing either to a rationalist or an intellectualist prejudice. The second case, in fact, is more surprising than the first, for if reason is in a certain sense opposed to sentiment, the Intellect remains neutral in this regard, just as light remains neutral with regard to colors; we intentionally say "intellectualist" and not "intellectual" for intellectuality contains no prejudices.

That a sentiment which is opposed to a truth is unworthy of esteem, everyone will concur, and such a sentiment is in fact the very definition of sentimentalism. When one rightly reproaches an attitude for being sentimental, this can only mean one thing, namely that the attitude in question contradicts a rational attitude and usurps its place; and let us recall that an attitude can be rational in a positive sense only when it is based either on intellectual knowledge or simply on adequate information about a real situation. An attitude cannot be termed rational just because it makes use of logic, since it is possible to reason in the absence of the necessary facts.

Just as intellectuality is, on the one hand, the nature of what is intellectual and, on the other, a tendency towards the Intellect, so likewise sentimentality means both the nature of what is sentimental and a tendency towards sentiment; as for sentimentalism, it systematizes an excess of sentimentality to the detriment of the normal perception of things: denominational and political fanaticisms fall in this category. If we draw attention to these distinctions, which in themselves are obvious, it is solely because of the frequent confusions that we cannot help but notice in this domain—though we are certainly not alone in so doing—and which run the risk of falsifying the notions of intellectuality and spirituality.

— ·:· —

"God is Love": if this saying is true—and it is so on divine authority—then sentiment is a normal and therefore positive dimension of the human microcosm, in which case all suspicions concerning it are absurd. *Ātmā* is *Sat*, *Chit*, and *Ānanda*: "Being", "Consciousness", and "Beatitude", or "Power", "Wisdom", and "Goodness"; in the microcosm, these aspects become will, intelligence, and sentiment. The desire to suppress sentiment thus amounts, ontologically speaking, to a desire to suppress the element *Ānanda*, neither more nor less.

Moreover, the opponents of sentiment—and thus basically of love—place themselves in a self-contradictory position, both from an existential and a psychological standpoint, firstly because nothing exists without love and secondly because no man can reject sentiments in his actual life, whether material or spiritual. Every man, on pain of hypocrisy, aspires to happiness, and happiness cannot be reduced to a mathematical equation.

The pinnacle of this energy termed sentiment is the love of God; in other words, this pinnacle is faith or devotion. Faith is the impetus that makes us live in God and for God; devotion is the reverential fear that is in conformity with the sense of the sacred and which encloses us in a contemplative climate of adoration and peace.

It might be objected that the love of God is above sentiments and that it engages more specifically the will, which has nothing sentimental about it; if such be the case, then one should not have spoken of the love of God, for love is unquestionably a sentiment; instead, one should have chosen another term. Sentiment, like mental intelligence, prolongs the Intellect—while limiting it—and consequently cannot be entirely cut off from it; thus there is no impenetrable barrier between the emotional love of God and the Intellect, the latter necessarily comprising a dimension of supernatural love.[3] If, on the one

---

[3] At this level, sentiment as a psychological phenomenon is transcended, but not as to its essential content nor as cosmic power.

hand, spiritual love cannot be an ordinary passion, given that its object is God and that it is the result—or the concomitant dimension—of an activity of the intelligence and of the will, on the other hand it is necessarily inspired by its supernatural source, which is the Holy Spirit and which is Love in itself.

There is the heart-as-knowledge and the heart-as-love; these are like the two faces of one and the same mystery.[4] It is to the loving heart that the following saying of Christ refers: "Much will be forgiven her, for she loved much"; and it is again to the heart, but in its distress, that this other saying refers: "Blessed are they that mourn, for they shall be comforted." One speaks of the heart that burns with love, and also of the heart that melts; it melts by drinking the wine of grace, and in melting it is itself the wine that is drunk by the Beloved.[5]

[4] The heart is sometimes considered as the seat of strength, which is entirely plausible since the heart is identified with the Intellect, which includes will and sentiment as well as intelligence, and which is thus the receptacle of all the faculties and all the virtues.

[5] Umar ibn al-Farid: "We have drunk to the memory of the Beloved, a wine that intoxicated us before the vine was created."

What Sincerity Is and What It Is Not

How often does one read or hear it said that someone is gravely mistaken, or that he is vice-ridden or criminal, but that he is "sincere" and is therefore "seeking God in his own way"—and other euphemisms of this sort—when what is really meant is this: fear not, he is making not the slightest effort either for truth or virtue. Such an opinion, which is truly perverse, is one manifestation among others of modern subjectivism, in which the most contingent of subjectivity takes precedence over objectivity, even in those cases where the objective is the very reason for being of the subjective, thus determining its worth. In other words, the now fashionable cult of sincerity, far from being moral or spiritual, is nothing other than a more or less cynical individualism, not without certain democratic overtones since, apparently, to wish to dominate and transcend oneself is to wish to place ourselves above others—as if the effort to better oneself somehow prevented others from doing the same.

Cynicism and hypocrisy are two forms of pride: cynicism is the caricature of sincerity or frankness, while hypocrisy is the caricature of scrupulousness or self-discipline, or of virtue in general. Cynics believe that to display shortcomings and passions is sincerity, whereas to hide them is hypocrisy; they do not dominate themselves and still less do they seek to transcend themselves; and the fact that they take their fault for a virtue is clear proof of their pride, precisely. Hypocrites, for their part, believe that it is virtuous to display virtuous attitudes or that a show of faith suffices for faith itself; their vice consists, not in manifesting the forms of virtue—which is a rule incumbent on everyone—but in believing that the manifestation is virtue itself and, above all, in mimicking virtues in the hope of being admired; but this is pride because it is individualism and ostentation. Pride is to overestimate oneself while underestimating others; and this is what the cynic does just as much as the hypocrite, either blatantly or subtly depending on the case.

All this amounts to saying that in cynicism as in hypocrisy, the autocratic, and thus tenebrous, ego takes the place of the spirit and of light; these two vices are acts of theft by which the passional and egoistic soul appropriates what belongs to the spiritual soul. Moreover, to present a vice as a virtue and, correspondingly, to accuse virtues of being vices, as is done by cynicism posing as sincerity, is nothing other than hypocrisy, and a particularly perverse form of it at that.

As for pride, it was defined very well by Boethius: "All the other vices flee from God; pride alone sets itself up against Him"; and by Saint Augustine: "Other vices attach themselves to evil, that evil may be accomplished; pride alone attaches itself to good, that good may perish." When God is absent, pride necessarily fills the void: it cannot but appear in the soul when nothing is there to refer to the Sovereign Good. Certainly, the virtues of worldly men or those of unbelievers have their own relative and indirect worth, but the same is true of physical qualities at their own level: the only qualities that contribute to the soul's salvation are those that are enhanced by the Truth and by the Way; no virtue cut off from these bases has any salvific power, which proves the relativeness, and the indirect scope, of purely natural virtues. A spiritual man does not feel that he owns his virtues; he renounces vices and extinguishes himself—actively and passively—in the divine Virtues, in the Virtues as such. Virtue is that which is.

A virtuous man conceals his faults for the following reasons: firstly, because he does not concede them any right to exist and because, after each lapse, he hopes it will be the last; a man cannot really be reproached for concealing his faults because he is striving not to sin and to behave correctly. Another reason is conformity to the norm: in order to be rid of a fault, one must not only have the intention to rid oneself of it for the sake of God and not just to please men, but one must also enter actively into the mold of perfection; and if it is clear that this must not be done just to please men, it is no less clear that it must be done also to avoid scandalizing them and setting a bad example; this is a charity demanded of us by God, since the love of God requires us to love our neighbor.

When so-called sincerity breaks the framework of traditional— or simply normal—rules of behavior, it betrays thereby its prideful nature; for the rules are venerable and we have no right to scorn them by placing our subjectivity above them. It is true that saints sometimes break these rules, but they do so from above, not from below—by virtue of a divine truth, not a human sentiment. Be that as it may, if a man of tradition effaces himself behind a rule of behavior, this is certainly not out of hypocrisy, but out of humility and charity: humility, because he realizes that the traditional rule is right and that it is better than he is; charity, because he does not wish to thrust on his neighbors the scandal of his own shortcomings, far from it: he intends to manifest a salutary norm, even if he is not yet personally up to its level.

— ∴ —

It is important to distinguish between sincerity as such, which encompasses and engages all of man—at least in moral terms—and fragmentary sincerity, which only deserves this name as a psychic phenomenon and within the subjective limits in which it occurs; quite paradoxically, this kind of good faith can graft itself as an autonomous detail on a substratum of bad faith, all the more so because in order to lie convincingly one must start by lying to oneself.

Too often mention is made of the sincerity of an error, but it is forgotten that true sincerity excludes persistence in a false idea because, precisely, it coincides with the love of truth: whosoever is fundamentally sincere is wary of his natural inclinations and will think twice before identifying them with objective reality. This is as much as to say that sincerity, inasmuch as it involves intelligence, coincides with objectivity—or at least with a sufficient objectivity from a point of view that may be relative but nonetheless valid—and this quality entails some degree of renunciation of self, hence a kind of death; as expressed in its own way, and to perfection, by this Hindu maxim: "There is no right superior to that of truth".

— ∴ —

The noble man is one who dominates himself and loves to do so; the base man is one who does not dominate himself and has a horror of doing so.[1] The spiritual man is one who transcends himself and loves

---

[1] Moreover, the noble man looks at what is essential in phenomena, not at what is accidental; he sees the overall worth in a creature and the intention of the Creator—not some more or less humiliating accident—and in so doing he anticipates the perception of the divine Qualities appearing through the forms. This is what is expressed by the words of the Apostle "for the pure all things are pure".

117

to transcend himself; the worldly man remains horizontal and hates the vertical dimension. And this is important: one cannot subject oneself to a demanding ideal—nor seek to transcend oneself for the sake of God—without bearing in one's soul what psychoanalysts term "complexes"; this amounts to saying that there are complexes that are normal for a spiritual man or simply for a decent man and that, conversely, the absence of "complexes" is not necessarily a virtue, to say the least. Doubtless, primordial man, or deified man, no longer has any complexes, but it is not enough to be free of complexes to be a deified or primordial man.

The root of all true sincerity is sincerity towards God, not towards what suits our own good pleasure; in other words, it is not enough to believe in God, one must also draw all the implications of this in our outer and inner behavior; and when we aspire to a perfection—since God is perfect and wants us to be perfect—we seek to manifest it even before we have realized it, and in order to realize it.

A man who submits to outward and inward norms, and thus who is striving in the way of perfection—or striving to eliminate imperfections—is well aware that among those who do not make this effort there are some who surpass him in natural qualities; but, endowed as he is with intelligence, without which he would not be man, he cannot fail to note that, whether he likes it or not, he is necessarily better than worldly men with respect to metaphysical truth and spiritual effort, and that any effort made for the sake of God is worth infinitely more than a mere natural quality that is never turned to spiritual account. For the rest, worldly people are always looking for accomplices in their dissipation and their ruin, and this is why spiritual people part company with them as much as possible, unless they have an apostolic mission; but, in this case, they will be most wary of imitating the bad behavior of the worldly and thus of going against what they preach.

By way of summary, we shall say that the content of sincerity is our tendency towards God and consequently our compliance with the rules that this tendency requires of us, and not our nature pure and simple with all its defects; to be sincere is not to indulge in vice before men, but to be virtuous before God, and accordingly to enter into the mold of virtues we have yet to assimilate, whatever men may think. It is true that certain saints—the "people of blame" in Sufism—have sought to create scandal in order to be scorned, which amounts in practice to scorning others, but moral or mystical egoism is oblivious of this; this attitude is nevertheless a two-edged sword, in extreme cases at any rate—those precisely which make it legitimate to speak of egoism—and not when it is simply a question of neutral attitudes intended to veil a perfection, or a desire for perfection. In any event, the imperatives of a particular mystical subjectivity cannot prevent the normal attitude from being that virtues should be practiced in equilibrium and dignity; and it is important not to confuse equilibrium with mediocrity, which derives from lukewarmness, whereas equilibrium derives from wisdom. The essence of dignity is not only our theomorphism, but humility together with charity; these two virtues compensate for the risks stemming from our quality as image of God, while at the same time participating in the divine Virtues, thus integrating them into our theomorphism. This theomorphism could well make us arrogant or egoistic, but when we grasp its true nature we see that it obliges us, on the contrary, to heed the perfections not only of the Lord but also of the servant; the whole mystery of the human *pontifex* lies in this complementarity.

It may be worth adding to these principial considerations that rules of behavior are at times subtle and complex and even paradoxical: for an old man to play with children involves no loss of dignity if he holds fast to the dignity incumbent on man as such; for a litigant to plead his right is not contrary to charity, provided he does not become unjust in his turn, be it merely out of pettiness.[2] Charity does not preclude holy anger, any more than humility precludes holy pride, or dignity precludes holy joy.

—— ⋅⋮⋅ ——

We have seen that hypocrisy consists, not quite clearly in adopting a superior mode of behavior with the intention of realizing and affirming

[2] The basis of charity is not only to understand that other men are ourselves—every man being "I"—but also to desire our own good; for if our immortal personality was not worthy of love, then neither would our neighbor's. "Hate thy soul" means: hate in yourself that which harms your ultimate interests.

it, but in adopting it with the intention of seeming to be more than one is. It is to be found, therefore, not in a behavior that may well be above the level of our present state, but in the intention to appear to be above others, even in the absence of witnesses, by way of intimate self-satisfaction; the virulence of the error resulting from the cult of sincerity prompts us once again to make this self-evident *distinguo*: if the mere fact of adopting a form of model behavior were hypocrisy, it would be impossible to make any effort towards goodness, and man would not be man.

Sincerity is the absence of falsehood in inward and outward behavior; to lie is deliberately to mislead; one can lie to one's neighbor, to oneself, and to God. But a pious man who covers his weakness beneath a veil of rectitude does not intend to lie, nor is he lying *ipso facto*; he does not want to manifest that which in fact he is, but he cannot help manifesting that which he wishes to be. And in so doing, he necessarily rejoins perfect truthfulness; for what we wish to be is, in a certain sense, what we are.

Veil of hypocrisy, veil of rectitude: in the first case, the veil is opaque and concealing; in the second case, it is transparent and transmitting. The "lowering of the veil" (*zawāl al-hijāb*), in the first case, is the rejection of hypocrisy; in the second case, it is the forsaking of effort, or rather the forgetting of the symbol, thanks to the liberating presence of the Real.

The Problem of Sexuality

The spiritual life in itself could never exclude a domain as fundamentally human as sexuality; sex is an aspect of man. Traditionally, the West is marked by a theology of Augustinian inspiration, which explains marriage from a more or less utilitarian angle, while neglecting the intrinsic reality of the matter. According to this perspective—leaving aside all apologetic euphemisms—sexual union in itself is sin; consequently, the child is born in sin, but the Church compensates, or rather overcompensates, for this evil with a greater good, namely baptism, faith, sacramental life. According to the primordial perspective, on the other hand, which is based on the intrinsic nature of these realities, the sexual act is a "naturally supernatural" sacrament. In primordial man sexual ecstasy coincides with spiritual ecstasy; it transmits to man an experience of mystical union, a "remembrance" of the divine Love of which human love is a distant reflection; an ambiguous reflection, certainly, since the image is at one and the same time both adequate and inverted. It is in this ambiguity that the whole problem resides: the primitive, "pagan", Greco-Hindu perspective—a *de facto* esoteric perspective in the Christian context—is based on the adequateness of the image, for a tree reflected in water is still a tree and not something else; the Christian, penitential, ascetical, and in fact exoteric perspective is on the contrary based on the inversion of the image, for a tree has its branches above and not below, so that the reflection is no longer the tree. But here is the great disparity between the two points of view: while esoterism accepts the relative and conditional justice of the penitential perspective, the latter could never accept the legitimacy of the "natural", primordial, and participative perspective; and this is exactly the reason why it can only be "esoteric" within a context that is Augustinian in style, although in itself it can nonetheless be integrated into an exoterism, as is proved, for example, by Islam.[1]

In a Christian atmosphere, sexuality in itself, hence isolated from all contextual bias, lends itself readily to the opprobrium of "bestiality", whereas in reality nothing that is human is bestial by its nature; that is why we are men and not beasts. Nevertheless, in order

---

[1] Islam being in this respect even more explicit than Judaism.

to escape from the animality in which we partake, it is necessary that our attitudes should be integrally human, namely in accordance with the norm our deiformity renders incumbent upon us; they must encompass both our soul and our spirit, or in other words, devotion and truth. Moreover, it is only the blind passion of fallen men that is bestial, and not the innocent sexuality of animals; when man is reduced to his animality, he becomes worse than the animals, who betray no vocation and violate no norm; we must not implicate the animal, which may be a noble creature, in the taboos and anathemas of human moralism.

If the sexual act were by its nature a sin—as basically the Christian and penitential perspective would have it[2]—this nature would be transmitted to the child that is conceived in it; if on the contrary the sexual act represents, through its profound and spiritually integral nature, an act that is meritorious because in principle sanctifying[3]—or a primordial sacrament evoking and actualizing in the required conditions a union with God—then the child conceived according to this nature will be hereditarily predisposed to spiritual union, no more and no less than he would be predisposed to sin in the opposite case; the fact that the act by itself is *de jure* if not *de facto* a sort of sacrament implies, moreover, that the child is a gift, and not the exclusive end of the act.[4]

The Church blesses marriage in view of the procreation of men, of whom believers will be made; it blesses it while taking upon itself the inevitable but provisional drawback of the "sin of the flesh". In which case, it is tempting to say that it is nearer to Saint Paul than to Christ; that is to say, Saint Paul, while inventing nothing—which is out of the question—nonetheless accentuated things in view of a particular application that was not necessary in itself. Unquestionably, Christ showed men the way of abstinence; but abstinence does not

---

[2] No doubt this perspective is not exclusively Christian, but we want to grasp it here in its best-known form.

[3] This is related to the fact that in several traditional worlds the sexual act of the prince is reputed to fertilize, through the woman, the soil of the country, or to increase the prosperity of the people.

[4] If the sexual act is a double-edged sword that can engender totally opposite eschatological consequences, depending on the objective and subjective conditions that accompany it, it may call to mind, *mutatis mutandis*, the sacraments which, in the absence of the required conditions, result not in grace but in condemnation.

necessarily signify that the sexual act is sinful by nature; it may signify on the contrary that sinners profane it; for in sexual union sinners rob God of the enjoyment that belongs to Him. Seen from this angle, the sin of Adam consisted in monopolizing enjoyment—in attributing to himself enjoyment as such, so that the fault lay both in the theft and in the manner of envisaging the object of the theft, namely a pleasure that is substantially divine. Thus his sin was to usurp the place of God while separating himself from the divine subjectivity in which man participated at the origin; it was to cease to participate in this divine subjectivity and to make himself absolute subject. The human subject, in making himself God in practice, at the same stroke limited and degraded the object of his happiness and even the whole cosmic ambience.

Clearly, there could not have been in the intention of Christ the sole concern not to see a natural and primordial sacrament profaned; there was also, and even above all, the offering of a spiritual means congenial to an ascetical perspective, for chastity is necessarily the ferment of a way, given precisely the ambiguity of sexual things. At Cana, Christ consecrated or blessed marriage, without one being able to say that he did so from the Pauline or Augustinian angle: he changed the water into wine, which is eloquent in its symbolism, and which refers with much more likelihood to the possibility of a union that is both carnal and spiritual than to the moral and social opportunism of the theologians; if it was a question of an exclusively carnal union, it would indeed no longer be human.[5]

Moreover, if procreation is such an important thing, it is impossible that the act which is its condition *sine qua non* should be nothing more than a regrettable accident, and that this act should not, on the contrary, possess a sacred character proportionate to the importance and holiness of procreation itself. And if it is possible to isolate—as do the theologians—procreation from the sexual act by stressing only the former, it must be equally possible to isolate the sexual act from procreation by accentuating the act alone in conformity with its own

---

[5] When the Church teaches that Mary was "conceived without sin", this refers to the fact that her soul was created without the stain of original sin; but many uninstructed believers think that this attribute refers to the extraordinary manner of her conception, realized without carnal union on the part of her parents—according to a tradition—or at least without desire or enjoyment in their union, and so without "concupiscence". If this interpretation is not theological, its existence is nevertheless significant, for such a sentiment is typical of the Christian perspective.

nature and its immediate context; this amounts to saying that love possesses a quality that makes it independent of its purely biological and social aspect, as moreover its theological and mystical symbolism proves. One can procreate without loving, and one can love without procreating; the love of Jacob for Rachel does not lose its meaning because Rachel was for a long time sterile, and the Song of Songs does not seek to justify itself by any demographic considerations.

Doubtless, Christ was not opposed to marriage, and he was perhaps no more opposed to polygamy either; the parable of the ten virgins seems to indicate this.[6] In the Christian world, polygamy should have been allowed for princes, if not for all believers; many wars and many tyrannical pressures on the Church would have been avoided—among others, the Anglican schism. Man must not put asunder what God has joined together, Christ said in condemning divorce; the marriages of princes, however, were for the most part the result of political bargaining, which has nothing to do with God, any more than it has to do with love. Polygamy, like monogamy, rests on natural factors: if monogamy is normal because the first marriage was of necessity monogamous and because femininity, like virility, resides entirely in a single person, then polygamy for its part is explained, on the one hand, by biological facts and by social or political opportuneness—at least in certain societies—and on the other hand by the fact that the infinitude which woman represents allows for a diversity of aspects; man is prolonged towards the periphery, which liberates, just as woman roots herself in the center, which protects.[7] To this it should be added,

---

[6] At least in a symbolical way, if one disregards the words "and of the bride" added by the Vulgate, and justified, so it appears, by a certain Jewish custom.

[7] Polyandry, on the other hand, finds no support in the facts of nature; extremely rare, it is doubtless to be explained by very special economic reasons and perhaps also by concepts proper to shamanism. There is also the case of sacred prostitution—hetaerae, hierodules, *devadāsīs*, geishas—in which woman becomes the center because she gives herself to a number of men; we are compelled to admit that this phenomenon is a possibility within the framework of archaic traditions, but it is at all events not possible in the later religions, apart from a few exceptions, which however are too marginal to warrant explicit mention.

leaving aside all considerations of opportuneness, that the more or less Nordic peoples tend to favor monogamy, and this for obvious reasons of climate and temperament, whereas the majority of Southern peoples seem to have a natural tendency towards polygamy, whatever be its form or degree. Be that as it may, it was an error, in the West, to impose on a whole continent a morality for monks: a morality that is perfectly legitimate in its methodic context, but which is nevertheless based on the error—as regards its extension to the whole of society—that sexuality is a kind of evil; an evil that should be reduced to a minimum and tolerated only by virtue of an approach that leaves out all that is essential.

No doubt a distinction should be made between a polygamy in which several women keep their personality, and a princely "pantagamy" in which a multitude of women represent femininity in a quasi-impersonal manner; the latter would be an affront to the dignity of human persons if it were not based on the idea that a given bridegroom is situated at the summit of humankind. Pantagamy is possible because Krishna is Vishnu, because David and Solomon are prophets, because the sultan is the "shadow of *Allāh* on earth"; it could also be said that the innumerable and anonymous harem has a function analogous to that of the imperial throne adorned with precious stones; a function that is analogous but not identical, for the throne made of human substance—the harem, namely—indicates in an eminently more direct and more concrete manner the real or borrowed divinity of the monarch. At a profane level, this pantagamy would not be possible; as to whether it is legitimate or permissible in any particular case, this is a question that can be settled only on the basis of the distinction between the individual, who may be unexceptional, and the function, which is sublime and may on that account attenuate human disproportions and illusions.

We have written the foregoing in order to explain existing phenomena and not to express preferences or their opposite; our personal sensibility is not at issue and may even be opposed to a particular moral or social solution, of which nevertheless we have sought to demonstrate the justification from a given point of view or in a given context.

—— ·:· ——

A very important possibility that must be taken into account here is abstinence within the framework of marriage; this moreover goes hand in hand with the virtues of detachment and generosity, which are the essential conditions for the sacramentalization of sexuality. Nothing is more opposed to the sacred than tyranny or triviality on the plane of conjugal relations; abstinence, a break in habits, and freshness of soul are indispensable elements of any sacred sexuality. In the direct daily interaction between two beings, there must be two equilibrium-producing openings, one towards heaven and the other on earth itself: there must be an opening towards God, who is the third element above the two spouses, without which the duality would become opposition; and there must be an opening or a void—an airing out, so to speak—on the immediate human plane, and this is absti-nence, which is both a sacrifice before God and a homage of respect and gratitude towards the spouse. For the human and spiritual dignity of spouses demands that they should not become a habit, should not be treated in a way that lacks imagination and freshness, thus allowing them to keep their mystery; this condition requires not only absti-nence, but also, and above all, loftiness of character, which results finally from our sense of the sacred or from our state of devotion.

Devotion, in fact, requires on the one hand respect for apartness, and on the other, sharing of intimacy; on the one hand, one must extinguish oneself and remain poor, and on the other, one must radiate or give; whence the complementarity of detachment and generosity. And pertinent to note in this context is that the patient and chari-table understanding of the spouse's physical temperament is a condi-tion not only of human dignity but also of the spiritual value of the marriage—periodic abstinence being, precisely, an expression of this understanding or of this tolerance.[8]

In order not to omit any possibility, we must even consider the case, however rare but in no wise illegitimate in itself, where this abstinence is definitive and where the ideal of a brother-and-sister relationship is combined with that of chastity;[9] in such a case, the tone

---

[8] It may be noted that the American Indians saw in sexual abstinence, to which they were sometimes constrained for practical reasons, a sign of strength and consequently of consummate virility.

[9] The marriage of Ramakrishna offers us an example of this. It would happen that the *Paramahamsa* would worship his wife without touching her; which is infinitely better than touching her without worshipping her.

will not be that of a pedantic or tormented moralism, but that of holy childlikeness. Obviously Platonic marriage presupposes rather special vocational qualifications, along with a spiritual point of view that supports this solution, in conformity with the words from Genesis: "It is not good that man should be alone; I shall make for him a help meet like unto him."[10]

— ∴ —

Certainly, the flesh was cursed by the Fall, but only in a certain respect, that of existential and formal discontinuity, not with respect to spiritual and essential continuity. The same remark applies to the natural form, that of the creature: the human body, male or female, is a theophany, and remains so in spite of the Fall;[11] in loving one another, the spouses legitimately love a divine manifestation, each according to a different aspect and a different relationship—the divine content of nobility, goodness, and beauty remaining the same. It is by basing itself on this relationship that Islam, on the one hand, implicitly recognizes the sacred character of sexuality in itself and, on the other hand—and by way of consequence—considers that every child is born *muslim* and that it is its parents who make of it an infidel, depending on the case.

Christian theology, by concerning itself with sin and seeing particularly in Eve and in woman in general the seductress, has been led to evaluate the feminine sex with a maximum of pessimism. According to some, it is man alone and not woman who was made in the image of God, whereas the Bible affirms, not only that God created man in His image, but also that "male and female created He them", which has been misinterpreted with much ingenuity. In principle, one might be surprised at this quasi-visual lack of intelligence on the part of the theologians; in fact, such a limitation has nothing surprising about

[10] This is also translated as "who will be meet for him" or "who will be worthy of him"; this passage, if one takes the trouble to understand it, rules out the pious misogyny and the holy heedlessness of some exegetes.

[11] "Whoever has seen me, has seen God": this *hadīth* applies first and foremost to the avataric person, but it applies equally—with obvious reservations—to the human form as such; in this case it is no longer a question of "such and such a man", but of "man as such".

it, given the voluntaristic and sentimental character of the exoterist perspective in general, hence one predisposed to prejudices and bias.[12] A first proof—if proof be needed—that woman is divine image like man, is that in fact like him she is a human being; she is not *vir* or *andros*, but like him she is *homo* or *anthropos*; her form is human and consequently divine. Another proof—but a glance ought to suffice—resides in the fact that, in relation to man and on the erotic plane, woman assumes an almost divine function—similar to the one that man assumes in relation to woman—which would be impossible if she did not embody, not the quality of absoluteness no doubt, but the complementary quality of infinitude; the Infinite being in a certain sense the *shakti* of the Absolute.

And this leads us to specify, in order to rectify the excessively unilateral opinions to which the question of the sexes has given rise, three relationships that govern the equilibrium between man and woman: firstly, the sexual, biological, psychological, and social relationship; then the simply human and fraternal relationship; and finally the properly spiritual or sacred relationship. In the first relationship, there is obviously inequality, and from this results the social subordination of woman, a subordination already prefigured in her physical constitution and her psychology; but this relationship is not everything, and it may even be more than compensated for—depending on the individuals and the type of contact—by other dimensions. In the second relationship, that of the human quality, woman is equal to man since like him she belongs to the human species; this is the plane, not of subordination, but of friendship; and it goes without saying that on this level the wife may be superior to her husband since one human individual may be superior to another, whatever be the sex.[13] Finally, in the third relationship there is, quite paradoxically, reciprocal superiority: woman, as we have said earlier, assumes in love a divine func-

---

[12] It may be objected that the doctors of the Church were inspired by the Holy Spirit; without a doubt, but this interpretation is conditional from the outset, if one may express it thus, for water takes on the color of its recipient. The Holy Spirit excludes intrinsic error and error that is harmful to the soul, but not necessarily every error that is extrinsic and opportune and thus in practice neutral as regards essential truth and salvation.

[13] The *Yoga Vāsistha* tells the story of the beautiful Queen Chudala, who realized the supreme Wisdom—that envisaged by Shankara—and who was the spiritual master of King Shikhidhwaja, her husband.

tion with regard to her partner, as does the man with regard to the woman.[14]

Apart from these three dimensions of the conjugal alliance, there are, as regards the actual choice of partner, two factors to be considered: affinity or resemblance, and complementarity or difference; love needs both of these conditions. Man naturally seeks—without having to explain or justify it—a human complement who is of his type and as a result with whom he can be at ease; but on the very basis of this condition, he will seek a complement who is different from himself, failing which it is not a complement, for the purpose of love is to allow human beings to complete one another naturally and not simply to repeat each other. It may happen that a person finds his partner in an individual from another race because this individual, in spite of the racial disparity, on the one hand fulfils this affinity in a decisive respect and on the other hand represents the ideal complement; in this case, it is not that the person preferred the other race *a priori*, which would scarcely have any meaning, but simply that destiny did not offer him the irreplaceable partner within the context of his own race. In principle, a great love depends on a choice, but in fact it depends largely on destiny: it is *karma* that decides whether the choice will be possible, that is to say, whether the man or the woman will or will not meet the ideal complement. Finally, the complementary type takes precedence over the degree of beauty: it is not perfect beauty that is the ideal, but perfect complementarity on the basis of perfect affinity; the man normally endowed with the sense of forms—or let us say, to the extent that he is able to take them into account—will prefer the lesser, but complementary, beauty to the greater beauty which for him is lacking in complementarity.

All these considerations result from a point of view that derives from the principle of natural selection, which in many cases can be neutralized by a moral and spiritual point of view, but without for

---

[14] So true is this that even Buddhism, which is ascetically hostile to sexuality in general and to the feminine sex in particular, could not help populating its heavens with feminine divinities, if such a formulation is permissible; it should be said that, in this case, we are dealing with Mahayanic and esoteric Buddhism. This same Buddhism gave rise to the Amidist marriage: Shinran, monk of the *Jōdo* school and founder of the *Shinshū* school, received advice from his master Honen to take a wife, so as to show thereby that the salvation through the direct way offered by Amida Buddha is accessible to married people as well as to celibates; always within the framework of the *Jōdo* initiation, which *a priori* is monastic.

all that losing its rights on its own level, which relates to the human norm, and thus to our deformity. At all events, it goes without saying, humanly speaking, that beauty— whatever be its degree—requires a moral and spiritual complement of which it is in reality the expression, and without which man would not be man.

If one looks at these things—on which we have dwelt at some length—without the slightest mistrust or hypocrisy, one will realize that they contain teachings which go beyond their immediate scope, and one will recognize without difficulty that, even without going beyond it, they hold all the interest the human condition deserves, this condition which is ours.

— ∴ —

Krishna, the great *avatāra* of Vishnu, had numerous wives, as did, moreover, at a period closer to ourselves, the prophet-kings David and Solomon; the Buddha, likewise a major *avatāra*, had none;[15] the same is true of Shankara, Ramanuja, and other minor incarnations, who nevertheless were Hindu by tradition like Krishna. This proves that if the choice of sexual experience or chastity may be a question of superiority or inferiority on the spiritual level, it can also be, for equivalent reasons, a matter of perspective and vocation; the whole problem comes down to the distinction between "abstraction" and "analogy", or to the opportuneness, be it intellectual, methodic, or yet psychological or quasi-existential, or perhaps merely social, of one or other of these options, which in principle are equivalent. The question that arises here is to know not only what man chooses, or what his particular nature requires or desires, but also and even above all how God wants to be approached: whether through the void, the absence of everything that is not He, or through the plenitude of His manifestations, or again through the void and through plenitude alternately, of which the hagiographies provide many an example. In the last analysis, it is God who is seeking Himself through the play of His veilings and unveilings, His silences and His words, His nights and His days.

Fundamentally, every love is a search for the Essence or the lost Paradise; the melancholy, gentle or powerful, which often appears in

[15] That is, he was married in his youth, while he was still *Bodhisattva* and not *Buddha*.

poetic or musical eroticism bears witness to this nostalgia for a far-off Paradise and doubtless also to the evanescence of earthly dreams, of which the sweetness precisely is that of a Paradise that we no longer perceive, or which we do not yet perceive. Gypsy violins evoke not only the chance fortunes of an all-too-human love, they also celebrate, in their profoundest and most poignant accents, a thirst for the heavenly wine that is the essence of Beauty; all erotic music, to the extent of its authenticity and nobility, rejoins the captivating and yet liberating notes of Krishna's flute.[16]

Like that of woman, the role of music is ambiguous, and so are the related arts of dance and poetry: there is either a narcissistic inflation of the ego, or an interiorization and a beatific extinction in the essence. Woman, incarnating *Māyā*, is dynamic in a double sense: either in the sense of an exteriorizing and alienating radiation, or in that of an interiorizing and reintegrating attraction; whereas man, in the fundamental respect in question, is static and unambiguous.

Man stabilizes woman, woman vivifies man; furthermore, and quite obviously, man contains woman within himself, and conversely, given that both are *homo sapiens*, man as such; and if we define the human being as *pontifex*, it goes without saying that this function includes woman, although she adds to it the mercurial character proper to her sex.[17]

Man, in his lunar and receptive aspect, "withers away" without solar-woman that infuses into the virile genius the life it needs in order to blossom; conversely, solar-man confers on woman the light that permits her to realize her identity by extending the function of the sun.

Chastity can have as its aim, not only resistance to the bondage of the flesh, but also, and more profoundly, an escaping from the polarity

---

[16] Visible forms manifest the heavenly essences by crystallizing them; music in a certain fashion interiorizes forms by recalling their quality as essence by means of a language made of unitive sweetness and limitlessness. Earthly beauty evokes in the soul the transfiguring "remembrance" of heavenly music, although with regard to this it may seem harsh and dissonant: "*Qualunque melodia più dolce suona / qua giù, e più a sé l'anima tira, / parebbe nube che squarciata tona, / comparata al sonar di quella lira / onde si coronava il bel zaffiro / del quale il ciel più chiaro s'inzaffira*" (Dante, *Paradiso* XXIII, 97-102).

[17] If woman is "of one flesh" with man—if she is "flesh of his flesh and bone of his bone"—this shows, in relation to the Spirit, which man represents, an aspect of continuity or prolongation, not of separation.

of the sexes and a reintegration of the unity of the primordial *pontifex*, of man as such; it is certainly not an indispensable condition for this result, but it is a clear and precise support for it, adapted to given temperaments and imaginations.

— ∴ —

If for Christianity, as for Buddhism in general, the sexual act is identified with sin—all euphemistic subtleties aside—this is easily explained by the fact that, the "spirit" being above and the "flesh" below, the most intense pleasure of the flesh will be the lowest pleasure in relation to the spirit. This perspective is plausible insofar as it takes account of a real aspect of things, that of the existential discontinuity between the phenomenon and the archetype, but it is false to the extent that it excludes the aspect of essential continuity, which precisely compensates, and on its level annuls, that of discontinuity. For if, on the one hand, the flesh as such is separated from the spirit, on the other hand it is united to it insofar as it manifests it and prolongs it, that is to say, insofar as the flesh is recognized as being situated on the unitive vertical axis or the radius, and not on the separative horizontal axis or the circle; in the first case the center is prolonged, and in the second it is concealed.

The possibility of benefiting from the mystery of continuity is something that depends either on the real and not imaginary contemplativity of the individual or on a religious system allowing an indirect and passive participation in this mystery; in which case, the risks of a centrifugal effect are neutralized and compensated by the general perspective and the particular dispositions of the religion, on condition, of course, that the individual submits to this in a sufficient manner. For the true contemplative, each pleasure that can be qualified as noble is a meeting with the eternal, not a fall into the temporal and the impermanent.

According to Meister Eckhart even the simple fact of eating and drinking would be a sacrament if man understood in depth what he was doing. Without entering into the details of this assertion, which in fact can be applied to a number of different planes—notably that of craftsmanship and art—we would say that in these cases the sacramental character has a significance that likens it to the "lesser mysteries"; sexuality, on the other hand, and this is what proves its dangerous ambivalence, refers to the "greater mysteries", as is indicated by the wine at Cana. Let us note in this connection that the passive complement of sexual union is deep sleep: here too there is a prefiguration of supreme union, with the difference nevertheless that in sleep the sacramental initiative is entirely from the side of God, who confers his grace on whoever may receive it; in other words, deep sleep is a sacrament of union to the extent that man is already sanctified.

In Islam there is a notion that offers a natural bridge between the sacred and the profane, or between the spirit and the flesh, and this is the notion of *barakah*, of "immanent blessing": it is said of every lawful pleasure[18] experienced in the name of God and within the limits allowed, that it carries a *barakah*, which amounts to saying that it has a spiritual value and a contemplative perfume, instead of being limited to a purely natural satisfaction, tolerated because it is inevitable or to the extent that it is so.

In order to properly understand the fundamental intention of the Christian point of view, one must take account of the following elements: the way towards God always involves an inversion: from outwardness one must move to inwardness, from multiplicity to unity, from dispersion to concentration, from egoism to detachment, from passion to serenity. Now, the leverage for Christianity is the opposition between worldly pleasure and sacrificial suffering, and this is what accounts from the outset for its prejudice against pleasure as such, although it is more of a methodic than an intellectual prejudice; but since Christianity is, by its very nature, a way rather than a doctrine—the patristic argumentation against the Greeks provides one more proof of this—it is led to put all the emphasis on that which in its eyes brings us most nearly, or alone brings us, to the redeeming God: God who is Himself the model of suffering and thereby of the way.

[18] This excludes vices contrary to nature and excesses—harmful to society as well as to the individual—which are obviously not capable of sacralization.

The obsessional and in fact defamatory suspicion of Christians with regard to all sacred sexuality is explained by this perspective. It may be objected that marriage is a sacrament; no doubt, but it is a sacrament with a view to procreation, and then to physical, psychic, and social equilibrium; it is not in view of love or union, in spite of the words of Christ that would allow for such an interpretation. To speak of exoterism is to speak of an outlook ruled by alternativism and exclusiveness, and thus too of simplification and stylization; as well as efficacy, certainly, but not total truth or unfailing stability.

We have alluded to the fact that anti-sexualism—apart from the fact that it is encountered more or less everywhere in one form or other—is likewise a prominent characteristic of Buddhism: in this perspective, based on subjectivity and immanence, woman appears *a priori* as the objective or outward element that takes us away from inward and immanent Bliss; woman is accident and attracts us towards accidentality, whereas the contemplative and interiorizing subjectivity of man pertains to the nirvanic Substance and opens onto it.

This provides us with the opportunity of making the following observation: if Buddhism denies the outward, objective, and transcendent God, this is because it puts all the emphasis on the inward, subjective, and immanent Divinity—whether it is termed *Nirvāna*, *Ādi-Buddha* or otherwise—which moreover makes it impermissible to describe Buddhism as atheistic. In the Amidist sector, Amitabha is the immanent Mercy that our faith can and must actualize in our favor; each beauty and each love is concentrated in this personification of Mercy. If it happens that some Buddhists assert that Amithaba does not exist outside ourselves or that he would not exist without us—analogous formulations are to be found in Eckhart and Silesius—they mean that his immanence and his saving efficacy presuppose our existence and our subjectivity, for one cannot speak of a content without a container; in short, if Buddhists seem to put man in the place of God transcendent, this is because man as concrete subjectivity is the container of immanent liberating Substance.

— ∴ —

In this context, as we were saying, woman appears as the exteriorizing and binding element: indeed feminine psychology, unless there is an appreciation of her spiritual worth, is characterized on the purely natural plane by a tendency towards the world, or towards the concrete and the existential if one will, and in any case towards subjectivity and sentiment, and then by a more or less unconscious guile in the service of this in-born tendency.[19] It is with regard to this tendency that Christians as well as Muslims have felt justified in saying that a holy woman is no longer a woman, but a man—an absurd formulation in itself, but defensible in the light of the axiom in question. But this axiom concerning the innate tendency of woman, precisely, happens to be relative and not absolute, given that woman is a human being like man and that sexual psychology is necessarily a relative thing; as much as one may wish to claim that Eve's sin was to beckon Adam to partake in the adventure of outwardness, one cannot forget that the role of Mary was the reverse and that this role also enters into the possibility of the feminine spirit. Nevertheless, the spiritual mission of woman can never be combined with a revolt against man, feminine virtue comprising submission in a quasi-existential manner: for woman, submission to man—not just to any man—is a secondary form of human submission to God. It is so because the sexes, as such, manifest an ontological relationship, and thus an existential logic, which the spirit may transcend inwardly but cannot abolish outwardly.

To allege that the woman who is holy has become a man by the fact of her sanctity amounts to presenting her as a denatured being: in reality, a holy woman can only be such on the basis of her perfect femininity, otherwise God would have been mistaken in creating woman—*quod absit*—whereas according to Genesis she was, in the intention of God, "a help meet like unto him"; and so firstly a "help" and not an obstacle, and secondly "like unto him", and not sub-human; to be accepted by God, she does not have to stop being what she is.[20]

---

[19] We are here in the realm of imponderables, but what is decisive is that the psychological differences between the sexes really exist, in a vertical or qualitative sense as well as in a horizontal or neutral sense. Perhaps one should add, in order to forestall easily predictable objections, that woman finds a means of manifesting her particular worldliness within the very framework of a *de facto* masculine worldliness; that is to say, generally human weaknesses do not abolish the specific—but certainly not ineluctable—weaknesses of the feminine sex. Finally, it is necessary to recall in this context that modern life ends by devirilizing men and defeminizing women, which is to the advantage of no one since the process goes against nature and transfers or even accentuates faults instead of correcting them.

[20] *Ave gratia plena*, the angel says to Mary. "Full of grace": this settles the question, given that Mary is a woman. The angel did not say *Ave Maria*, because to him *gratia plena* is the name that he gives to the Virgin; this amounts to saying that *Maria* is synonymous with *gratia plena*.

The key to the mystery of salvation through woman, or through femininity, if one prefers, lies in the very nature of *Māyā*: if *Māyā* can attract towards the outward, it can also attract towards the inward.[21] Eve is Life, and this is manifesting *Māyā*; Mary is Grace, and this is reintegrating *Māyā*. Eve personifies the demiurge under its aspect of femininity; Mary is the personification of the *Shekhinah*, of the Presence that is both virginal and maternal. Life, being amoral, can be immoral; Grace, being pure substance, is capable of reabsorbing all accidents.

Sita, the wife of Rama, seems to combine Eve with Mary: her drama, at first sight disappointing, describes in a certain fashion the ambiguous character of femininity. In the midst of the vicissitudes of the human condition, the divinity of Sita is significantly maintained: the demon Ravana, who had succeeded in abducting Sita—following a fault on her part—believes that he has ravished her, but he has ravished only a magical appearance, without having been able to touch Sita herself. The fault of Sita was an unjust suspicion and her punishment was likewise such a suspicion: this is the form taken here by the sin of Eve; but at the end of her earthly career, the Ramayanic Eve reintegrates the Marial quality: Sita, the incarnation of Lakshmi,[22] disappears into the earth, which opens for her, and this signifies her return to divine Substance, which the earth visibly manifests.[23] The name of Sita, in fact, means "furrow": Sita, instead of being born of woman, emerged from the Earth-Mother, that is to say, from *Prakriti*, the metacosmic Substance at once pure and creating.

---

[21] When it is said that *Samsāra* is *Nirvāna* and vice versa, this means that there is only *Nirvāna* and that *Samsāra* is its radiance, which is both centrifugal and centripetal, projecting and reabsorbing, creating and saving.

[22] Lakshmi is a divine but already cosmic personification of *Prakriti*, the feminine pole of Being, of which she manifests the aspect of goodness, beauty, and happiness.

[23] The negative symbolism of the earth—arising from the fact that it is "below" and that it suggests downward movement, heaviness, and darkness—is neutralized here by the positive symbolism of the earth, that of stability, of fertility, or substantiality and hence of purity, which it seems to manifest by the springs that gush forth from its bosom. Substantiality likewise entails the aspects of depth and strength: by "descending", Sita reintegrates the depths of her divine substance, which coincides with the power of Lakshmi.

The Hindus excuse Sita by emphasizing the fact that her fault[24] was due to an excess of love for her spouse Rama; by universalizing this interpretation, one can conclude that the origin of evil is not curiosity or ambition as in the case of Eve, but an immoderate love, and thus the excess of a good.[25] This would seem to rejoin the biblical perspective in the sense that the sin of the first couple was to divert love: to love the creature more than the Creator, to love the creature outside the Creator and not in Him. But in this case the "love" is more of a craving on the part of the soul than a form of worship; a desire for novelty or fullness of experience rather than an adoration; hence a lack of love rather than a deviated love.

The condition *sine qua non* for the innocent and natural experience of earthly happiness is the spiritual capacity of finding happiness in God, and the inability to enjoy things outside of Him. We cannot validly and enduringly love a creature without carrying him within ourselves by virtue of our attachment to the Creator; not that this inward possession must be perfect, but it must at all events present itself as an intention that allows us to perfect it.

The state—or the very substance—of the normal human soul is devotion or faith, and this comprises an element of fear as well as an element of love; perfection is the equilibrium between the two poles, and this brings us back once again to the Taoist symbolism of *yin-yang*, which is the image of balanced reciprocity: we mean that the love of God, and by reflection the love of the husband or the wife, entails an element of fear or respect.

---

[24] Namely a defamatory suspicion cast on the virtuous Lakshmana, who refused to go in search of Rama since his mission was to protect Sita; he finally obeyed, and this allowed Ravana to abduct the heroine.

[25] The *Rāmāyana*, in narrating the incident, specifies that the mind of a woman is "covered with clouds" when the interest of the beloved is at stake; her trust is "inconstant" and her tongue "venomous"; the compensatory quality being the love of her *alter ego*, and consequently the perfect gift of self. In another place, the *Rāmāyana* points out the gentle wisdom of the wife in contradistinction to the unreflecting anger of the warrior.

To be at peace with God is to seek and find our happiness in Him; the creature that He has conjoined to us may and must help us to reach this with greater facility or with less difficulty, depending on our gifts and with grace, whether merited or unmerited.[26] That being said, we evoke the paradox—or rather the mystery—of attachment in view of detachment, or of outwardness in view of inwardness, or again, of form in view of essence. True love attaches us to a sacramental form while taking us away from the world, thus rejoining the mystery of exteriorized Revelation in view of interiorizing Salvation.[27]

---

[26] According to a well-known *hadīth*, "marriage is half of the religion".

[27] For as the *Veda* declares: "Verily it is not for love of the husband that the husband is dear, but for love of *Ātmā* that is in him. Verily it is not for the love of the wife that the wife is dear, but for the love of *Ātmā* that is in her" (*Brihadāranyaka Upanishad*, II, 4:5).

Dimensions of the Human Vocation

Injustice is a trial, but a trial is not an injustice. Injustices come from men, whereas trials come from God; what, on the part of men, is injustice and therefore evil, is trial and destiny on the part of God. One has the right, or possibly even the duty, to fight a particular evil, but one must resign oneself to a trial and accept destiny; in other words, it is necessary to combine the two attitudes, given that every injustice that we suffer at the hands of men is at the same time a trial that comes to us from God.

In the horizontal or earthly dimension, one can escape from evil by fighting it and overcoming it; in the vertical or spiritual dimension, by contrast, we can escape, if not from the trial as such, at least from its weight, and this we do by accepting an evil as the divine will, while transcending it inwardly as cosmic play, just as one can transcend spiritually any other manifestation of *Māyā*. For the din of the world does not enter the divine Silence that we carry within our own depths and into which, like accidents into substance, both the world and the ego are extinguished and absorbed.

Man has the duty to resign himself to the will of God, but by the same token he has the right to transcend spiritually the suffering of the soul to the extent that this is possible for him; and this, precisely, is not possible without a prior attitude of acceptance and resignation, which alone brings out fully the serenity of the intelligence and which alone opens the soul to help from Heaven.

It is plausible that God can send us sufferings so that we may grasp all the better the worth of His liberating Grace, and so that we may strive with all the more fervor to respond to the requirements of His Mercy. When man is unaware that he is drowning, he does not bother to call for help; now salvation is premised on our call, and there is finally nothing more consoling than this cry of trust or certitude.

— ·⁝· —

It is important not to confuse the two dimensions of which we have just spoken: that God should send us a trial does not prevent this from possibly being an injustice on the human plane; and that men should treat us unjustly does not prevent this from being justice on the part of God. Thus we must avoid two errors: believing that an evil, on its own plane, is something good because God sends it to us, or because God permits it, or because everything comes from God; and believing that a trial as such, is an evil, because it is so in its form, and because we suffer from it. It would be equally false to believe that we directly deserve an injustice because God permits it, for if this were the case, there would be no injustice and the unjust would be just; it would be equally false to imagine that we do not deserve a trial because we have done nothing that, logically, would have provoked it.

In reality, the cause of a trial is inscribed in our very relativity, hence in the fact that we are contingent beings or individuals; there is no need to have recourse to the transmigrationist theory of good or bad *karma* to know that contingency entails fissures, and that it does so in succession as well as in simultaneity. The cosmic possibility fashioning individuality is what it must be, in its limitation as well as in its positive content, and in its possibilities of transcending itself: finite and passible in its contours, it is infinite and impassible in its substance, and this is why trials carry within themselves the virtuality of liberation. They are thus the messengers of a liberty which, in our immutable and immanent reality, has never ceased to be, but which is darkened by the clouds of ever-shifting contingency, which the intelligent soul can be faulted in a certain manner for identifying itself with.

It is correct to say that no one escapes his destiny; but it is worth adding a conditional reservation, namely that fatality comprises different degrees, because our nature does so. Our destiny is dependent on the personal level—high or low—at which we position ourselves, or in which we enclose ourselves; for we are what we want to be and we undergo what we are. Concretely, this means that destiny may change, if not as to style at least as to mode or intensity, depending on the change of level that spiritual ascension may bring about in us.[1]

This explains why Muslims, who are acutely aware of predestination (*qadar*), can nevertheless on certain occasions pray that God may erase the evil that is inscribed on the tablet of their destinies. In a general manner, they could not pray—logically and reasonably—

---

[1] For example, a slight accident may replace a serious accident; spiritual death may replace physical death; an initiatic pact may take the place of a marriage pact, or vice versa.

for anything whatsoever if there were not in predestination certain margins, modes, or degrees of application, in short a kind of internal life, required by the divine Freedom, which compensates for the implacable crystallinity of "what is written". This also explains why astrological data remain fixed only to the extent that man neglects or refuses to transcend himself; it may be difficult to grasp these things with the mind, perhaps, but they are no more mysterious than the boundlessness of space and time, or the empirical uniqueness of our ego, and other paradoxes of nature that we have no choice but to accept.

To transcend oneself: this is the great imperative of the human condition; and there is another that anticipates it and at the same time prolongs it: to dominate oneself. The noble man is one who dominates himself; the holy man is one who transcends himself. These are the two dimensions—one horizontal and one vertical—to which we alluded when speaking of injustices and trials: the first dimension is that of earthly and outward man, and the second that of celestial or inward man. The obligation to dominate oneself, and all the more so to transcend oneself, is engraved in the intelligence and the will of man, because this intelligence is total, and this will is free: being total and free, the human soul has no other positive choice than to dominate itself in order to transcend itself. Our intelligence and our will are proportioned to the Absolute, meaning that our vocation as man is determined existentially by this relationship; without this, man would not be man. Nobility and holiness are the imperatives of the human state.

Man must dominate himself because, as center, he is called on to dominate the periphery; if God in Genesis conferred on man dominion over all other earthly creatures, this means that man, being responsible and free, must above all dominate himself, for he too possesses in his soul a periphery and a center; no one can govern others without knowing how to govern himself. Man is by definition a total, although reduced, cosmos, and this is expressed by the very term "microcosm"; now, the spirit must dominate the passional powers of the soul and hold in check its tenebrous elements, so that the microcosm may realize the perfection of the macrocosm.[2] On the plane of everyday experience, it is only too obvious that reason must dominate sentiment and imagination, and that in its turn it must obey the Intellect, or faith; the latter plays the role of the Intellect in the non-metaphysician, which in no wise means that it is absent in the metaphysician; in his case faith is the psychic prolongation or the *shakti* of knowledge, and not a simple *credo quia absurdum est*.[3]

But self-domination also depends on an outward reality, namely the fact that an individual is part of a society; since human intelligence is capable of transcendence and thereby of objectivity, man escapes from animal solipsism and realizes that he is not the only one who is "myself"; this entails, normally or vocationally, the virtue of generosity, by which man proves that his will is really free. The freedom of the will results directly from the totality of the intelligence: given that intelligence is capable of objectivity and transcendence, the will is necessarily capable of freedom.

If our intelligence obliges us to dominate ourselves, because the higher must rule the lower and because the spirit within us is threatened by passions and vices, intelligence obliges us *a fortiori* to transcend ourselves: for this intelligence, such as we have defined it, cannot but realize that man does not have his end in himself, and consequently can only find his meaning and his plenitude in that which constitutes his *raison d'être*. Transcendence is not merely the result of human reasoning; it is clearly the opposite that is true: if man is capable of reasoning according to the facts of transcendence and if this reasoning becomes obvious to his mind inasmuch as the mind is faithful to its vocation, this is because transcendence is engraved in the very substance of human intelligence, or one might even say: because our intelligence is made of transcendence. Our deiformity entails that our spirit is made of absoluteness, that our will is made of freedom, and that our soul is made of generosity; to dominate oneself and to transcend oneself is to remove the layer of ice or of darkness that imprisons man's true nature.

[2] Or of "Universal Man", as the Sufis would say. The Universe, in perfect hierarchy and equilibrium, is personified in the Prophet.

[3] We quote this phrase of Tertullian's in its elementary meaning, but it lends itself to a subtler interpretation that relates it to the *credo ut intelligam* of Saint Anselm. In fact, the dividing line between discernment and faith is a complex matter and is repeated at different levels.

The Supreme Commandment

"Hear, O Israel: the Lord our God is one Lord. And thou shalt love the Lord thy God with all thine heart, and with all thy soul, and with all thy might" (Deut. 6:4-5). This fundamental expression of Sinaitic monotheism contains the two pillars of all human spirituality, namely metaphysical discernment on the one hand and contemplative concentration on the other; or in other words: doctrine and method, or truth and way. The second element is presented under three aspects: according to a certain rabbinical interpretation, man must firstly "unite himself with God" in his heart, secondly "contemplate God" in his soul, and thirdly "accomplish in God" with his hands and through his body.[1]

The Gospel gives a slightly modified version of the Sinaitic enunciation, in the sense that it makes explicit an element that in the *Torah* was implicit, namely "mind"; this term is found in each of the synoptic Gospels, whereas the element strength is only found in the versions of Mark and Luke,[2] which may indicate a certain change of accent or perspective with regard to the "Old Law": in contrast with the element "soul", the element "mind" is now highlighted and gains in importance over the element "strength", which refers to works; there is in this a sign of a tendency towards an interiorization of activity. In other words, whereas for the *Torah* the "soul" is both active or operative and passive or contemplative, the Gospel seems to denote by the term "soul" the passive contemplative element, and by the term "mind" the active operative element; it may be supposed that this is to mark the superiority of inward activity over outward works.

Thus the element "strength" or "works" seems to have a different emphasis in Christianity than in Judaism: in the latter, "mind" is in a certain fashion the inward concomitant of outward observance, whereas in Christianity works appear rather as the exteriorization, or the external confirmation, of the activity of the soul. Jews contest

---

[1] In this we may distinguish, either three ways, or three modes that are inherent in every way.

[2] Mark 12:30: ". . . with all thy heart, and with all thy soul, and with all thy mind, and with all thy strength"; Luke 10:27: ". . . with all thy heart, and with all thy soul, and with all thy strength, and with all thy mind."

the legitimacy and efficacy of this relative interiorization;[3] conversely, Christians readily believe that the complication of outward prescriptions (*mitzvoth*) does harm to the inward virtues;[4] in reality, if it is true that the "letter" can kill the "spirit", it is no less true that sentimentalism can kill the "letter", quite apart from the fact that no spiritual fault is the exclusive prerogative of any religion. At all events, the sufficient reason for a religion is precisely to put the emphasis on a given spiritual possibility; and this possibility will serve as the framework for those possibilities that are apparently excluded, inasmuch as they are destined to be realized; thus, of necessity, one finds in each religion elements that seem to be reflections from the other religions. What can be said is that Judaism, in its basic framework, is a *karma-mārga* rather than a *bhakti*, whereas the relationship is inverse in Christianity; but *karma*, "action", necessarily comprises an element of *bhakti*, "love", and vice versa.

These considerations, as well as those to follow, can serve as an illustration of the fact that, of necessity, the profoundest truths are already to be found in the fundamental and initial formulations of the religions. Esoterism, in fact, is not an unpredictable doctrine that can only be discovered, should the occasion arise, by means of detailed researches; what is mysterious in esoterism is its dimension of depth, its particular developments, and its practical consequences, but not its starting points, which coincide with the fundamental symbols of the religion in question;[5] moreover its continuity is not exclusively "horizontal" as is that of exoterism, it is also "vertical", in the sense that esoteric mastery is related to prophecy, without for all that departing from the framework of the mother-religion.

---

[3] The Pauline interpretation of circumcision is a patent example of this transposition.

[4] Hasidism would suffice to prove the contrary, were proof needed for something so obvious.

[5] This is why it is vain to ask "where Christian esoterism has gone" and to suppose, for example, that it is founded on the Kabbalah and the Hebrew language; Christian esoterism can only be founded on the Gospel and on the symbolism of the dogmas and the sacraments—and by extension on the "Old Testament" in translation, notably on the Psalms and the Song of Songs—although it can certainly annex, "on the side", elements from Jewish and Hellenic esoterism; it even does so of necessity, since these elements are within its reach and correspond to certain vocations.

— .:. —

In the Gospels, the law of the love of God is immediately followed by the law of the love of one's neighbor, which is enunciated in the *Torah* in the form: "Thou shalt not hate thy brother in thine heart: thou shalt in any wise rebuke thy neighbor, and not suffer sin upon him. Thou shalt not avenge, nor bear any grudge against the children of thy people, but thou shalt love thy neighbor as thyself. I am the Lord" (Lev. 19:17-18).[6] Thus, a triple Law follows from the biblical passages quoted: firstly, recognition by the intelligence of the unity of God; secondly, union, both volitive and contemplative, with the One God;[7] and thirdly, transcending the misleading and distorting distinction between "I" and "the other".[8]

Love of one's neighbor receives all its meaning through the love of God: it is impossible to abolish the separation between man and God—to the extent that it can and must be abolished— without also abolishing in a certain fashion, and bearing in mind all the aspects comprised in the nature of things, the separation between the *ego* and the *alter,* in other words, it is impossible to realize consciousness of the Absolute without realizing consciousness of our relativity. To understand this well, it is sufficient to consider the illusory, and illusion-producing, nature of egohood: there is indeed something thoroughly absurd in believing that "only I" am "I"; only God can say this without contradiction. It is true that we are condemned to this absurdity, but we are so only existentially, and not morally; what determines that we are men and not animals is precisely the concrete awareness that we have of the "I" of other people, hence of the relative falseness of our own ego; now, we must understand the implications of this and correct spiritually what is unbalanced and deceptive in our existential egohood. It is in view of this imbalance that it is said: "Judge not that

[6] Or again: "But the stranger that dwelleth with you shall be unto you as one born among you, and thou shalt love him as thyself: for ye were strangers in the land of Egypt: I am the Lord your God" (Leviticus 19:34).

[7] For—in Vedantic terms—"the world is false, *Brahma* is true".

[8] For "all things are *Ātmā*". Consequently: "Inasmuch as ye have done it unto one of the least of these my brethren, ye have done it unto Me" (Matt. 25:40); "He that hath pity upon the poor lendeth unto the Lord; and that which he hath given will He pay him again" (Proverbs 19:17).

ye be not judged", and also: "Thou considerest not the beam that is in thine own eye", or again: "All things whatsoever ye would that men should do to you, do ye even so to them" (Matt. 7:3, 12).

After proclaiming the supreme Commandment, Christ added that the second Commandment was "like unto" the first, which implies that the love of one's neighbor is essentially contained in the love of God and that it is real and acceptable only insofar as it derives from the latter, for "he that gathereth not with me, scattereth abroad"; the love of God may thus sometimes contradict our love for men, as in the case of those who must "hate father and mother in order to follow Me", although men can never be frustrated by such an option. It is not enough to love one's neighbor, we must love him in God, and not against God, as atheistic moralists do; and in order to love him in God, we must love God.

What enables divine injunctions to be both simple and absolute is that any adaptations required by the nature of things are always implied, and cannot but be so; thus, charity does not abolish natural hierarchies: the superior treats the inferior—when the relationship of hierarchy applies—as he himself would like to be treated if he were the inferior, and not as if the inferior were a superior; or again, charity does not imply that we should share in the errors of others, or that others should escape a punishment that we would have deserved ourselves, if we had shared in their errors or their vices, and so on.

In this vein of thought, the following remark could be made: the prejudice is well known that would have contemplative love justify itself and excuse itself before a world that scorns it, and that would have the contemplative become needlessly involved in activities that take him away from his goal; those who think in this manner are obviously unaware that contemplation represents for human society a sort of sacrifice that is beneficial for it and of which it is in real need. The prejudice in question is analogous to the one that condemns the ceremonial splendor of sacred art, sanctuaries, priestly vestments, and liturgy: here again there is a refusal to understand, firstly, that not all riches belong to men,[9] but that some belong to God, and do so for the sake of everyone; secondly, that sacred treasures are offerings or

---

[9] The notion of poverty, moreover, lends itself to many fluctuations, given the artificial and inexhaustible nature of the needs of "civilized" man. There are no "underdeveloped" peoples, there are only overdeveloped peoples.

sacrifices that are due to His greatness, His beauty, and His glory; and thirdly, that in a society, the sacred must of necessity make itself visible, so as to create a presence or an atmosphere without which it fades from men's minds. The fact that a spiritual individual may be able to do without forms is beside the question, for society is not this individual; and the individual needs society in order to blossom, just as a plant needs earth in order to live. Nothing is viler than envy with regard to God; poverty dishonors itself when it covets the gold decoration of sanctuaries;[10] it is true that there have always been exceptions to the rule, but they have no connection with the cold and strident demands of iconoclastic utilitarians.

— .·. —

In the *Torah* there is a passage that has been much misused in order to support an argument in favor of a so-called "vocation of the earth" and a consecration of the devouring materialism of our age: "Be fruitful and multiply, and replenish the earth, and subdue it: and have dominion over the fish of the sea, and over the fowl of the air, and over every living thing that moveth upon the earth" (Genesis 1:28).[11] Now, in fact this command only defines human nature in its relationships with the earthly environment or, in other words, it defines the rights resulting from our nature; God says to man: "Thou shalt do such and such a thing", as He would say to fire to burn and to water to flow; every natural function necessarily derives from a divine Command. By this imperative form of the divine Word, man knows that if he dominates on earth, it is not through abuse, but according to the Will of the Most-High and therefore according to the logic of things; but this Word in no wise means that man must abuse his capacities by devoting himself exclusively to the inordinate, enslaving, and finally

---

[10] It will be recalled that in the *Torah* these gold decorations are prescribed by God Himself. And it is significant that neither Saint Vincent de Paul nor the holy Curé d'Ars—both so ardently concerned with the welfare of the poor but never forgetting the spiritual welfare without which material welfare has no meaning—ever dreamt of begrudging God His riches; for the Curé d'Ars, no expense was too great for the beauty of the house of God.

[11] Rabbinical exegesis no doubt explains the meaning of this enumeration, but it is not this aspect that concerns us here.

destructive exploitation of earthly resources. For here, as in other cases, it is necessary to understand the words in the context of other words that necessarily complete them, which is to say that the passage quoted is intelligible only in the light of the supreme Commandment: "Thou shalt love the Lord thy God with all thy heart, with all thy soul, and with all thy might." Without this key, the passage on fruitfulness could be interpreted as forbidding celibacy and excluding all contemplative concerns; but the supreme Commandment shows precisely what are the limits of this passage, what is its necessary basis, and its total meaning: it shows that the right or the duty to dominate the world hinges upon what man is in himself.

The equilibrium of the world and creatures depends on the equilibrium between man and God, and so on our knowledge, and on our will, with regard to the Absolute. Before asking what man must do, it is necessary to know what he is.

—— ⋮ ——

We have seen that the supreme Commandment comprises as it were three dimensions, namely: firstly, the affirmation of divine Unity, and this is the intellectual dimension; secondly, the obligation of loving God, and this is the volitive or affective dimension; and thirdly, the obligation of loving one's neighbor, and this is the active and social dimension; this third mode is indirect, and its plane of application is outward, while necessarily having its roots in the soul, in the virtues, and in contemplation.

As for the first dimension, which constitutes the fundamental enunciation of Judaism[12]—prefigured in the ontological testimony of the burning bush[13]—it comprises two aspects, one concerning intellection and the other faith; as for the second dimension, we will recall that it comprises the three aspects "union", "contemplation", and "accomplishment", the first relating to the heart, the second to the soul or the mental element, or to virtues and thought, and the third to the body. And finally the third dimension, love of one's neighbor,

---

[12] "Hear, O Israel, the Lord our God is one Lord."

[13] "And God said unto Moses, I am that I am" (Exod. 3:14).

derives from the generosity necessarily engendered by the knowledge and the love of God; it is thus both condition and consequence.

Having enunciated the two Commandments—unconditional and "vertical" love of God and conditional and "horizontal" love of one's neighbor[14]—Christ adds: "On these two commandments hang all the law and the prophets" (Matt. 22:40). In other words, the two Commandments on the one hand constitute the *Religio perennis*—the primordial, eternal, and *de facto* underlying[15] Religion[16]—and on the other hand are to be found, by way of consequence, in all manifestations of this *Religio* or of this *Lex*, namely in the religions that govern humanity; herein therefore is contained a doctrine proclaiming both the unity of the Truth and the diversity of its forms, and at the same time defining the nature of this Truth by means of the two Commandments of Love.

---

[14] The Decalogue contains, and develops, these two crucial Commandments.

[15] "The Lord possessed me (Wisdom) in the beginning of His way, before His works of old. I was set up from everlasting, from the beginning, or ever the earth was" (Proverbs 8:22-23).

[16] We say "primordial Religion", and not "Tradition", because the first of these terms has the advantage of expressing an intrinsic reality (*religere* = "to bind" the earthly with the heavenly), and not simply an extrinsic reality like the second (*tradere* = "to hand down" scriptural, ritual, and legal elements). Moreover, one may with reason ask if there could be any question of "tradition" in an age in which spiritual knowledge was innate or spontaneous, or again, if the necessity of a "tradition", and thus of an outward handing down, does not *ipso facto* involve the necessity of a plurality of formulations.

The True Remedy

According to the unanimous conviction of ancient Christianity and of all other traditional humanities, the cause of suffering in the world is the degeneration of man and not a simple lack of knowledge and organization. No progress nor any tyranny will ever succeed in ending suffering; only holiness on the part of everyone would attain this to a certain extent, were it in fact possible to realize this goal and thus to transform the world into a community of contemplatives and a new earthly Paradise. This assuredly does not mean that man should not, in keeping with his nature and simple common sense, seek to overcome the evils that occur in his life; to do this, he needs no divine or human injunction. But to seek to establish in a country a relative well-being in view of God is one thing, and to seek to establish perfect happiness on earth and apart from God is another; this second aim is doomed to failure from the start, precisely because the lasting elimination of our miseries depends on our conformity to divine Nature, or on our fixation in the "kingdom of God which is within you". As long as men have not realized sanctifying "inwardness", the abolition of earthly trials is not only impossible, it is not even desirable; for the sinner—outward man—needs suffering to expiate his faults and tear himself from sin, or to escape from the "outwardness" from which sin derives.[1] From the spiritual point of view, which alone takes account of the real cause of our calamities, evil is not by definition that which causes us to suffer, but that which, even with a maximum of comfort or pleasure, or of "justice" if one likes, frustrates a maximum of souls from achieving their final end.

Fundamentally, the whole problem may be reduced to the following nucleus of questions: what good is it to eliminate effects if the cause remains and continues to produce similar effects over and over? And even more urgently: what is the use of eliminating the effects of

---

[1] It is from this idea that, among the majority of ancient peoples, is derived the obligation to be a warrior and so continually risk one's life on the battlefield; the same perspective is found in the warrior castes of all the great peoples. Without the heroic virtues, it is believed, man declines and the whole of society degenerates; the only man who can escape this constraint may be the saint, which amounts to saying that if all men were contemplatives, the harsh law of collective heroism would not be necessary.

evil to the detriment of the elimination of the cause itself? And finally, what is the use of eliminating them while replacing the cause by another and far more pernicious one, namely hatred of the Sovereign Good and passion for impermanent things? In a word: if one fights the calamities of this world outside the total truth and the ultimate good, incomparably greater calamities will be created, beginning, precisely, with the negation of this truth and the forfeiture of this good; those who are set on liberating man from an age-old "frustration" are in fact those who impose on him the most radical and the most irreparable of frustrations.

No doubt, it is in the nature of man to strive to improve the world, but it is necessary to do this in a fully human and consequently divine manner. "He that gathereth not with me, scattereth abroad": these words, like many others, seem to have become a dead letter; and yet a new encyclical tells us: "The Church must scrutinize the signs of the times and interpret them in the light of the Gospel." Meanwhile it is the mathematical opposite that is being done.

——— ·⦂· ———

"Seek ye first the kingdom of God and His righteousness and all these things shall be added unto you": this saying is the very key to the problem of our earthly condition, as are the words: "The kingdom of Heaven is within you."

To the question "what is sin", it may be replied first of all that this term refers to two planes or two dimensions: the first of these planes requires "obedience to the commandments", and the second, following the words of Christ to the rich young man, requires that one should "follow me", in other words, establish oneself in the "inward dimension" and so realize contemplative perfection; the example of Mary takes precedence over that of Martha. Suffering in the world is due, not only to sin in the basic sense of the word, but also and above all to the sin of "outwardness", which moreover engenders all the others, inexorably so; a perfect world would be, not only that of men who abstained from the sins of commission and omission, as did the rich young man, but above all that of men living "towards the Inward", and firmly established in the knowledge—and consequently in the love—of the Unseen that transcends everything and encompasses everything. There are three degrees to be observed here:

the first is abstention from sin-as-action, such as murder, theft, lying, omission of sacred duty; the second is abstention from sin-as-vice, such as pride, passion, avarice; the third is abstention from sin-as-a-state, in other words from this very "outwardness" that is at once dispersion and hardening and which gives rise to all vices and all transgressions. The absence of this sin-as-a-state is nothing else than "love of God" or "inwardness", whatever be its spiritual mode; only this inwardness would be capable of regenerating the world, and this is why it is said that the world would have collapsed long ago but for the presence of the saints, be it visible or hidden.

Sin-as-vice and even more so sin-as-a-state constitute intrinsic sin; these two degrees meet in pride, the emblematic notion that includes everything that imprisons man in outwardness and keeps him away from divine Life. As regards the first degree—transgression—whether there is manifest sin depends on the intention, namely whether there is real opposition to a revealed Law; in itself, it can happen that a forbidden act becomes permissible in certain circumstances, for it is always permissible to lie to a bandit or to kill in legitimate self-defense; but apart from such circumstances, the illegal act is always connected to intrinsic sin, it becomes integrated with sin-as-vice and thereby with sin-as-a-state, which is nothing other than "hardness of heart" or the state of the "heathen", according to biblical language.

There is no possible partnership between the principle of good and organized sin; that is to say, the powers of the world, which are inevitably sinful powers, organize sin in order to abolish the effects of sin. It seems that the new "pastoralism" specifically wants to speak the "language" of the "world", which has become an honorable entity, without there being any discernible reason for this unexpected promotion; now, to wish to speak the language of the "world", or that of "our time"—another empty argument that carefully avoids proving anything whatsoever—is to make truth speak the language of error and virtue the language of vice.[2]

---

[2] "But into whatsoever city ye enter, and they receive you not, go your ways out into the streets of the same, and say, even the very dust of your city, which cleaveth on us, we do wipe off against you; notwithstanding be ye sure of this, that the kingdom of God is come nigh unto you. But I say unto you, that it shall be more tolerable in that day for Sodom, than for that city" (Luke 10:10-12). This passage, like the one that forbids the "casting of pearls before swine", shows clearly that there are limits to everything, even "pastoralism".

To understand religion is to accept it without imposing on it casually insolent conditions; to set conditions on it is obviously to fail to understand it and to render it subjectively ineffective; the absence of bargaining is part and parcel of the integrity of faith. To set conditions—be this on the plane of individual or social "well-being" or on that of the liturgy, which one would like to make as flat and trivial as possible—is to be fundamentally unaware of what religion is, what God is, and what man is; it is to reduce religion in a trice to a neutral and inoperative backdrop, which it could never be in any way, and from the outset to take away all its rights and its whole reason for being. Profane humanitarianism, which official religion intends to blend itself with more and more, is incompatible with the total truth and consequently also with true charity, for the simple reason that the material well-being of earthly man is not the whole of well-being and does not coincide, in fact, with the overall interest of the immortal human person. The norm is a sober well-being—not artificially puffed up—whose spiritual dangers man compensates by an inward ascesis; all the traditional civilizations in their normal state tend to realize this basic well-being, which is a contingent favor, and this ascesis, which is an unconditional requirement;[3] true happiness—or integral well-being—can only come from this equilibrium, every question of destiny and subjective disposition apart.[4]

"Seek ye first the kingdom of God. . .". To remember this constantly anew is the first duty of men of religion, and if there is a truth particularly suited to "our time", it is this more than any other.

—— ·⋮· ——

The true remedy, as we have said, is to seek first the kingdom of God; however, man is so made that this truth can in certain cases give rise to conflicts of functions, duties, or vocations; this is illustrated by a curious paradox in the *Divine Comedy* that is sufficiently instructive to warrant dwelling on it a little. It is true that it is not normally our

---

[3] The Oriental civilizations, in their cyclical decadence, have more or less disfigured or corrupted principles; modern Western civilization, for its part, denies them, which amounts to killing the patient in order to end the disease; the *kali-yuga* is everywhere.

[4] And since we are speaking of the collectivity, we are not speaking of saints.

practice to enter into the details of historical or personal phenomena, but we think an exception can be made in this case, all the more as it provides a concrete example of the typical interweaving of elements found in Providence.

One of the contradictions, real or apparent, to be found in the *Divine Comedy* is the fact that Dante places in hell a saint, namely Pope Celestine V, whom the poet reproaches for having abdicated and for having thus betrayed his charge. Here is the story, one that is well known but inevitably lost sight of by many people: the holy see having remained vacant for more than two years—following the death of Nicholas IV towards the end of the thirteenth century—the cardinals elected the hermit Pier Angelerio from Murrhone in the Abruzzi, an aged holy man who had founded the Celestine Order;[5] the reason for this unexpected election was that the hermit had threatened them with hell-fire if they delayed any longer in electing a pope. From the moment of his election, the holy man—who took the name of Celestine V—was held more or less prisoner in Naples by King Charles II and the Colonna clan, protagonists of the moral and political reform of Christianity. The new pope soon proceeded to nominate some cardinals of the same tendency, which was the only thing to do, but which aroused vehement protests from the opposing "worldly" party, represented especially by the Caetani clan; and it was a cardinal of this family who entreated the pope to abdicate in his favor, and who, having become pope in his turn—under the name of Boniface VIII— held his predecessor prisoner in Rome; it was there that Celestine died after two years of captivity.

In the first passage of the *Inferno* that refers to Celestine V, Dante "sees and recognizes" in the first circle of hell, reserved for the sins of omission, "the shadow of him who from cowardice made the great refusal" (III, 58-60); in a second passage, Boniface VIII speaks of the "two keys that my predecessor held not dear" (XXVII, 103-105); while in a third passage, it is Boniface VIII himself who is reproached for "having taken the Beautiful Lady (the Church) by fraud (from Celestine V), and thereafter having abused her" (XIX, 55-57). Dante's attitude towards Celestine V may appear excessive, but one must take into account the following factors: first of all, the canonization of the

---

[5] A branch of the Benedictines, which spread widely in the fourteenth century; it still has monasteries in Italy to this day.

hermit pope, which was promulgated in the pontificate of Clement V, took place, as far as one can tell, after the completion of the *Inferno;* secondly, Dante avoids mentioning Celestine V by name, and some have even supposed that in the first passage quoted Dante is speaking, not of this pope, but of Esau or Diocletian, both of them more or less traitors to their charge;[6] finally, only this first passage places the pope in hell—assuming it is the pope who is referred to—whereas the other two passages place Boniface VIII in hell, and the allusions to Celestine V—incontestable in these instances—do not imply that he too is damned.

Be that as it may, if Dante did not hesitate to make the insinuations just mentioned, this can be explained by considerations of both a spiritual and political nature, which were to the discredit of Boniface VIII, and also, from another point of view, by the haughty and combative nature of the poet;[7] now, the election of Boniface was made possible only by Celestine's abdication, an unprecedented act in the history of the papacy. The hermit-pope has been reproached for having fallen, without resistance, under the influence of the Colonna—a reproach that is in no wise conclusive, for the Colonna were on the side of the *spirituali* and, like the pope, hated the ambitions and insatiable worldliness of the clergy; Celestine V had no motive, to say the least, for opposing rightful tendencies that were in conformity with his own sentiments, merely because his quasi-jailers also subscribed to them.

Celestine V could in principle have achieved his plans for the renewal of the Church, but he quickly came up against unsuspected

---

[6] An obvious reproach in the case of the brother of Jacob, but not in the case of the Roman emperor.

[7] One may well feel surprised that Dante had no compunction in placing in hell contemporaries or controversial great men from the past, and in describing the pains of hell in a singularly detailed fashion; and that in so doing he did not shrink from assuming responsibility for imaginative coagulations that were necessarily both conjectural and bold. In this there may doubtless be seen a mark of the European spirit, which is very inventive but not very sensitive to the subtle hazards of the magic of words and images; but one may also suppose that Dante felt himself at even greater liberty to imagine a hell that was too concrete and sentences that were too peremptory, in that his intention was to compensate the darkness of the *Inferno* by the liberating light of the *Paradiso;* this moreover seems to be suggested by the crossing of the river Lethe towards the end of the *Purgatorio,* the quintessential meaning of this symbolism being the reabsorption of accidentalities into pure Substance.

difficulties of a kind largely unimaginable for a man of his purity; it was for having missed this opportunity, and for having missed it in favor of one of the chief representatives of the worldly tendency, that Dante could not forgive him.[8]

—— ·:· ——

It remains to be explained why Celestine V, a virtuous man if there ever was one, shrank from what Dante considered to be an imperative duty; the reasons for his doing so were of no interest to the eagle of Florence, or at least they escaped him at the moment of writing the *Inferno*, but they do explain and excuse the attitude of the holy pontiff, who *a priori* was hardly a man of this lower world. By this we mean that he was a born contemplative, that is to say a contemplative not by conversion, but by nature. In the language of *gnosis*, he was what is called a "pneumatic", namely a being who is drawn by Heaven in a "supernaturally natural" manner; the name of *Coelestinus*, chosen by the new pope and given to the monastic order which he founded, is also an indication of this. Now, the "pneumatic" lives from the memory of a lost paradise; he seeks only one thing, a return to his origin, and having himself a quasi-angelic nature, he is to a large extent unaware of the average nature of men. Incapable of knowing in advance that the general run of men are wild beasts, Celestine V— with a holy naivety—believed them to be similar to, or even better than himself; he was unaware to what extent passions, ambitions, and other illusions dominate intelligences and wills, and to what extent men are capable of false pretenses—which incidentally proves their culpability. He had to become pope to find this out.

A companion of the young Saint Thomas Aquinas told him, in the presence of other young monks, to look out of the window to

---

[8] Another holy pope whom we are surprised to meet in the *Inferno* (XI, 6-10) is Anastasius II, accused of having fallen into heresy under the influence of Photinus, apostolic vicar in Thessalonica; in reality, this pope—keen to come to an understanding with Constantinople—had done no more than receive Photinus with kindness; but this incident contributed to a subsequent confusion between Anastasius II and the emperor Anastasius who was a partisan of the Monophysite heresy. Given this misunderstanding, the case of the fifth century pope does not pose the same problem as that of the hermit-pope who was Dante's contemporary.

see a flying ox; this the saint did, without of course seeing anything. Everyone began to laugh, but Saint Thomas, imperturbable, made this remark: "A flying ox is less astonishing than a lying monk". There is no occasion to reproach pure souls for having a certain credulity which, in fact, is to their credit, all the more in that their humility inclines them to overestimate others, provided that any evidence to the contrary is not more than obvious.

Pier Angelerio accepted the tiara because he believed that this was the will of God; but what Providence wanted for him was a spiritual experience and not the pontificate; an experience that at the same time was an instruction for others in incorruptibility, and not an example of weakness, still less of cowardice. God also wished to show that there are vocations that are normally mutually exclusive— except in the case of very rare gifts, found especially in Prophets—and that no vocation is more pleasing to him than that of contemplation, which includes all others in a potential manner. Moreover, Celestine V would have been an ideal pope in the normal ambience that Dante wished for, that is to say, under the protection of a powerful emperor fully conscious of his charge, and consequently freed from the political hassles that the Roman pontiffs had to struggle with; it was undoubtedly from this normal point of view that the hermit of the Abruzzi accepted the tiara and it was because of the same point of view that the Florentine poet did not forgive him for having renounced it. The whole problem here lies in the definition of "duty": the imprescriptible vocation of the contemplative—of the "pneumatic" whose spiritual ascent results from his very substance and not from a choice or a conversion as in the case of the "psychic"[9]—may possibly be reconcilable with an activity in the world, quite obviously, but in many cases—for a variety of reasons—this is not so in fact. At all events, it is through the duties specific to him that the contemplative fully satisfies the love of God, and thereby the love of men, the latter being contained in the former.

[9] The "pneumatic" may incarnate either an attitude of knowledge or of love, although the former manifests more directly his essential nature; he is not necessarily a great sage, but he is necessarily a pure and quasi-angelic man. Be that as it may, these gnostic terms can be understood with different nuances, independently of the speculations of Valentinus.

Dante's intention was to replace the illegitimate worldliness of the popes with the legitimate lay status of the emperors, this lay status being entirely relative and in a certain manner sacerdotal in its turn. Now, Celestine V was the very type of a spiritual pope; it is certainly not a pontiff of his sort who would have favored the worldly and humanist revolution of the Renaissance, thus inaugurating the self-destruction of Christianity. Naturally Dante could not foresee the nature of the cultural revolution of the Medici and the Borgias, but he perceived its principle; he could see distant consequences in proximate causes. The state of urgency, he thought, did not permit considerations of personal vocation, not even in the case of a saint like Celestine V.

What Dante foresaw, his contemporaries did not know or did not want to know; the incorrigible brawlers of the Middle Ages imagined that they could kill and plunder each other indefinitely in the name of God and the angels and the saints; they could not sense that this very contradiction, if it exceeded certain limits, would ultimately culminate in the destruction of their supremacy and their form of government, and at the same time of Western Christendom. Dante had been called a "dreamer" because his plan for the empire was never realized; if this were the case then every man who counsels wisdom and prudence is retrospectively a dreamer if he is not obeyed; and as no sage is ever obeyed fully, every sage would be a dreamer. If the norm is a dream, it is certainly no dishonor to dream.

There was not—and could not be—between Dante and Celestine V any objective divergence on the subject of the true remedy for the evils of this world here below; but there was a subjective divergence of temperament and vocation, in the sense that Dante, while knowing perfectly the rights of pure contemplativity, considered he could not grant the saintly pope the benefit of these rights, and this for reasons of his public duties. Be this as it may, in order to maintain the world in equilibrium, or in order even to improve it in a particular sector, it is not enough that there should be men capable of taking effective measures in keeping with spiritual principles, it is also necessary that there should be saints who, like the "motionless mover" of Aristotle, realize only the "one thing necessary", namely that which constitutes the reason for being of every human city. The sap of human "usefulness" is the divine "uselessness"; this idea evokes the whole mystery of sacrifice, and above all that of the sacred in itself; of the sacred that determines all measures and at the same time escapes all measures.

Criteria of Worth

What constitutes the effective—and not merely virtual—spiritual worth of a man, for whom the question can or must be asked? Is it his intelligence, his discernment, his metaphysical knowledge? Obviously not, if this knowledge is not combined with a will to realize and an overall virtue, which are at least sufficient. Is it his realizational will, his power of concentration? No, if this is not combined with the necessary minimum of doctrinal knowledge and virtue. And spiritual worth likewise does not consist in virtue, if this virtue is not accompanied by a doctrinal understanding that is at least satisfactory and by an equivalent realizational effort.

All this amounts to saying that the spiritual worth of a man does not consist in his possessing an eminent degree either of discernment, or of concentration, or yet of virtue, but in his possessing at least a sufficient degree of these three capacities. Now, this sufficient degree implies that the capacity in question offers the essential: it is therefore necessary that knowledge, in order to be sufficient, contain that which is indispensable, and the same is true for effort and virtue, *mutatis mutandis*.

Obviously the most brilliant intellectual knowledge is useless in the absence of a corresponding realizational initiative and in the absence of the necessary virtue; in other words, knowledge is nothing if it is combined with spiritual laziness and with pretension, egoism, hypocrisy. Likewise, the most prestigious power of concentration is nothing if it is accompanied by doctrinal ignorance and moral insufficiency; likewise again, natural virtue is but little without doctrinal truth and spiritual practice, which bring out its value in view of God and which thus restore its whole reason for being.

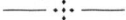

The indispensable doctrinal knowledge is the capacity to distinguish the Absolute from the contingent. Then one must know that the contingent is prefigured in the Absolute, and that the Absolute projects itself into contingency; it is a question, in the first case, of the heavenly *Logos* and, in the second, of the earthly *Logos*. And it is obviously essential to know the eschatological implications of the divine Nature, for man knows nothing if he does not accept the immortality of the soul and the requirements the human vocation entails.

Regarding concentration, which is the operative prolongation of knowledge, it is closely linked with intention, to the point of having no value except through it. A man who would practice concentration to his fullest powers with the intention of obtaining the gift of miracles or the prestige of holiness, would gain nothing and lose everything; on the contrary, a man who failed to concentrate—despite the utmost goodwill—but who did so with a spiritually satisfactory intention, would be accepted by Heaven. In any case, the legitimacy of the intention produces in the end a sufficient concentration: the person who is chased by a bull flees without having to make an effort of concentration; and likewise for lovers who make haste to meet; the efficacy, and hence the concentration, is in the sincerity of the intention, and the intention is determined by the reality of the situation. The man who prays because he really wants to escape from hell, or because he has a nostalgia for Paradise, or because he loves God and loves to pray, or because the reality of God is too concretely compelling for his mind to ignore it—such a man will realize fervor effortlessly and thus concentration, single-mindedness, and contemplative inwardness.

As for virtue, which is the moral sap of every spiritual operation, this is essentially generosity, and so the gift of self towards God and the opening of one's soul towards one's neighbor; to speak of generosity is to speak of detachment, for the greedy and petty man cannot be generous. Generosity, by its very nature, implies an intuition of the good intentions of others: that is to say, the generous man will never attribute a bad interpretation to good intentions, although it may happen that he attribute a good interpretation to bad intentions, for which he will not be blamed by God so long as this misinterpretation is due to an accidental and excusable misunderstanding and not to an obstinacy contrary to the truth. Many men are in hell because they gratuitously suspected honest men; but not a single honest man is in hell because he let himself be deceived.

Virtue, to be such, is objective—it conforms to the real and not to illusion; generosity is never indulgence or weakness; its internal strength is the gauge of its virtue. One must be generous towards one's neighbor when he is the victim of an error or a defect, but never when he identifies himself with them; one can be generous with passion, but not with pride; or again, one can be generous in one and the same case once or twice, but not a third time. Just as one cannot be generous with the devil, since one cannot convert him, so one cannot be generous with men who share his spirit; nevertheless, one has the moral right to overestimate them *a priori*—this is all to our honor—but one never has the right to underestimate men of goodwill.

It would be wrong to conclude that men who do not at a first glance have the discernment to detect the devil under a particular guise are influenced by him owing to the mere fact of their mistake, for their guilelessness is natural and respectable; however, those who act like the devil are affected by him, even if they think they are combating him and can recognize him right away under a given guise. In a word, it is better to have a generosity that inadvertently absolves a guilty party, than to have a fiery and acerbic "critical sense" that drags innocents into the wake of its condemnation.

Poverty before God becomes richness before men: in other words, receptivity towards God becomes radiance and generosity towards men. This radiance is always determined by the truth, not by a gratuitous subjectivity, and therefore comprises an aspect of adamantine rigor; a rigor which, in certain cases, is the only charity possible.

— .:. —

Certainly, the ideal is that a man should realize to an eminent degree the three conditions or capacities—namely, intellectual discernment, spiritual effort, and moral beauty—or that he should realize two or a single one to this degree, while possessing the other—or the others— to a sufficient degree; but when it is simply a question of knowing whether a man is spiritual or not, whether he is sincere or worldly, such peak accomplishments do not have to enter into consideration. Without question, it is infinitely better to realize the equilibrium of the three capacities, at least to a sufficient degree, than to lack one of them while at the same time possessing a brilliant hypertrophy that is rendered problematical by the very fact of its isolation.

An objection could be made to this system of criteria, namely that the spiritual worth of a man is not always obvious and that it is impossible to detect it in people who are not well known, but this is beside the point, for we are only considering cases where a spiritual or psychological situation does become manifest or must indeed become so, and where moreover we have the right or even the duty to know about it. It is not a question of wondering about people who do not concern us, either practically or theoretically, but of guarding ourselves against errors with regard to people who might be overlooked because their talents are modest, or who, on the contrary, enjoy an undeserved prestige because their talents are exceptional. Man is exposed to the gravest spiritual harm either by failing to recognize a superior soul because of a slight imperfection, or by paying homage to an inferior soul because of a striking quality which in fact is inoperative.

Our three criteria indicate the very foundation, and in a sense the basis, both essential and minimal, of the human vocation; and this is bound to be spiritual if man is truly man. The summit of the first condition—doctrinal understanding—is a direct intellection that is manifested by a permanent inspiration and which is close to prophecy; the lower limit of doctrinal understanding is knowledge of the truths that are indispensable for salvation, or a sufficient knowledge of the basic tenets of metaphysics.

The summit of the second condition—realizational tension—is a permanent state of union with God; the lower limit of this tension being a legitimate and sincere intention and the effort resulting therefrom.

Finally, the summit of the third condition—moral conformity—is perfect beauty of soul: a nobility that enables man to see things from above, not only on the plane of doctrinal abstractions, but also on that of intimate sentiments. It is to perceive with the sensitive soul the relativity and evanescence of things, and at the same time, in an opposite and complementary respect, to perceive the absoluteness and infiniteness—and hence the permanence—which things in their fashion manifest and allow to shine through; from this it ensues that the noble soul always possesses something unconditional and adamantine, and at the same time something unlimited and radiant; and this radiance shows itself specifically in generosity. As for the lower limit of virtue, this is basic generosity, or the capacity to put moral dignity above self-interest, which proves that man is really man, and that he is so by vocation, and not by accident.[1]

All of this criteriology is no doubt fairly elementary, but it is nonetheless sufficient from the point of view of its own principles; schemas have a right to exist, even though they are nothing but ellipses. At all events, the criteria in question—and this stems from their own nature—provide not so much an instrument for assessing others as a means of evaluating oneself, at least *a priori* and provided that one is not having to protect oneself against the illusions of others. This nevertheless does not authorize us to lose sight of the fact that potentially other people are in us and we are in other people so that we are never absolved from perfecting in ourselves what we see as being imperfect around us.

---

[1] It should be mentioned that the moral worth of a man reveals itself notably—on the basis of general and obvious factors—by the ease with which he accepts justifiable criticisms, and, what is more, tolerates slight exaggerations in such criticisms; also by the impartiality with which he examines even unjustified criticisms, if they are not too implausible; and by the prudence and sense of proportion that he shows when circumstances oblige him to criticize others, something that he will do without needing to show hesitation when the case is clear, for virtue cannot require indulgence for the "wolves in the fold". The overall attitude that we have just described comes from detachment, and thus also from generosity, the two virtues being connected; they are none other than humility and charity: objectivity both extinctive and radiant.

Part III

Aesthetic & Theurgic Phenomenology

Foundations of an Integral Aesthetics

Esoterism comprises four principal dimensions: an intellectual dimension, represented by doctrine; a volitive or technical dimension, which encompasses the direct and indirect means of the way; a moral dimension, which concerns the intrinsic and extrinsic virtues; and an aesthetic dimension, to which pertain symbolism and art from both the subjective and objective point of view.

Exoterically, beauty represents either an excusable or an inexcusable pleasure, or an expression of piety and thereby the raiment of a theological symbolism; esoterically, it serves as a spiritual means in connection with contemplation and interiorizing "reminiscence". By "integral aesthetics" we mean in fact a science that takes account not only of sensible beauty but also of the spiritual foundations of this beauty,[1] foundations which explain the frequent connection between the arts and initiatic methods.

Aesthetics as such, being the science of the beautiful, concerns the laws of objective beauty as well as those ruling the sensation occasioned by the beautiful. Something is objectively beautiful when it expresses in one fashion or another an aspect of cosmic splendor which, in the final analysis, is divine, and when it does so in accordance with the principles of hierarchy and equilibrium this splendor comprises and requires; the perception of beauty, being a strict adequation and not a subjective illusion, essentially entails, on the one hand, a sense of satisfaction for the intelligence, and on the other, a sentiment at once of security, infinity, and love. Of security: because beauty is unitive and excludes, by means of a kind of musical evidence, the fissures of doubt and worry; of infinity: because beauty, by its very musicality, melts all hardness and limitations, thus freeing the soul from its constrictions, be it only in a minute or remote manner; of love: because beauty conjures love, that is to say, it draws the soul to union and hence to unitive extinction. All of these factors produce

---

[1] One must not confuse aesthetics with aestheticism: the second term refers to an artistic and literary movement in England in the nineteenth century. But the term can also refer to an excessive preoccupation with aesthetic values real or imaginary, or at any rate very relative. That said, one must not too readily cast aspersions upon romantic aesthetes, who had the merit of a nostalgia that was very understandable in a world that was sinking into a hopeless mediocrity and a cold and inhuman ugliness.

a sense of satisfaction for the intelligence, which spontaneously senses in beauty—inasmuch as it understands it—the truth and the good, or reality and its liberating power.

—— ·⦙· ——

The Divine Principle is the Absolute and, being the Absolute, it is the Infinite; it is from Infinity that manifesting or creating *Māyā* arises; and this Manifestation realizes a third hypostatic quality, namely Perfection. Absoluteness, Infinity, Perfection; and consequently: beauty, inasmuch as it is manifestation, requires perfection, and perfection, for its part, is realized through absoluteness on the one hand and through infinity on the other: in reflecting the Absolute, beauty realizes a mode of regularity, and in reflecting the Infinite, it realizes a mode of mystery. Beauty, being perfection, is regularity and mystery; it is through these two qualities that it stimulates and at the same time appeases the intelligence, and also the sensibility that is in conformity with the intelligence.

In sacred art, one finds everywhere and of necessity, regularity and mystery. According to a profane conception, that of classicism, it is regularity that produces beauty; but the beauty concerned is devoid of space and depth, because it is without mystery and therefore without any vibration of infinity. It can certainly happen in sacred art that mystery predominates over regularity, or vice versa, but the two elements are always present; it is their equilibrium that creates perfection.

Cosmic Manifestation necessarily reflects or projects the Principle both according to absoluteness and according to infinity; conversely, the Principle contains or prefigures the root of Manifestation, and so of Perfection, and this is the *Logos*. The *Logos* combines *in divinis* regularity and mystery, it is so to speak the manifested Beauty of God; but this manifestation remains principial, it is not cosmic. It has been said that God is a geometer, but it is important to add that He is just as much a musician.

Absolute, Infinite, Perfection: the first could be represented by a point, the second by the radii extending from it, and the third by the circle. Perfection is the Absolute projected, by virtue of Infinitude, into relativity; it is by definition adequate, but it is not the Absolute, or in other words, it is such and such an Absolute—namely, the manifested Absolute—but not the Absolute as such; and by "manifested Absolute" one must always understand: manifested in such and such a way. The Infinite is divine Femininity, and it is from it that Manifestation proceeds; in the Infinite, Beauty is essential, and so formless, undifferentiated, and unarticulated, whereas in and through Manifestation it coagulates and becomes tangible, not only because of the very fact of exteriorization, but also, and positively, by virtue of its content, image of the Absolute and factor of necessity, and so of regularity.

The cosmic, or more particularly the earthly, function of beauty is to actualize in the intelligent creature the Platonic recollection of the archetypes, all the way out into the luminous Night of the Infinite.[2] This leads us to the conclusion that the full understanding of beauty requires virtue and is identifiable with it: that is to say, just as it is necessary to distinguish, in objective beauty, between the outward structure and the message in depth, so there is a *distinguo* to make, in the meaning of the beautiful, between the aesthetic sensation and the corresponding beauty of soul, namely such and such a virtue. Aside from any question of "sensible consolation", the message of beauty is both intellectual and moral: intellectual because it conveys to us, in the world of accidentality, aspects of Substance, without however having to address itself to abstract thought; and moral, because it reminds us of what we must love, and consequently be.

—— ·⁝· ——

In conformity with the Platonic principle that like attracts like, Plotinus states that "it is always easy to attract the Universal Soul . . . by constructing an object suited for undergoing its influence and receiving its participation. Now the image-like representation of a thing renders it always suitable for undergoing the influence of its model; it is like a mirror that is capable of capturing the thing's appearance."[3]

---

[2] According to Pythagoras and Plato, the soul has heard the heavenly harmonies before being exiled on earth, and music awakens in the soul the remembrance of these melodies.

[3] This principle does not prevent a heavenly influence manifesting itself incidentally or accidentally, even in an image that is extremely imperfect—works of perversion and subversion being excluded—through pure mercy and by virtue of the "exception that proves the rule".

This passage enunciates the crucial principle of the almost magical relationship between the appropriate conformity of the recipient and the predestined content, or between the adequate symbol and the sacramental presence of the prototype. The ideas of Plotinus must be understood in the light of those of the "divine Plato": now, Plato approved the fixed types of the sacred sculptures of Egypt, but he rejected the works of the Greek artists who imitated nature in its outward—hence insignificant—accidentality, while following their individual imagination. This verdict immediately excludes from sacred art the productions of an exteriorizing, accidentalizing, sentimentalist, and virtuoso naturalism, which errs through abuse of intelligence as much as by omission of the inward and the essential.

Likewise, and for even stronger reasons: the inadequate soul, that is to say, the soul not in conformity with its primordial dignity as "image of God", cannot attract the graces that favor or even constitute sanctity. According to Plato, the eye is "the most solar of instruments", which Plotinus comments on as follows: "The eye would never have been able to see the sun if it were not itself of solar nature, any more than the soul could see the beautiful if it were not itself beautiful." Now, Platonic Beauty is an aspect of Divinity, and this is why it is the "splendor of the True": this amounts to saying that Infinity is in some fashion the aura of the Absolute, or that *Māyā* is the *shakti* of *Ātmā*, and consequently that every *hypostasis* of the absolute Real—whatever be its degree—is accompanied by a radiance that we might seek to define with the help of such notions as "harmony", "beauty", "goodness", "mercy", and "beatitude".

"God is beautiful and He loves beauty", says a *hadīth* that we have quoted more than once:[4] *Ātmā* is not only *Sat* and *Chit*, "Being" and "Consciousness"—or more relatively: "Power" and "Omniscience"—but also *Ānanda*, "Beatitude", and thus Beauty and Goodness;[5] and

---

[4] Another *hadīth* reminds us that "the heart of the believer is sweet, and it loves sweetness (*halāwah*)". The "sweet", according to the Arabic word, is at the same time the pleasing, coupled with a nuance of spring-like beauty; which amounts to saying that the heart of the believer is fundamentally benevolent because, having conquered the hardness specific to egoism and worldliness, it is made of sweetness or generous beauty.

[5] When the Koran says that God "has prescribed for Himself Mercy (*Rahmah*)", it affirms that Mercy pertains to the very Essence of God; yet, the notion of Mercy only accounts, in a partial and extrinsic way, for the beatific nature of the Infinite.

what we want to know and realize, we must *a priori* mirror in our own being, because in the domain of positive realities[6] we can only know perfectly that which we are.

—— ·:· ——

The elements of beauty, be they visual or auditive, static or dynamic, are not only pleasant, they are above all true and their pleasantness comes from their truth: this is the most obvious, and yet the least understood truth of aesthetics. Furthermore, as Plotinus remarked, every element of beauty or harmony is a mirror or receptacle that attracts the spiritual presence corresponding to its form or color, if one may express it thus; while this applies as directly as possible to sacred symbols, it is also true, in a less direct and more diffuse way, in the case of all things that are harmonious and therefore true. Thus, an artisanal ambience made of sober beauty—for it is not a question of sumptuousness except in very special cases—attracts or favors *barakah*, "blessing"; not that it creates spirituality any more than pure air creates health, but it is at least in keeping with it, which is much, and nothing could be more normal, humanly speaking.

Despite these facts, which should be more than obvious and which are corroborated by all the beauties that Heaven has bestowed on the traditional worlds, some will doubtless ask what connection there can be between the aesthetic value of a house, of an interior decoration, or of a tool and spiritual realization: when did Shankara ever concern himself with aesthetics or morality? The answer to this is that the soul of a sage of this scope is naturally beautiful and exempt from all pettiness, and that furthermore, an integrally traditional environment—especially in a milieu like that of the brahmins—largely if not absolutely excludes artistic or artisanal ugliness; so much so that Shankara had nothing to teach—nor *a fortiori* to learn—on the subject of aesthetic values, unless he had been an artist by vocation and profession, which he was not, and which his mission was far from demanding.

[6] This reservation means that we do not know privative realities—which, precisely, manifest unreality—except by contrast; for example, the soul understands moral ugliness to the extent that it itself is morally beautiful, and it cannot be beautiful except by participation in divine Beauty, namely Beauty in itself.

Certainly, the sensation of the beautiful may in fact be merely a pleasant experience, depending on the degree of receptiveness; but according to its nature and of course by virtue of its object, it offers to the Intellect, along with its musicality, an intellectual satisfaction, and thus an element of knowledge.

It is necessary here to clear up an error which would have it that everything in nature is beautiful because it belongs to nature, and that everything in traditional production is likewise beautiful because it belongs to tradition; and that as a result, ugliness does not exist either in the animal or the vegetable kingdoms since, apparently, every creature "is perfectly what it should be", which has really no connection with the aesthetic question; likewise it is said that the most magnificent of sanctuaries possesses no more beauty than some tool or other, always because the tool "is everything that it should be". This is tantamount to maintaining not only that an ugly animal species is aesthetically the equivalent of a beautiful species, but also that beauty is such merely due to the absence of ugliness and not due to its own content, as if the beauty of a man were the equivalent of that of a butterfly, or of a flower, or a precious stone. Beauty, however, is a cosmic quality that cannot be reduced to abstractions foreign to its nature; likewise, the ugly is not only that which is not completely what it is supposed to be, nor is it only an accidental infirmity or a lack of taste; it is in everything that manifests, accidentally or substantially, artificially or naturally, a privation of ontological truth, of existential goodness, or, what amounts to the same, of reality. Ugliness is, very paradoxically, the manifestation of a relative nothingness: of a nothingness that can affirm itself only by denying or eroding an element of Being, and thus of beauty. This amounts to saying that, in a certain fashion and elliptically speaking, the ugly is less real than the beautiful, and in short that it exists only thanks to an underlying beauty that it disfigures; in a word, it is the reality of an unreality, or the possibility of an impossibility, like all privative manifestations.

—— .∴. ——

The argument that aesthetic quality is far from always coinciding with moral quality and that consequently it is superfluous—an argument that is correct in its observation but false in its conclusion—overlooks an obvious fact, namely that the ontological and in principle spiritual merit of beauty remains whole on its own level; the fact that an aesthetic quality may not be fully enhanced does not mean that it could not and should not be, and it would then prove its spiritual potentiality and so its true nature. Inversely, ugliness is a privation even when it is allied to sanctity, which cannot make it positive, but which obviously neutralizes it, just as moral badness sterilizes beauty, but without abolishing it as far as its existential, but not volitive, aspect is concerned.[7]

The dilemma of moralists trapped in "black or white" alternatives is resolved metaphysically by the complementarity between transcendence and immanence: according to the first perspective nothing is really beautiful because God alone is Beauty; according to the second, every beauty is really beautiful because it is that of God. Thus every beauty is at once a closed door and an open door, that is to say, an obstacle and an instrument: either beauty takes us away from God because it is entirely identified in our mind with its earthly support, which then assumes the role of idol, or beauty brings us closer to God because we perceive in it the vibrations of Beatitude and Infinitude that emanate from divine Beauty.[8]

Very paradoxically, what we have just said also applies to the virtues; the Sufis insist on this. Like physical beauties, moral beauties are both supports and obstacles: they are supports thanks to their profound nature, which belongs to God ontologically, and obstacles to the extent that man attributes them to himself as merits, whereas they are only openings towards God in the darkness of human weakness.

Virtue cut off from God becomes pride, as beauty cut off from God becomes idol; and virtue joined to God becomes sanctity, as beauty joined to God becomes sacrament.

---

[7] This is all the difference, in a face, between the features as such and the expression, or between the form of a body and its gestures, or again, between the form of an eye and its gaze. Nevertheless, even the gaze of a morally imperfect person can have beauty when it expresses the spring of youth, or simply happiness, or a good sentiment, or sadness; but all of this is a question of degree, either of the natural beauty or of the moral imperfection.

[8] Ramakrishna, when he saw a flight of cranes, a lion, a dancing-girl, used to fall into ecstasy. This is what is called "seeing God everywhere"; not by deciphering symbolisms, of course, but by perceiving the essences.

The Degrees of Art

Traditional art derives from a creativity that combines heavenly inspiration with ethnic genius, and does so in the manner of a science containing rules and not by way of individual improvisation; *ars sine scientia nihil.*

The work of the artist or craftsman comprises two perfections, a perfection of surface and perfection of depth. At surface level, the work must be well done, in conformity with the laws of the art and the demands of the style; in depth, it must be able to communicate the reality that it expresses. This explains why traditional art is related to esoterism as regards its form and to spiritual realization as regards its practice; for the form expresses the essence, and an understanding of the form evokes and requires transcending it in view of the essence or archetype.

The artist, in fashioning the work—the form—fashions himself; and as the purpose of the form is to convey the essence or celestial content, the artist sees this *a priori* in the formal container; in realizing the form from the starting point of the essence, he becomes the essence by realizing the form.

No doubt, a distinction should be made, within the framework of a traditional civilization, between sacred art and profane art. The purpose of the first is to transmit spiritual truths, on the one hand, and a celestial presence, on the other hand; sacerdotal art has in principle a truly sacramental function. The function of profane art is obviously more modest: it consists in providing what theologians term "sensible consolations", in view of an equilibrium conducive to the spiritual life, rather in the manner of the flowers and birds in a garden. Art of whatever kind—and this includes craftsmanship—is there to create a climate and forge a mentality; it thus rejoins, directly or indirectly, the function of interiorizing contemplation, the Hindu *darshan:* contemplation of a holy man, a sacred place, a venerable object, a divine image.[1]

---

[1] When one compares the tumultuous and heavily carnal paintings of a Rubens with noble, correct, and profound works such as the profile of Giovanna Tornabuoni by

In principle, and in the absence of opposing factors capable of neutralizing this effect, the aesthetic phenomenon is a receptacle that attracts a spiritual presence; while this applies in the most direct way possible to sacred symbols, where this quality is superimposed on sacramental magic, it likewise holds good, though in a more diffuse manner, for all elements of harmony, that is of truth become sensible form.

— .:. —

No art in itself is a human creation; however, what distinguishes sacred art is that its essential content is a revelation, that it manifests a properly sacramental form of heavenly reality, such as the icon of the Virgin and Child, painted by an angel, or by Saint Luke inspired by an angel, or such as the icon of the Holy Face, which dates back to the holy shroud and to Saint Veronica; or such as the statue of Shiva dancing, or the painted or carved images of the Buddhas, *Bodhisattvas*, and Taras. Ritual psalmody in a sacred language—notably Sanskrit, Hebrew, and Arabic—and then, in some cases, the calligraphic copying—likewise ritual—of the sacred Books fall in the same category, according to the broadest possible interpretation of this denominator; architecture, or at least the decoration of sanctuaries, liturgical objects, and sacerdotal vestments are in general of a less direct order. It would be difficult to do justice in a few lines to all possible types of sacred expression, which comprises such diverse modes as recitation, writing, architecture, painting, sculpture, dance, the art of gestures, clothing; in what follows we shall be concerned only with the plastic arts, or even with painting alone, the latter being moreover the most immediately tangible and also the most explicit of the arts.

Besides the icons of Christ and the Virgin, there are also a multitude of other hieratic images that relate facts of sacred history or the

Ghirlandaio or the "Red and White Plum Blossoms" on a pair of screens by Korin, one may wonder whether the term "profane art" can serve as a common denominator for productions so dissimilar in quality. In the case of noble works imbued with contemplative spirit one would prefer to speak of "extra-liturgical art", without having to specify whether it is profane or not, or to what extent it is. Moreover, one must distinguish between normal profane art and a profane art that is deviated and which therefore can no longer serve as a basis for comparison.

lives of the saints; likewise in Buddhist iconography, after the central images come the numerous representations of secondary personifications; it is this more or less peripheral category that may be termed indirect sacred art, even though there may not always be a strict dividing line between it and direct or central sacred art. The function of this ramification—apart from its didactic significance—is to enable the spirit of the central images to shine through a diverse imagery that captures the movement of the mind by infusing into it the radiance of the Immutable, thereby imposing on the moving soul a tendency towards interiorization; this function is thus entirely analogous to that of hagiography or even to that of tales of chivalry, not forgetting fairy tales whose symbolism, as is well known, belongs to the realm of the spiritual and so to that of the sacred.

Sacred art is far from always being perfect, although it is necessarily so in its principles and in the best of its productions; nevertheless, in the great majority of imperfect works, the principles compensate for the accidental weaknesses, rather as gold, from a certain point of view, can compensate for the but slight artistic value of a given object. Two pitfalls threaten sacred art and traditional art in general: a virtuosity exerting itself towards the outward and the superficial, and also a conventionalism devoid of intelligence and soul; but this, it must be stressed, rarely deprives sacred art of its overall efficacy, not least its capacity to create a centering and interiorizing atmosphere. As for imperfection, one of its causes can be the inexperience, or else the incompetence of the artist; the most primitive of works are rarely the most perfect, for in the history of art there are periods of apprenticeship just as later there are periods of decadence, the latter often being due to virtuosity. Another cause of imperfection is unintelligence, either individual or collective: the image may be lacking in quality because the artist—the word here having an approximate meaning—is lacking in intelligence or spirituality, but it may likewise bear the imprint of a certain collective unintelligence that comes from the sentimental conventionalization of common religion; in this case, the collective psychism clothes the spiritual element with a kind of "pious stupidity", for if there is a naiveté that is charming, there is also a naiveté that is annoying and moralistic. This must be said lest anyone should think that artistic expressions of the sacred dispense us from discernment and oblige us to be prejudiced, and so that no one should forget that in the traditional domain in general, there is on all planes a constant struggle between a solidifying tendency and a tendency towards transparency, which draws the psychic back to the spiritual. All of this may be summed up by saying that sacred art is sacred in itself, but that it is not necessarily so in all its expressions.

Sacred art is vertical and ascending, whereas profane art is horizontal and equilibrating. In the beginning, nothing was profane; each tool was a symbol, and even decoration was symbolistic and sacral. With the passage of time, however, the imagination increasingly spread itself on the earthly plane, and man felt the need for an art that was for him and not for Heaven alone; the earth too, which in the beginning was experienced as a prolongation or an image of Heaven, progressively became earth pure and simple, that is to say that the human being increasingly felt himself to possess the right to be merely human. If religion tolerates this art, it is because it nevertheless has its legitimate function in the economy of spiritual means, within the horizontal or earthly dimension and with the vertical or heavenly dimension in view.

Nevertheless, it must be reiterated here that the distinction between a sacred and a profane art is insufficient and too hasty when one wishes to take account of all artistic possibilities; it is therefore necessary to have recourse to an additional distinction, namely that between a liturgical and an extra-liturgical art: in the first, although in principle it coincides with sacred art, there may be modalities that are more or less profane, just as inversely, extra-liturgical art may comprise some sacred manifestations.

The term "sensible consolation", wrongly applied by theologians to sacred art itself, as also, moreover, to the beauties of virgin nature—as if beauty had nothing to transmit other than consolation[2]—is better suited to the simpler types of art and the secondary charms of nature. The purpose of such arts is to convey a climate of holy childlikeness, which the culture maven poisoners—always aggressive and megalomaniac—will doubtless qualify as "maudlin affectation", which is nothing but a slanderous misuse of language; in reality art has no right—insofar as it is unpretentious, and even without this reser-

---

[2] It is true that this notion of "consolation" has a deeper import in the mystical realm.

vation—to be grandiloquent and titanesque, the mission of the artist being to produce work that is sane and balanced and not an expression of a soul's feckless turmoil.

Certainly the artist does not fashion his work with the sole intention of producing a spiritually or psychologically useful object; he also produces it for the joy of creating by imitating, and of imitating by creating, that is to say, for the joy of bringing out the existential intention of the model, or in other words, of extracting the very quintessence from this model; at least this is the case in some instances, because generalizations about this would be disproportionate and pretentious. In other instances, the work of the artist is, on the contrary, an extinction through love, the artist dying, so to speak, in creating: he achieves a form of union by identifying himself with the admired or beloved object, recreating it according to the music of his own soul. In other instances yet—although all these modes may or must be combined with one another in different degrees—the artist is fascinated by the manner in which the object can be adapted to a given material or a given technique: Japanese engravers confer on Mount Fuji and other views a quality that makes one think of the wood that they use; the painters of screens present rivers and the moon against a gilded background that enhances them by giving them in addition a celestial perfume.

Be that as it may, the "sensible consolation" is in the work before appearing in the result; the sanctification of the religious artist precedes that of the spectator. Every legitimate art satisfies both emotivity and intelligence, not only in the finished work, but also in its execution.

There is likewise in art a desire to set down in some medium the visual, auditive, or other forms that escape us, and which we wish to retain or possess; this desire for materializing or possessing them in some fashion goes together, quite naturally, with a desire for assimilation, because an attribute must not only be beautiful, it must also be entirely ours, which brings us back directly or indirectly, depending on the case, to the theme of union and love.

— ⋮ —

The Hindu, or more particularly the Vishnuite miniature, is one of the most perfect extra-liturgical arts there is, and we have no hesitation in saying that some of its productions are at the summit of universal painting. An heir to sacred painting, of which the Ajanta frescoes offer us a final vestige, Hindu miniature has undergone Persian influences, but it remains essentially Hindu and is in no wise syncretistic;[3] it has in any event achieved a nobility of draughtsmanship, coloring, and stylization in general, and over and above this, a climate of candor and holiness, which are unsurpassable and which, in the best of its examples, transport the viewer into an almost paradisal atmosphere, a sort of earthly prolongation of heavenly childlikeness.

The Hindu miniature, whether centered on Krishna or on Rama, is a visualization of those spiritual gardens that are the *Mahābhārata*, the *Bhāgavata Purāna*, and the *Rāmāyana*, but it also conveys musical motifs in a romanticized style, as well as the contradictory sentiments that love may provoke in various situations; most of these subjects hold us, willingly or not, under the spell of Krishna's flute. Some of these paintings, in which a maximum of rigor and musicality is combined with a vivid spiritual expressiveness, pertain unquestionably to sacred art inasmuch as the label "profane" can no longer be applied to them; *spiritus ubi vult spirat*. This is a possibility that we also encounter in other domains, for example, when we are forced to admit that the *Bhagavad Gītā*, which logically pertains to secondary inspiration, is in reality an *Upanishad*, and thus a revelation of a supereminent degree, or when a particular saint, belonging socially to a lower caste, is recognized as personally possessing the rank of brahmin.

All these remarks apply likewise to that other summit of painting realized by the Japanese screen; apart from the fact that this genre, in many of its productions, consciously prolongs the Zen-like or more or less Taoist painting of the kakemonos, whose content is a landscape or plants, as well as other subjects that need not enter into consideration here, it often attains a degree of perfection and profundity that renders it inseparable from Buddhist or Shintoist contemplativity.

Another type of extra-liturgical art whose powerful and candid originality is particularly appealing is Balinese art, in which one finds Hindu motifs combined with forms specific to the Malay genius; the fact that this genius—apart from the Hindu influence—has expressed itself principally in the sphere of craftsmanship and in that of archi-

---

[3] Whether it be a case of art, doctrine, or anything else, there is syncretism when there is a cobbling together of disparate elements, but not when there is a unity that has assimilated elements stemming from diverse origins.

tecture made of wood, bamboo, and straw, does not prevent one from granting it qualities that sometimes attain to great art; there can be no doubt that from the point of view of intrinsic values, and not merely from that of a particular taste, a splendid barn in Borneo or Sumatra has much more to offer than does the plaster-nightmare of a Baroque church.[4]

—— ·:· ——

Regarding the styles just mentioned, we find ourselves at the diametrical opposite, not of certain medieval miniatures no doubt, nor of the noblest and most spring-like works of the Quattrocento, but of the dramatic titanism, or the fleshly and vulgar delirium of the megalomaniacs of the Renaissance and the seventeenth century, infatuated with anatomy, turmoil, marble, and gigantism.

Non-traditional art, about which a few words must be said here, encompasses the classical art of antiquity and the Renaissance, and extends up to the nineteenth century which, reacting against academicism, engenders impressionism and other analogous styles; this reaction rapidly deteriorates into all sorts of perversities, either "abstract" or "surrealistic"—although it is really of "subrealism" that one ought to speak here. It goes without saying that worthwhile works are to be found incidentally in impressionism as well as in classicism—in which we include romanticism, since its technical principles are the same—for the cosmic qualities cannot but manifest themselves even in this realm, and a given individual aptitude cannot but lend itself to this manifestation; but these exceptions, in which the positive elements succeed in neutralizing erroneous or insufficient principles, are far from being able to compensate for the serious drawbacks of extra-traditional art, and we would gladly do without all its productions if it were possible to rid the world from the heavy burden of the West's cult of culture, with its vices of impiety, dispersion, and poisonousness. The least that one can say is that it is not this kind of grandeur that brings us closer to Heaven. "Suffer the little children to come unto me and forbid them not; for of such is the Kingdom of Heaven."

---

[4] The same can be said of Shinto sanctuaries, which have been described as "barns", especially those at Ise.

This cult of culture is practically synonymous with civilizationism, and hence with implicit racism; according to this prejudice, Western humanity proves its superiority by the "Greek miracle" and all its consequences, and thus by the anthropolatry—it is not for nothing that one speaks of humanism—and cosmolatry that characterize or rather constitute the classicist mentality. Now, the "Greek miracle" is first and foremost an abuse of the intelligence, which could not have occurred if awareness of the sacred had not gradually crumbled—despite Orphism and Platonism—in large sections of the ruling class under the pressure of an increasingly profane outlook, that is to say of an exteriorized and exteriorizing intelligence both unstable and adventuresome and infatuated with novelties; in keeping with this mentality, the moderns see in the most exteriorized and most enterprising mind a superior intelligence or even intelligence as such.

As we believe we have mentioned on other occasions, what must be blamed in artistic naturalism is not its exact observation of nature, but the fact that this observation is not compensated and disciplined by an equivalent awareness of that which transcends nature, and so of the essences of things, as happens for example in Egyptian art; in all sacred arts it is style that corrects the risk of outwardness, contingency, and accidentality deriving from the imitation of nature, in that style indicates a mode of inwardness; we would even say that an awareness of essences to a certain extent compromises or delays, if not a sufficient observation of outward things, at least their strict translation into graphic terms, although—and one must insist on this—there is no incompatibility in principle between exact draughtsmanship and contemplativity, which confer on a drawing the imprint of inwardness and essentiality. This combination, moreover, is prefigured by the almost inward quality of normative forms, a quality, precisely, that requires an artistic treatment capable of enhancing it through the laws of the fixative or crystallizing dimension that is figurative art.

A perfect equilibrium between a noble naturalness and an interiorizing and essentializing stylization is a precarious but nonetheless possible phenomenon. It goes without saying that essentiality or the "idea" takes precedence over naturalness; the intuition and expression of supra-nature takes precedence over the observation and imitation of nature. To each thing its rights, according to its place.

—— ·:· ——

A naturalistic work of art of the most academic kind can be perfectly pleasing and nobly suggestive by virtue of the natural beauty that it copies, but it is nevertheless deceptive to the very extent that it is exact, that is to say, to the extent that it seeks to pass off a flat surface for three-dimensional space, or inert matter for a living body. In the case of painting, it is necessary to respect both the flat surface and immobility: therefore it is necessary that there should be neither perspective, nor shadows, nor motion, except in the case of a stylization which, precisely, permits the integration of perspective and shadows in the work, while conferring on motion an essential, and thus a symbolic and normative quality. In the case of sculpture, not only is it necessary to respect the immobility of matter by suppressing motion or by reducing it to an essential, balanced, and quasi-static type, it is also necessary to take account of the particular material substance used. When expressing the nature of a living body, or some essential aspect of its nature and thereby some underlying "idea", it is important to take account of the nature of clay, wood, stone, or metal; hence, wood allows different modalities from those allowed by mineral substances and, amongst the latter, metal enables different qualities of expression to be brought into relief than does stone.

Stylization, as we have seen, permits a maximum of naturalism when it knows how to impose on it a maximum of essentiality; in other words, a summit of creative exteriorization calls for a summit of interiorizing power and consequently requires a mastery of the means whereby this power can be realized. In the majority of cases art stops half-way and there is nothing wrong in this, since there is concretely no reason why it should be otherwise; traditional art fulfils its role perfectly; art is not everything, and its productions need not be absolute. But this is independent of the principle that sacred art must satisfy every sincere believer; in other words, it fails in its mission if its crudeness, or on the contrary its superficial virtuosity, leaves unsatisfied or even troubles believers of good will, namely those whom humility preserves from all intolerance and worldly acrimony.

We have already remarked that there is a relative but not irremediable incompatibility—an incompatibility of fact and not of principle—between the spiritual content or the radiance of a work of art and an implacable and virtuosic naturalism: it is as if the science of the mechanism of things killed their spirit, or at least ran the grave risk of killing it. On the one hand we have an execution that is naive, but filled with graces and diffusing an atmosphere of security, happiness, and holy childlikeness; while on the other hand—in classical antiquity and from the Cinquecento onwards—we have on the contrary an execution that is scientifically perfected to a high degree but the content of which is human and not heavenly—or rather it is "humanistic"—and the work suggests, not a childlikeness still close to Heaven, but an adulthood fallen into disgrace and expelled from Paradise.

When calling the art of copying nature an abuse of intelligence, we have indicated its analogy with modern science: artistic naturalism, like exact science, comprises valid aspects since each is true in a certain respect, but in fact, the average man is incapable of completing this wholly outward truth, or these respective truths, by means of their indispensable complements, without which science and art cannot realize the equilibrium that is in conformity with the total reality that logically determines them. Everyone today is aware that the efficacy of the experimental sciences is no longer an argument in their favor, since the calamities they engender result precisely from their efficacy; likewise, even though artistic naturalism is capable of displaying a maximum of adequation, it is exactly for this reason, given the use that has been made of it for all too long, that it has ended up depriving souls of a healthy nourishment in keeping with their true needs.

Not least, an element that in one way or another has powerfully contributed to the ruination of art is the search for originality and ambition; by and large and despite some laudable exceptions, this is all it takes to deprive art of that atmosphere of candor and peaceful happiness, or of sanctity, which is part of its reason for being.

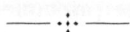

The analogy between artistic naturalism and modern science enables us to insert a comment here. We do not reproach modern science for being a fragmentary, analytical science, lacking in speculative, metaphysical, and cosmological elements, or for originating from the residues or remains of ancient sciences; we reproach it for being subjectively and objectively a transgression and for leading subjectively and objectively to disequilibrium and hence to disaster.

Conversely, traditional sciences do not have our unmixed admiration; the ancients too had their scientific curiosity; they too operated by means of conjectures and, whatever their sense of metaphysical or mystical symbolism may have been, they were sometimes—indeed often—mistaken in fields in which they wished to acquire a knowledge, not of transcendent principles, but of physical facts. It is impossible to deny that on the level of phenomena, which nevertheless is an integral part of the natural sciences, to say the least, the ancients—or Easterners—have had inadequate conceptions, or that their conclusions were often exceedingly naive. Now, we certainly do not reproach them for having believed that the earth is flat and that the sun and the vault of heaven revolve around it, since this appearance is natural and providential for man; but one can reproach them for a number of false conclusions drawn from certain appearances, in the illusory belief that they were practicing, not symbolism and spiritual speculation, but phenomenal or indeed exact science. One cannot, after all, deny that the purpose of medicine is to cure, not to speculate, and that the ancients were ignorant of many things in this field in spite of their great knowledge in other sectors; that said, we are far from contesting that traditional medicine had, and has, the immense advantage of a perspective that includes the whole man; that it was, and is, effective in cases in which modern medicine is impotent; nor are we contesting that modern medicine contributes to the degeneration of the human species and to over-population; or that an absolute medicine is neither possible nor desirable, and this for obvious reasons. But let no one say that traditional medicine is superior purely on account of its cosmological speculations and in the absence of certain effective remedies, and that modern medicine, which has these remedies, is merely a pitiful residue because it is ignorant of these speculations; or that the doctors of the Renaissance, such as Paracelsus, were wrong to uncover the anatomical and other errors of Greco-Arab medicine; or, in an entirely general way, that traditional sciences are marvelous in all respects and that modern sciences, chemistry for example, are no more than fragments and residues.

No piece of knowledge about the phenomenal order is bad in itself; but the key question is that of knowing, firstly, whether this knowledge is reconcilable with the purpose of human intelligence, secondly, whether in the last analysis it is truly useful, and thirdly, whether man can bear it spiritually; now, it has been proven a thousand times over that man cannot bear a body of knowledge that ruptures a certain natural and providential equilibrium, and that the objective consequences of this knowledge correspond exactly to its subjective anomaly. Modern science could not have developed except as the result of a forgetting of God, and of our duties towards God and towards ourselves; in an analogous manner, artistic naturalism, which first made its appearance in antiquity and was rediscovered at the beginnings of the modern era, can be explained only by the explosive birth of a passionately exteriorized and exteriorizing mentality.

If the deviation of art is a possibility, the rejection of art is another. To speak of a great civilization that rejects, not one particular kind of art, but all art, is a contradiction in terms; the more or less iconoclastic point of view of a Saint Bernard or a Savonarola cannot be the attitude of a whole urban civilization. But this point of view, or a point of view that is in practice analogous, can exist traditionally outside a civilization of this type, for example in the nomadic or semi-nomadic world of the North American Indians; they, although not all the aboriginal inhabitants of America, are indeed more or less hostile to the plastic arts, as doubtless were also their distant and fellow nomads the ancient Mongols, and perhaps also the ancient Germans and Celts. Thus, according to the Indians, virgin nature, which is sacred, is of an unparalleled beauty, and it contains every conceivable type of beauty; it is thus vain and indeed impossible to seek to emulate the works of the Great Spirit. It is curious to note that the classical world, that of naturalism and anthropolatry, sees itself as a conqueror before nature; the cult of man leads to contempt for surrounding nature, whereas for the Indian, as moreover for Far-Easterners, nature is a mother, and also a fatherland, of which man is indeed the center, but not the absolute proprietor, and still less the enemy.

The exclusion of plastic arts in the religious naturism of the American Indians results from a real and thus legitimate aspect of things; it could therefore not fail to assert itself in one or several parts of the globe; history proves that this perspective, while it obviously has nothing exclusive about it, nevertheless has a solid basis; to notice this, it is enough to consider all the deviations of the "creative genius" and of all the evils afflicting the world of civilizationism.

This point of view asserted itself moreover in the ancient world, at least partially: the prohibition of images by Judaism and Islam proceeds in fact from an analogous or symbolically equivalent perspective, and it makes itself felt in the world as a sort of beneficent aeration or as a factor of equilibrium. The difference is that in the case of the American Indians, the motivation for the rejection or abstention lies in the inimitability of nature—apart from practical reasons that are in any case relative—whereas in the case of the monotheistic Semites it lies in the sins of luciferianism, magic, and idolatry.

It must nevertheless be admitted that the Indians of whom we are speaking did not completely abstain from figurative drawings: they decorated their tents with a kind of pictography representing men and animals, and sometimes they might also carve their calumets in the simplest way, but in both cases the art is integrated into objects that are both useful and sacred, and therefore conforms to the sobriety and holy poverty of a world that is committed to taking no thought for the morrow.

Islam tolerates—in certain countries or in certain settings—miniatures of a very decorative style, on condition that God never appear in them, and that the face of the Prophet be left blank or covered by a veil; painting is accepted, albeit without enthusiasm, because things that are painted "project no shadow", the miniatures having in addition the advantage of being small, and thus hardly cumbersome.

The Semites reproach the iconodules for worshipping wood, stone, and metal, and images made by man; they are right when they are speaking either of their own past or present paganism, or that of their habitual pagan neighbors, but not when they include in their reproach Christian or Asiatic iconodules. The sacred images of these communities are, precisely, not made by human hand; Christians express this by attributing the first icon to an angel, with or without the participation of Saint Luke. As for the inert matter that the idolaters seem to worship—although in reality it contains a magical power—it ceases to be inert in sacred art because it is inhabited by a heavenly or divine presence; the sacred image is created by God, and it is sanctified and as if vivified by His presence.

The *de facto* ambiguity of beauty, and consequently of art, comes from the ambiguity of *Māyā*: just as the principle of manifestation and illusion both takes one away from the Principle and leads back to it, so too earthly beauties, including those of art, can favor worldliness as well as spirituality, which explains the diametrically opposite attitudes of the saints towards art in general or a given art in particular. The arts reputed to be the most dangerous are those engaging hearing or movement, namely poetry, music, and dance; they are like wine, which in Christianity serves as the vehicle for a deifying sacrament, whereas in Islam it is prohibited, each perspective being right despite the contradiction. That the intoxicating element—in the broadest sense—lends itself particularly to sanctification, is something that Islam recognizes in its esoterism, in which wine symbolizes ecstasy and in which poetry, music, and dance have become ritual means in view of "remembrance".

Beauty, whatever use man may make of it, belongs fundamentally to its Creator, who through it projects into the world of appearances something of His being. The cosmic, and more particularly, the earthly function of beauty is to actualize in the intelligent and sensitive creature the recollection of the essences, and thus to open the way to the luminous Night of the one and infinite Essence.

The vocation *sine qua non* of man is to be spiritual. Spirituality is exercised on the planes that constitute man, namely intelligence, will, affectivity, production: human intelligence is capable of transcendence, of the absolute, of objectivity; the human will is capable of liberty, and thus of conformity to what is grasped by the intelligence; human affectivity, which is joined to each of the preceding faculties, is capable of compassion and generosity, owing to the objectivity of the human mind, which frees the soul from its animal egoism. Finally, there is a specifically human capacity for production, because of which man has been called *homo faber*, and not merely *homo sapiens*: it is the capacity for producing tools and constructing dwellings and sanctuaries, and if need be for making clothes and creating works of art, and for spontaneously combining in these creations symbolism and harmony. The language of harmony may be simple or rich, depending on needs, perspectives, and temperaments; decoration too has its purpose, both from the point of view of symbolism, and from that of musicality. This amounts to saying that this fourth capacity must also have a spiritual content on pain of not being human; thus its role is simply to exteriorize the three preceding capacities by adapting them to material or cultural needs, or let us simply say by projecting them into the sensible order otherwise than by rational discourse or writing. Exiled as we are on earth—unless we are able to content ourselves with that shadow of Paradise that is virgin nature—we must create for ourselves surroundings that by their truth and their beauty recall our heavenly origin and thereby also awaken our hope.

When creating, man must project himself into matter according to his ideal and spiritual personality, not according to his fallen state, so that he may afterwards be able to repose his soul and his spirit in a framework that reminds him in a gentle and holy manner of what he must be.

—⁖—

The two Hindu notions of *darshan* and *satsanga* sum up, by extension, the question of human ambience as such, and so also that of art or craftsmanship. *Darshan* is above all the contemplation of a saint, or of a man invested with a priestly or princely authority, and recognizable by the vestimentary symbols or other that manifest it; *satsanga* is the frequentation of holy men, or simply men of spiritual tendency. What is true for our living surroundings is likewise true for our inanimate surroundings, whose message or perfume we unconsciously assimilate to some degree or another. "Tell me whom thou frequentest and I shall tell thee who thou art."

Art refers essentially to the mystery of the veil: it is a veil made of the world and ourselves and it is thus placed between us and God, but it is transparent to the extent that it is perfect and communicates to us what at the same time it conceals. Art is true, that is to say a transmitter of Essence, to the extent that it is sacred, and it is sacred, and thus a means of remembrance and interiorization, to the extent that it is true.

The Role of Appearances

For exoterism, appearances are unimportant, unless Revelation and Tradition takes them into consideration to some degree or another; for principial esoterism, on the contrary, appearances have all the importance resulting from their nature on the one hand, and from that of man on the other. For an absurd appearance is an error, and many errors in history would have been avoided had one not created a framework of appearances that favored them, and made them appear as truths or at least as very venial sins. Certainly, it is the spirit that counts, not forms, when such an alternative arises; in normal conditions, however, it arises seldom, and in any case the primacy of the spirit does not require falseness on the part of forms, to say the least.

Perfect virtue encompasses everything that lies within our reach, just as the total truth encompasses everything that is.

When 3 is multiplied by 4, the product is 12; it is neither 11 nor 13, but expresses exactly the conjugated powers of the multiplicand and multiplier. Likewise—metaphorically speaking— when the Christian religion is multiplied by Western humanity, the product is the Middle Ages; it is neither the age of the barbarian invasions nor that of the Renaissance. When a living organism has reached its maximum of growth, it is what it should be; it should neither stop short at the infant stage nor should it grow on indefinitely. The norm does not lie in hypertrophy, it lies at the exact outward limit of normal development. The same holds good for civilizations.

If we compare Saint Louis and Louis XIV, we could of course confine ourselves to saying that they represent different ages, which is either a truism or an error; it is a truism to assert that every man lives in his own age, and it is an error to declare that the difference between the two French kings, or more precisely between the worlds in which they live and which they incarnate, is only a difference of time. The real difference is that Saint Louis represents Western Christianity in the full development of its normal and normative possibilities, whereas Louis XIV represents something entirely different, namely that substitute for religion, or for Christendom, that is so-called "Civilization"; admittedly, Christianity is still included in this but the emphasis is elsewhere: it lies now on the titanesque and worldly humanism which, following the example of ancient Rome, is strangely hostile to virgin nature.

Outward forms offer criteria in this regard. It is either false or insufficient to claim that Saint Louis wore the costume of his period and that, *mutatis mutandis*, Louis XIV did the same; the truth is that Saint Louis wore the dress of a Western Christian king, whereas Louis XIV wore that of a monarch who was already more "civilized" than Christian—the first attribute referring, needless to say, to "civilizationism" and not to civilization in the general sense of the word. The appearance of Saint Louis is that of an idea that has reached the fullness of its ripening; it marks, not a phase, but something complete, a thing that is entirely what it ought to be.[1] The appearance of a king of the Renaissance or of the age immediately following is the appearance, not of a thing, but of a phase—although one is not really speaking here of a phase, but of an extravagant episode; whereas we have no difficulty in taking seriously the appearance not only of a Louis IX, but also of a Pharaoh, an Emperor of China, or for that matter, an American Indian chief, it is impossible to escape an impression of ridiculousness emanating from the famous portraits of certain kings. These portraits, or rather these poses and these accoutrements, depicted so humorlessly and pitilessly, are supposed to combine all imaginable sublimities, but cannot be fitted together into a single formula, for it is impossible to have everything at one and the same time; the hieratic and as it were incorporeal splendor of a Christian emperor cannot readily be combined with the paradisal and naked splendor of an ancient hero.

Saint Louis, or any other Christian prince of his time, could well figure amongst the kings and queens—in the form of columns—of the cathedral of Chartres; the later kings, those more marked by an invasive worldliness, would be unthinkable as sacred statues.[2] This is not to say

---

[1] The appearance of Clovis or Charlemagne might be that of a perfect Germanic type or of a perfect monarch, but it could not epitomize Western Christendom in an age when its constituent elements were as yet uncombined and had not yet interpenetrated.

[2] The column statues of Chartres have the value of a criterion of formal orthodoxy, equal to that of an iconostasis: no exhibition of individualism or of profanity could ever find a place amongst them.

that all the princes of the Middle Ages were individually better than those of the Renaissance and later ages, but this is obviously not the question; it is a question here exclusively of demeanor and dress insofar as these are adequate manifestations of a norm that is both religious and ethnic, and thus of an ideal that joins the divine with the human. The king, like the pontiff, is not merely an official, he is also, by the very reason of his central position, an object of contemplation, in the sense of the Sanskrit term *darshan*: to benefit from the *darshan* of a saint is to be penetrated by the intangible aspects of his appearance, if not by the symbolism of his pontifical robes, as the case may be. Saint Louis is one of those sovereigns who spiritually incarnate the ideal that they represent so to speak liturgically, whereas the majority of the other medieval princes represent this ideal at least in the second way which, let it be said once more, is far from being without importance from the point of view of the concrete intelligibility of the royal function, which is full of hidden meanings at once earthly and heavenly.

— ·|· —

When one compares the different European costumes over the centuries, one is struck by the irruption of worldliness that occurs towards the end of the Middle Ages, and one is astonished that believing men, who are supposed to fear God, could have been to such a degree dupes of their vanity, their self-satisfaction, and their lack of critical sense and spiritual imagination, or indeed dignity. Female dress, whether that of princesses or simply that of ordinary women, retains its sober beauty up to the end of the fourteenth century approximately, then becomes complicated, pretentious, and extravagant—with certain intermittent exceptions, often overly sumptuous nonetheless—to reach, in the eighteenth century, an inhuman limit of puffed-up excess and perversity; then, after the French Revolution, one returns to ancient simplicity, but only to slide thereafter into new excesses, whose more or less democratic spirit does not prevent complication and grotesqueness, in short, a worldly pretentiousness deprived of all innocence. As regards male dress, it too also undergoes a near sudden fall in the fifteenth century: it loses its religious character and its sober dignity and becomes either affected—"courtly", if one will—but in any case tainted with narcissism, or else driven by pure fantasy, so much so that the men of those times, if they do not look like dandies, make one think of court jesters. All this is explained in part by the unrealistic and clumsy scission between a religious world and a secular world, the latter never having been integrated normally into religion, whence the Renaissance on the one hand and the Reformation on the other. The specifically worldly character of male dress subsequently becomes even more accentuated and gives rise, throughout history and in the same way as female dress, to an unbalanced lurching between contrary excesses, ending with the sort of barbarous nothingness that prevails in our own age.[3]

In saying this, we know only too well that visual criteria are devoid of significance for the "man of our time", who is nevertheless a visual type by curiosity as well as from an incapacity to think, or through lack of imagination and also through passivity; in other words, he is a visual type in fact but not by right. The modern world, sliding hopelessly down the slope of an irremediable ugliness, has furiously abolished both the notion of beauty and the criteriology of forms; this is, from our point of view, yet another reason for using the present argument, which is like the complementary outward pole of metaphysical orthodoxy, for, as we have mentioned elsewhere in this connection, "extremes meet". There can be no question, for us, of reducing cultural forms, or forms as such, objectively to chance and subjectively to tastes; beauty is the splendor of the true, it is an objective reality that we may or may not understand.[4]

---

[3] What we say of clothes holds good equally for interior layouts and decorations of abodes, especially furniture. It is hardly believable that the same men that made the marvels of sober majesty that are Gothic and Nordic furniture, could have created and tolerated the lacquered and gilded horrors of the courtly and bourgeois furniture of the eighteenth century; that the noble and robust gravity of the works of the Middle Ages could have given way to the wretched affectation of later works; in short, that utility and dignity should have been replaced by a hollow, chattering, and swaggering luxuriousness.

[4] What is admirable in the Orthodox Church is that all its forms, from the iconostases to the vestments of the priests, immediately suggest the ambience of Christ and the Apostles, whereas in what might be called the post-Gothic Catholic Church too many forms are expressions of ambiguous civilizationism or bear its imprint, that is, the imprint of this sort of parallel pseudo-religion that is "Civilization" with a capital C: the presence of Christ then becomes largely abstract. The argument that "only the spirit matters" is "hypocritical angelism", for it is not by chance that a Christian priest wears neither the toga of a Siamese monk nor the loin-cloth of a Hindu ascetic. No doubt the "cloth doth not a monk make"; but it expresses and manifests him, as well as providing him with the importance his role demands!

—— .:. ——

One may wonder what would have become of Latin Christianity if the Renaissance had not dealt it a death blow. Doubtless it would have undergone the same fate as the Eastern civilizations: it would have fallen asleep on top of its treasures, becoming in part corrupt and remaining in part intact. It would have produced, not "reformers" in the conventional sense of the term—which is without any interest, to say the least—but "renewers" in the form of a few great sages and a few great saints. Moreover, the aging of civilizations is a human phenomenon, and to fault it excessively is to find fault with man as such.

Be that as it may, we should like to point out here that the chronic disequilibrium characterizing Western humanity has two principal causes, the antagonism between Aryan paganism and Semitic Christianity on the one hand, and the antagonism between Latin rationality and Germanic imaginativeness on the other.[5] The Latin Church, with its sentimental and unrealistic idealism, has created a completely unnecessary split between clergy and laity, whence a perpetual uneasiness on the part of lay people towards the clergy; it has moreover imposed on the Germanic peoples, but without taking account of their needs and tastes, too many specifically Latin solutions, forgetting that a religious and cultural framework, in order to be effective, must adapt itself to the mental requirements of those upon whom it is imposed. And since, in the case of Europeans, their creative gifts far exceed their contemplative gifts, it can be said that the West excels in "destroying what it has worshipped"—whereas, the role of Christianity should have been to re-establish equilibrium by accentuating contemplation and channeling creativity; hence, the history of Western civilization is made up of cultural betrayals that are difficult to understand—one is astonished at so much lack of understanding, ingratitude, and blindness—and, quite naturally, these betrayals appear most visibly in their formal manifestations, in other words, in the human ambience which, in normal conditions, ought to

---

[5] From the point of view of spiritual worth, it is contemplativity that is decisive, whether it is combined with reason or with imagination, or with this or that type of sensitivity.

suggest a sort of earthly Paradise or heavenly Jerusalem, with all their beatific symbolism and with all their stability.

The Renaissance, at its apogee, replaces happiness with pride; the Baroque reacts against this pride or this crushing coldness with a false happiness, cut off from its divine roots and full of a vainglory that is tormented while at the same time delirious. The reaction to this reaction was a pagan classicism leading to the bourgeois ugliness, both shapeless and mediocre, of the nineteenth century; this has nothing to do with the real people or with a popular craftsmanship that is still authentic, and which more or less escaped the march of history, bearing witness to a rustic wholesomeness far removed from all civilizationist affectation.[6]

As for the modern world, it represents a possibility of disequilibrium and deviation that could not fail to be manifested when its time was ripe; but the metaphysical ineluctability of a phenomenon should not prevent us from noticing what it is in itself, nor does it authorize us to take it for what it is not, especially since the truth is by definition constructive, either directly or indirectly. Even the most ineffective truth in appearance, though failing to change the world, will always help us in some way or other to remain, or to become, what we ought to be in the face of God.

---

[6] Popular art, moreover, can often be the vehicle for primordial symbols, solar most notably; this feature is found in peoples situated as far as possible from one another, sometimes in forms that are identical down to the last detail.

The Function of Relics

It is in the nature of man—since he combines the outward with the inward—to avail himself of sensory supports towards the progress of his spirit or for the equilibrium of his soul. These supports are either artistic, and thus symbolistic and aesthetic, or theurgic; in the latter case their function is to act as a vehicle for benefic, protective, and sanctifying forces; the two types can moreover be combined. We wish to speak here of the second category, or more precisely of a particular case, that of relics, whose function indeed pertains to theurgy, at least indirectly; we say theurgy, and not magic, given that the forces acting in this case have their reason for being and their essential source in divine Grace and not in human art.[1] In order to deal with this subject, it may suffice to reply to two objections, one regarding the authenticity of relics, and the other their efficacy.

Let us first of all recall that the origin of the cult of relics stems from the bodies of the saints, then parts or pieces of these bodies, then objects that have touched them, and later objects that have touched those first objects; this last category is, for obvious reasons, limitless since it is possible to place fabrics on relics of "major eminence", such as on the Holy Tunic kept at Treves. The important thing to bear in mind, however, is that the cult of relics, far from being a fairly recent abuse, as most Protestants suppose, goes back to the period of the catacombs and represents an essential element in the devotional and charismatic economy of Christianity.

There are two notions at the origin of relics, the one theological and official, and the other more popular, at least *a posteriori* and *de facto*. Theologically, the cult of relics, as that of images, is based on the respect due to the saints as glorious members of Christ, and on the idea that, in venerating the saints through their relics, one will be inspired by their love of God, or love God through them; as for the popular perspective, this cult is based simply on the beneficent and possibly miraculous power inherent in the bodies of the blessed and which cannot but impart itself to some extent—depending on the

---

[1] At the summit of this phenomenological category is situated the sacramental order, whose nature is nevertheless such that, from a stricter point of view, it constitutes a separate category.

importance of the saint—to objects that have been in contact with these bodies. We say "popular" for simplicity's sake even though this term does no more than recognize a state of fact; the idea of a miraculous presence in relics was, in fact, taught by Saint Cyril of Jerusalem and other Church Fathers, while the thesis of the moral function of relics—also dating from the earliest days—was upheld especially by the Scholastics.

Three different powers are to be distinguished in a relic: firstly, there is the beneficent influence inherent in the object itself; secondly, there is a superadded psychic energy coming from the devotees as the result of intense and prolonged adoration; thirdly, there is the aid that may be granted by the saint, from Heaven itself, independently of the two preceding factors but combining with them, if necessary. The presence of a theurgic power is more certain with corporeal remains, such as bones or blood, but it is no less probable with objects formerly belonging to saintly individuals; in the case of quasi-divine persons, such as Christ and the Blessed Virgin, the inherence of a theurgic power in the very least object that touched them is even absolutely clear. However, this power does not work blindly: its positive or negative manifestation—as the case may be—depends on the nature of the person who benefits by it or who is subjected to it, and also upon all kinds of circumstances, both subjective and objective.

A very particular instance of relics is that of heavenly objects sent down to earth, such as the black stone of the Kaaba or the pillar of Saragossa; the applicability here of the term "relic" (*reliquia* = "remains") may well be questioned, but all things considered it must be admitted that the term has *de facto* a very broad meaning that can apply to any sensory object carrying a celestial presence. Tradition relates that the pillar (*el pilar*) was carried to Saragossa by angels; the Blessed Virgin, at that time still alive on earth, accompanied them and stood upon the pillar, and then departed with the angels after giving certain commands to the Apostle Saint James.[2] The pillar, of heavenly origin, descended into earthly matter; it thus underwent in its passage a kind of "transubstantiation"—the same observation applies to the black stone at Mecca—just as, conversely, earthly bodies raised up to Heaven, those of Jesus and Mary for example, undergo an ascendant "transubstantiation". We are aware, in saying this, that the starting

---

[2] The pillar was touched by Mary, as was the black stone by Abraham; in this sense the term "relic" is fully justified, given the "avataric" quality of the holy personages.

point of modern science is to deny suprasensory cosmic dimensions outside space—although even the most ordinary magic cannot be explained except by one of these dimensions—but we cannot at this point expound the doctrine of cosmic degrees, which we have explained on other occasions;[3] quite clearly, it is impossible to discuss the significance of relics without presupposing an adequate knowledge of this doctrine, or at least the fundamental notion of the levels of universal Existence.

The cult of relics is encountered in various forms in all religions; Buddhist *stūpas* are no more than great reliquaries. Even Islam, which is hardly inclined to this type of cult, cannot forego it completely, if only because the Prophet, and the saints after him, left behind them objects that it is impossible not to venerate.[4] What corresponds most directly in Islam to the cult of relics is the veneration of the Prophet's tomb at Medina and the tombs of saints, starting with those of the great Companions; most of these tombs are at the same time mosques, sometimes renowned for the miracles that occur there,[5] after the fashion of the Christian churches built from the first centuries onwards over the tombs of martyrs. The same idea of combining the body of a saint with a sanctuary is found in the Christian custom of encasing a relic within an altar; every altar is in principle a mausoleum.

The rejoinder to the objection that relics are ineffectual has been given above; it remains to consider the objection that they are not genuine. In reply to this difficulty, it may be said in the first place that the guarantee of authenticity lies in the very principle of the cult of relics, without which the cult, which is in fact universal, would not

---

[3] See our book *Logique et transcendance*, chap. "Le symbolisme du sablier", and also *Forme et substance dans les religions*, chap. "Les cinq Présences divines".

[4] Certain objects once belonging to the Prophet are conserved in Istanbul in the old palace of the sultans; in an Islamic climate they cannot occasion an organized cult, but Muslims nevertheless contemplate them with veneration possibly murmuring meanwhile the *salāt ʿalā 'n-Nabī*, or perhaps too by formulating requests in prayers.

[5] This calls to mind the house of the Blessed Virgin at Ephesus, where Catholics celebrate Mass while Muslims pray in the adjoining room; the various *ex-votos* show that the Virgin grants miracles to each of those communities.

exist anywhere; the next point to be made is that the canonical, and hence traditional, nature of the cult constitutes a guarantee of the authenticity and legitimacy of relics in the eyes of anyone who knows what a religion is. There is, in fact, in the charismatic economy of every intrinsically orthodox religion, a protective power that keeps a watchful eye on the integrity of the various elements of worship, even if they are no more than secondary, and this power results from the presence of the Holy Spirit, and is thus not unconnected with the mystery of infallibility.

These fundamental facts do not prevent our admitting that, in the Middle Ages when the need to possess relics became all but insatiable, some unscrupulous or unbalanced people started falsifying them; but, aside from the fact that the victims of these frauds were particular individuals and not the custodians of sanctuaries, this abuse does not logically permit doubts about the genuineness of relics canonically recognized. The question still remains, however, as to whether canonically recognized relics did not occasionally include an unauthentic one as the result of error if not fraud; despite guarantees resulting from the nature of things and despite administrative safeguards,[6] mistakes are always possible in exceptional cases, for almost metaphysical reasons that need not be discussed here. In this event, the grace inherent in the religion intervenes in another way: in response to the fervor in the adoration of a relic, the saint invoked will make himself present therein,[7] exactly as a saint can choose to make himself present in a painted or sculptured image that likewise has no link back to the personality of the saint on earth.[8]

---

[6] Since the Middle Ages, "pious frauds" have obliged the Church to draw up rules to safeguard the cult of relics: their identity and integrity had to be certified by a seal-bearing official, that is, they had to be recognized by the bishop and approved by the Pope. It should also be noted that the Church in the Middle Ages had to act with equal severity against superstitious abuses and even against sacrilegious practices with a magical intent.

[7] According to an opinion that is current in the Maghreb and doubtless also in other Muslim lands, there are saints whose function it is to take responsibility for prayers made over a false tomb or an empty tomb—or other mistakes of this kind—which in its way explains the fact that prayers combined with a false support, but legitimate as regards form and meaning, are not invalidated by the material error.

[8] The same is true of miraculous medallions, for example, which are not relics of the Blessed Virgin, but objects made at her behest and then charged with her beneficent power; likewise also for miraculous waters.

The miraculous images of the Virgin are such, not because Mary once actually touched them physically, but because she was willing to bestow her grace upon them; as much could be said, *mutatis mutandis*, of certain saints subsequently declassified due to archeological scruples—supposing these scruples can be justified.[9] There are cases where the question of historicity is best put on hold, since it is not always possible—to say the least—to prove the non-historical nature of persons or events situated in the mists of an inaccessible past; besides, it is an unrealistic prejudice to take only written documents into account and to disdain oral traditions, even to the point of forgetting their existence or their very possibility. When it comes to ancient cults, not well supported historically, but deep-rooted and hence efficacious, the Holy Spirit, or what Muslims would call the *barakah*, must be "given a free hand" and the temptation to dot all the i's—too often inspired by an inferiority complex—must be resisted; one must have a feeling for the concrete meaning of sacred phenomena, and trust in the paracletic and charismatic power that animates the body of religion and of which we spoke above.[10] All this is rendered yet more plausible by the fact that side by side with its need for transparency, Heaven loves a certain indetermination or asymmetry, as many of the elements in religion bear witness, and above all the Scriptures themselves.

—— ·:· ——

Iconoclasts of all kinds need to be reminded that it is better to love God through a saint than not to love him at all; or, again, that it is better to remember this love thanks to a saint, his relic, his image, than to disdain these supports whilst forgetting to love God; this is what

[9] A saint like Saint Philomena should have been allowed to "rest in peace", from the moment she manifested her person through the miracles of Ars; it is a tautology to add that she did this with Heaven's acquiescence, without troubling herself with the *nihil obstat* of "exact science".

[10] A certain lack of the "sense of *barakah*", which is curiously typical of the Latin world, is shown likewise at the level of sensible forms, which should be those of sacred art; we are thinking here not only of the unspeakable harm stemming from the Baroque style, but also of the ponderous and pedantic manner in which certain holy places are fitted out, frequently dominated by a crude and obnoxious clutter of metallic assemblages that cannot but disturb the outpouring of heavenly influences. If there are two great incompatibles, they are indisputably "civilization" and Paradise.

the reformers who rejected images and relics lost sight of without being able to put anything of like value in their stead—and without even suspecting there was anything there to replace—because, in rejecting these supports, they simultaneously rejected sainthood; quite different is the case of the Muslims, who accept sainthood outright and hence venerate the tombs of saints. Muslims are, moreover, "aniconists" rather than "iconoclasts"—somewhat as Buddhists are "nontheists" and not "atheists"—and the primordial proof of this is that the Prophet, upon the capture of Mecca, protected with his own hands an image of the Virgin and Child that was in the Kaaba; in other words, Islam does not set out heretically to attack traditional images that already existed—the crude idols of the Bedouins had nothing sacred about them—but simply forbids the making of images *a priori* in order to facilitate one particular mode of awareness of the Transcendent, which, in emphasizing omnipresence and essentiality, does in fact preclude all visible supports.

What does correspond to Western iconoclasm in the context of Islam is Wahhabism, which destroys mausoleums, seeing in them manifestations of idolatry;[11] but to compare it with Protestantism is however not permissible, since Wahhabism, which is extreme Hanbalism, upholds all the essential elements of dogma and practice. Thus it is deeply significant that Wahhabi iconoclasm stopped short before the tomb of the Prophet in Medina, which is the supreme relic in the Muslim universe, summarizing for Islam the mystery of the presence on earth of celestial humanity.

---

[11] Iconoclasts of every kind readily assert, sometimes not without demagogy, that if images, relics, and *koubba*s are destroyed, the people will put God in the place of these "idols"; but they forget one thing: namely that the people will not do so. Doubtless, the people can do without these supports when abstraction is at the very foundation of the religion, but not when abstraction is imposed after the fact.

An Elementary Criteriology of Celestial Apparitions

According to a *hadīth* the devil cannot assume the physical appearance of the Prophet. In itself, this is entirely plausible; yet, one may nonetheless ask what is the usefulness of this information given the fact that, after the Companions had disappeared, there was no longer—and there is no longer—any witness to this appearance.

The practical import of the *hadīth* is as follows: if the devil were to take on the appearance of a deified man or of an angel, he would inevitably betray himself by some discordant detail; this would no doubt pass unnoticed by those whose intention lacks both disinterestedness and virtue and who, placing their desires above the truth, basically wish to be deceived, but not by those whose intelligence is serene and whose intention is pure. The devil cannot assume objectively an entirely adequate likeness of an "angel of light", but he can do so subjectively by flattering—and so corrupting—the viewer who has laid himself open to illusion; this explains why, in a climate of individualistic and passional mysticism, all celestial apparitions are sometimes rejected; a measure of prudence that would have no point outside such a climate and that is, in itself, at the very least exaggerated and problematical.

The right attitude towards an apparition—or some other grace—that God does not impose upon us with an irresistible certitude, is one of deferential neutrality, and possibly of pious expectancy; but even when a grace is accompanied by certitude, one must take care not to base oneself exclusively upon it for fear of lapsing into the error many false mystics have been guilty of at the beginning of their careers; for the decisive basis of the spiritual way is always an objective value, but for which there could be no question of a "way" in the proper sense of the term. This amounts to saying that with respect to graces or visions one must be neither discourteous nor credulous, and that it suffices to take one's stand upon the unshakable elements of the way, namely the elements of Doctrine and of Method, which are established *a priori* on a basis of absolute certitude and which will never be disavowed by authentic manifestations of grace.[1]

---

[1] In the same vein of thought, there is the problem of the question addressed ritually to God, the Muslim *istikhārah*. For this procedure to be valid it is necessary that the intention should be a pure one and then that the interpretation should be correct, and this

Those who are in the grip of illusion do not know, and do not wish to know, that the devil can give them sound inspirations with the sole aim of gaining their trust, so as to be able finally to lead them into error, and that he can tell them the truth nine times the more easily to deceive them on the tenth occasion, and that he deceives above all those who are seeking the confirmation or fulfillment of illusions to which they are attached.[2] This applies to visions as well as to auditions or other messages.

One particular type of grace is ecstasy. Here too one must distinguish between the true and the false, or between the supernatural and the morbid—even the demonic. A very rare and, at the same time, most paradoxical exception, is accidental ecstasy, something which, in this context, cannot be left unmentioned. It may happen that someone entirely profane has a real ecstatic experience, without understanding how or why; such an experience is unforgettable and has a more or less profound effect upon the character of the person concerned. This is a matter of a cosmic accident due to a far distant cause, which is to say that it lies in that individual's destiny, or in his *karma*—merits acquired in the past, in a pre-terrestrial realm—as Hindus and Buddhists would say. But it would be a serious mistake to see in such an experience a spiritual acquisition of a conscious and active character, when such an event can only be a call to an authentic way in which one starts again from nothing: *quaerite et invenietis.*

None of this has any direct bearing on celestial apparitions, but ecstasy is nonetheless a way of "seeing God", through a veil either woven with symbols or fashioned from ineffable light. It may coincide

depends on a variety of conditions, both subjective and objective. For example, one cannot ask Heaven if such and such a dogma is true or whether or not the spiritual master is right or not, for this would manifest either an attitude of unbelief or insubordination, contradicting the principle *credo ut intelligam* which, precisely, applies in such cases.

[2] The satanic origin of a message is immaterial when it is benefic, but the devil will give such a message only to those whom he expects to deceive thereafter, otherwise he would have no interest in doing so, to say the least. In this general context let us also recall the fact that according to certain ancient maxims that are well known, "heresy resides in the will and not in the intelligence", and that "to err is human but to persevere in error is diabolical".

moreover with a vision, and in that case it will be the subjective pre-condition for a supernaturally objective mode of perception—just as sleep may be—that is to say, it will be the already celestial meeting point in view of a contact between earth and Heaven.

— ·:· —

Among real or apparent graces there are also "powers" such as those of healing, forecasting, suggestion, telepathy, divination, and the performance of minor miracles. These powers may indeed be direct gifts from Heaven, but in this case they are related to some degree of sanctity; otherwise they are merely natural, though rare and out of the ordinary. Now in the opinion of the most diverse spiritual authorities one should treat them with great circumspection, paying no attention to them, all the more as the devil may get involved in this and has every reason to do so. Gratuitous powers, even if the indication *a priori* of some election on the part of Heaven, can cause the downfall of those who become attached to them to the detriment of the pur-gative asceticism required in all spirituality; many a heretic and false spiritual master started on his way by becoming the dupe of some power with which nature had endowed him. For the truly spiritual man, powers such as these are seen at the outset as a temptation and not as a favor; he will not dwell on them, if only for the simple reason that no saint will take his own sanctity as axiomatic. Man does not have access to the standards that are God's—except in abstract terms or through a particular grace deriving from a dignity already prophetic by nature—for no man can be both judge and party in his own cause.

It therefore goes without saying that powers may be just as pre-carious as visions, and as authentic as them, depending on human predisposition and according to the will of God. The criterion of supernatural power resides in the character of the man concerned, and nobility of character is also, and essentially so, one of the criteria of sanctity; which is tantamount to saying that powers cannot on their own be proofs of spiritual election.[3]

---

[3] The twin pillars of the virtuous character are humility and charity; one could also say, patience and generosity, or detachment and goodness. According to a saint, the devil has said that he can do everything—except humble himself. The underlying meaning: everything that is outward, for what is inward is precisely humility or sincerity.

— ∴ —

According to a well-known principle, angels always speak in the doc-trinal or mythological language of those whom they are addressing, provided this language is intrinsically orthodox; however, there are here two elements of possible contradiction, namely differences of religion and differences of level. Consequently, a celestial being may manifest himself not only in terms of a particular religion or of a particular denomination, but also in terms of a given degree of uni-versality; and just as esoterism on the one hand prolongs while on the other contradicts exoterism—the former attitude referring to the truth that saves and the latter to the formalism that limits—so too celestial manifestations may in principle contradict each other within the framework of one and the same religion, according to whether they take account of this particular cosmos or, on the contrary, express the one and universal Truth.

Having said this, it is necessary to understand that the spokesmen of Heaven never give lessons in "universalist erudition"; for instance, they will never speak either of *Vedānta* or of Zen in a Semitic setting, any more than they will speak of Spanish mysticism or of Hesychasm in a Hindu or Buddhist setting. But, to repeat, there is nothing abnormal in Heaven favoring by supernatural signs a specific spiritual perspective, while favoring in the same manner another one that sur-passes it, provided both perspectives are intrinsically legitimate and even though both are situated in the same religious cosmos.

— ∴ —

The question of the apparition of a deified man—of an *Avatāra*, if one will—raises another problem, that of the distinction between a visionary dream and an ordinary dream. Celestial beings appear only in visionary dreams, not in ordinary ones, but this does not mean that all celestial manifestations in the context of an ordinary dream are diabolical, for they may be merely natural: just as we can dream of something that preoccupies us, so we can dream innocently of a saint, without the absence of any spiritual cause implying the presence of a malefic one. The situation is quite different when the apparition is self-contradictory in itself, or when the context is discordant, for then a satanic element has mingled with the merely natural cause, unless this very element is actually the cause of the mirage; if such is the case, the dream may even be taken for a visionary one, but it is precisely its content that betrays its origin.

Contrary to what occurs in ordinary dreams, visionary dreams are absolutely homogeneous and of a crystalline precision; they leave behind them, upon awakening, an impression of freshness, luminosity, and happiness, unless their content conveys a threat from Heaven and not a consolation or an encouragement, as is more often the case. In keeping with their supernatural character, visionary dreams are more or less rare, for Heaven is not prolix and there is no reason why man should receive frequent celestial messages.[4]

At this point, mention should be made about the relation between the dreaming and the waking states, for there are those who will contend that the dream-experience does not concern the waking ego. Indeed, some modern Vedantists claim that the two states in question are wholly unrelated, that the dreaming ego is not in any way the same as the waking one, that the two states are closed systems, and that it is incorrect to take the waking ego as the point of reference for the dreaming consciousness;[5] and that consequently the latter is in no way inferior to the former nor less real.[6]

This extravagant and pseudo-metaphysical opinion is contradicted, in the first place, by the fact that, on awakening, we remember our own dream and not that of someone else; secondly, by the fact that the inconsistent and fluid character of dreams, on the one hand, and their reference to our objective experiences, on the other, prove their subjectivity, their passivity, and their contingency; and, thirdly, by the fact that, while dreaming, we can perfectly well be aware that we are dreaming and that it is we—and not someone else—who are

---

[4] An exception must be made for ongoing messages, those taking the form of a habitual dialogue between a celestial personality and the privileged soul, as was the case with Sister Consolata; but there is then only an interior dialogue, without any visual manifestations.

[5] Like Kant, Siddheswarananda, for instance, seems to think that his own experiences limit those of others.

[6] Some have even gone so far as to claim that dreaming is superior to the waking state since it comprises possibilities that are excluded by the physical world, as though these possibilities were anything but purely passive and as though the objective and decisive reality of the waking state did not compensate infinitely for the dream possibility of rising into the air; or again, as if one could not just as well dream of being paralyzed.

dreaming. Proof of this is that it can happen that we awaken of our own free volition when the development of the dream takes a disturbing turn; by contrast, no one would think of making an effort to emerge from the waking state—however disagreeable the situation—in the hope of awakening into some paradisal state with the conviction that one had emerged from an accident of one's own imagination, whereas in reality the terrestrial world continues to be what it is. Certainly the universe is a kind of illusion with respect to the Principle, but on the plane of relativity the objective world is not an illusion with respect to a particular subjectivity.[7]

"And behold the angel of the Lord appeared unto him in a dream, saying, Joseph, thou son of David, fear not to take unto thee Mary thy wife. . . . Then Joseph being raised from sleep did as the angel of the Lord had bidden him." And again: "Behold the angel of the Lord appeareth to Joseph in a dream, saying, Arise, and take the young child and his mother, and flee into Egypt. . . . When he arose, he took the young child and his mother by night, and departed into Egypt". These passages from the Gospel show as clearly as one could wish the conti- nuity—evident in itself—between the dreaming and the waking states or between the ego of the sleeper and that of the man who is awake; the fact that it is here a question of a visionary dream, therefore of an intrinsically objective phenomenon rather than of an ordinary one, in no way detracts from the force of the argument, given that the framework of the phenomenon is the dreaming consciousness and not the waking one. The angel, instead of making himself physically vis- ible, has so to speak mirrored himself in the psychic substance of the sleeping person; this precisely is what characterizes visionary dreams, which thus combine an objective phenomenon with an eminently subjective state of consciousness, that is to say one that is withdrawn

---

[7] Shankaracharya, so misunderstood by some of his interpreters, is of the same opinion when he specifies, in his commentaries on the *Vedānta Sūtras*, that "the world of the intermediate state (the dream) is not real in the same way that the world woven of ether and of the other elements is real". He says also that "the visions of a dream are acts of memory, whereas the visions of the waking state are acts of immediate con- sciousness (acts of perception); and the distinction between memory and immediate consciousness is recognized by everyone as being based on the absence or presence of the object". And finally: "This drifting (in dreams), based only on mental impressions (*vāsanā*), is not real." All this, obviously, concerns ordinary dreams, not visionary ones, the objective reality of which is evident, given their supernatural cause.

from the external world.[8] Here objective reality enters the dream-world, either unveiled or clothed in symbolism.

The question of knowing which detail would be inconsistent with the authenticity of a celestial apparition depends either on the nature of things or else on a particular religious perspective or a particular level of this perspective. That is to say, there are elements that in themselves, and from every religious or spiritual point of view, are incompatible with celestial apparitions, whereas there are others that are so only in the framework of a given perspective or a given spiritual viewpoint; for example, according to Catholic criteriology, total nudity is excluded so far as the messengers of Heaven are concerned,[9] whereas in Hinduism it has either a neutral or a positive character. The reason for the Catholic attitude is that Heaven can neither wish to arouse concupiscence nor do anything to offend modesty—although, even in the climate of Christianity, there is here some latitude—whereas the Hindu attitude can be explained by the sacred character of nudity, which is based on the body's theomorphism, that is to say upon its "humanized divinity" as it were; in this case metaphysical transparency compensates for the ambiguity of the flesh, which, in any case, both Hindus and Muslims regard as something natural and not sinful.[10] As for discordant elements that are intrinsically incompatible with a celestial manifestation, there are first of all—and quite obviously—elements of ugliness or grotesque features, not just in the actual form of the apparition but also in its movements or even simply in the setting and atmosphere; then there is the question of discourse, both from the point of view of content and of style, for Heaven neither

[8] It is true that all knowledge, consciousness, or perception is subjective by definition, but what counts is the direct objective cause, not the subjective phenomenon as such, when it is a matter of distinguishing a real experience from an imaginary one.

[9] So far as women are concerned, probably even partial nudity, except in the case of *lactatio*, as indicated by Saint Bernard's vision and also as depicted in certain icons.

[10] It will no doubt be objected that the same is true for Christians; but while this is so in theory it is not so in practice, collective sentiments not always being at the level of theological niceties. The opinion of modernists has nothing to do with authentic Christian sensibility.

lies nor is it "chatty".[11] "God is beautiful and He loves beauty", the Prophet said; loving beauty, God also loves dignity, He who combines beauty (*jamāl*) with majesty (*jalāl*). "God is love", and love excludes, if not holy wrath, most certainly ugliness and pettiness.

A decisive criterion of authenticity, on the basis of necessary extrinsic criteria, is the spiritual or miraculous efficacy of the apparition: if nothing spiritually positive results from the vision, then it is of doubtful validity to the very extent that the visionary himself is imperfect, but without necessarily being false even in such a case as this, for the motives of Heaven may escape men; if, on the contrary, the visionary draws a permanent grace from the vision to the point of becoming a better person,[12] or if the vision is the source of miracles without being accompanied by any discordant elements, in that case there can be no doubt one is dealing with a true celestial apparition. *A fructibus eorum cognoscetis eos.*

Our attitude regarding celestial manifestations depends finally on our understanding of the relationship between transcendence and immanence, and also between necessity and contingency, which brings us back to the mystery of the Veil. On the one hand, when we perceive a celestial sign, we must not lose sight of the fact that it is a veil, albeit luminous; on the other hand, knowing that it is a veil, we must not forget, *a fortiori*, that its reason for being is the transmission of truth and presence and that in this respect the sign is as if transubstantiated, and that therefore it is itself truth and presence. On the one hand, the Virgin personifies and manifests the Mercy of God; on the other, the divine Mercy is personified in the Virgin and is manifested by her; not in the sense that every positive phenomenon necessarily manifests God because in reality there is nothing but He, but in the sense that God makes Himself manifest in an eminently direct way in the midst of His indirect and ordinary manifestations, which pertain to the natural, not the supernatural, realm.

---

[11] Which cuts short a whole series of apparitions or "messages" of which one hears talk in the second half of the twentieth century.

[12] Either because he modifies his habitual behavior or else undergoes a change in his character, the former being an extrinsic result, the latter an intrinsic one; in any case, neither change is entirely disconnected from the other.

When perceiving the symbol or the support, one can see God either after or before the form: after, because the form evokes God; before, because God has made Himself form. The mystery of the Veil contains the whole mystery of *hypostasis*, and thereby that of theophany.

The Sun Dance

Theurgic phenomenology encompasses not only sacred symbols, the supports of heavenly fluids, and subjective graces, but also, and even above all, rites in which man actively cooperates with a salvific theurgy. By "phenomenology" we simply mean the study of a category of phenomena, and not a particular philosophy that claims to resolve everything by observing or exploring in its fashion the phenomena that present themselves to our attention, without our being able to account for this central and ungraspable phenomenon that is the mystery of subjectivity; if we are dwelling a little on this question, it is because the standpoint we are adopting provides a key to the theme we intend to discuss.

The scission into subject and object is the result of relativity: without this scission, or polarity, there would be neither limitation nor diversity, and thus no phenomenon. Now, the subject can only grasp its own nature by recognizing it in the object and by discovering the object within itself, namely in the subject, which is the interiorized object just as the object is the exteriorized subject. The subject grasps its own reality in two stages, that is to say, through adequacy and through totality: it grasps it adequately by and in the highest object to which human intelligence is proportioned, namely the absolute Object; and it grasps it totally by the contemplative assimilation of this Object, which entails the emptiness and extinction of the subject: emptiness from the point of view of the mental artifices that compromise the perception of the pure Object, and extinction from the point of view of the passional elements that limit and darken this mirror that the subject embodies. The knowledge the subject realizes takes place in the coincidence between the transcendent Object and pure subjectivity, for the subject as such reveals a dimension of the immanent Object and, in so doing, is revealed as absolute Subject, having been objective only due to its veiling.

The transcendent Object, which by virtue of its absolute and infinite character awakens in the subject the consciousness of "immanent transcendence"—if recourse to such a paradox is permissible—may be the idea of the Absolute, of God, of the Great Spirit, but it can also be manifested in the form of a symbol, such as the sun. The sun is our macrocosmic heart; the heart is the sun of our microcosm; by knowing the sun—by knowing it in depth—we know ourselves. To know the divine Object is to die for it and in it, so that it may be born in us; the Sun Dance of the Indians of North America provides a striking example of this.

There are men who worship the sun because it is a manifestation of God; there are others who refuse to worship it because it is not God, as the fact of its setting would seem to validate. The worshippers of the sun could rightly contend that it does not set, but that it is the rotation of the earth that creates this illusion; and their point of view could be compared to that of esoterism, which on the one hand is aware of the theophanic and as it were sacramental nature of the great phenomena of the visible world, and on the other hand knows the real and total nature of things and not a particular aspect or appearance only.

But a third possibility should also be mentioned here, that of idolatry: there are men who worship the sun, not because they know that it manifests God, or that God is manifested by it, nor because they know that it is motionless and that it is not it that sets,[1] but because they imagine that God is the sun; in this case, exoterist condemners of the sun find it easy to loudly protest about paganism. They are relatively right, while ignoring that idolatry—or more precisely heliolatry—can only be a degeneration of a legitimate attitude; not an exclusive attitude, no doubt, but in any case one that is aware of the real situation, both from the point of view of the subject as well as from that of the object.

Strictly speaking, the prostration in front of the Kaaba, or in the direction of the Kaaba, could be interpreted as an act of idolatry, seeing that God is outside space and that the Kaaba is a spatial and material object. If this reproach is absurd, the analogous reproach addressed to worshippers of the Principle "through" the sun, or the Christian, Hindu, or Buddhist venerators of images, is so also, from the point of view of the principle and without taking into account differences of level that are always possible. One Sufi declared that

---

[1] The fact that the sun moves in its turn, as seems to be the case, does not enter into consideration in a symbolism that is limited to our solar system.

the Kaaba revolved around him, the true Kaaba having been realized in his heart.

Like the Aryan mythologies—Hindu, Greco-Roman, and Nordic—hyperborean shamanism, to which the tradition, both differentiated and homogeneous, of the Indians of North America belongs, distinguishes itself by its sacred interpretation of virgin nature: in it, nature plays the role of Temple, as well as of divine Book.[2] In this there is an element of esoterism—obviously so, since we are dealing here with a surviving remnant of the primordial religion—that monotheistic and Semitic exoterism had to exclude by reason of the fact that it was obliged to oppose the naturalism of religions that had become pagan, but which, on the plane of the *religio perennis* or simply of truth as such, retains all its rights even within the framework of the Abrahamic monotheisms; for no one can prevent nature in general and its noble contents in particular—despite a certain universal but completely relative curse—from manifesting God and being the instruments of graces, which they can communicate in certain conditions both objective and subjective.[3]

One example of these graces, which we intentionally take from Islam, precisely because this religion is particularly abstract and iconoclastic, is the "mercy" (*rahmah*) that resides in rain, or which God sends by means of rain; thus the Prophet was fond of baring his head beneath the rain because of the blessing it carried. Now, the sun also transmits a blessing, but Islam makes no use of this for reasons of perspective, that is to say because the sun, in the mindset of the Arabs, ran the risk of usurping the place of God. Completely different is the perspective of the Hindus, who worship Surya, the male Sun, or

---

[2] Thus, the American Indians have the merit of always having been the defenders of nature and of human kinship with it. Their spokesmen declare today: "We do not want equality, but the possibility of living our life; we refuse the way of the whites. Our values are founded on respect for nature: according to us, man belongs to the earth, not the earth to man."

[3] Be that as it may, the biblical injunction to "have dominion over the earth" does no more than define man; this injunction, which was meant *a priori* for the Semitic nomads, runs no risk of being misinterpreted—in the sense of a declaration of war against nature—except in a European, Aristotelian, and civilizationist climate.

of the Japanese, whose worship is addressed to Amaterasu, the solar Goddess:[4] in these traditional worlds, and in many others, man seeks to benefit from the solar power and possesses the means to do so.[5]

The great sacrificial Dance of the North American nomadic Indians, which is consecrated to the solar Power, formerly included secondary rites that varied considerably depending on the tribes: all sorts of mythological elements entered into its composition to the point, in some cases, of nearly relegating the sun to a background role. But this complexity, normal in a fragmented and shifting world like that of the American Indians, is not of a kind to invalidate the fundamental content of the ritual cycle in question; this content has in fact survived all the tribulations that the Plains Indians have had to suffer since the beginning of the nineteenth century.

The Sun Dance has essentially two meanings, one outward and the other inward: the first is diverse, the second unchanging. The more or less outward intention of the Dance may be a personal vow, or the prosperity of the tribe, or, more profoundly—with the Cheyenne for example—the desire to regenerate the entire creation; the inward and unchanging intention is to be united with the solar Power, to establish a link between the Sun and the heart, in other words, to realize a ray that attaches earth to Heaven, or to reactualize this ray that is pre-existent but has been lost.[6] This strictly "pontifical" (*pontifex*) operation is based on the equation "heart-Sun": the Sun is the Heart of the

[4] The relationship between the sun and the tree—ritually actualized in the Sun Dance—occurs also in Shinto, according to which the primordial "pillar", joining Heaven and Earth and called "the ladder of Heaven", is the first of all created things; Amaterasu being, despite mythological fluctuations, the principal Divinity. This recalls the *Virgen del Pilar* at Saragossa: the Virgin—whose solarity is emphasized by a glowing halo—stands on a pillar of heavenly origin.

[5] For the Hindus, especially the *Sauras*, the sun is the "Eye of the world"; according to the *Rig Veda*, it is the soul "of things that move as well as of those that are still"; in other words, it manifests the universal Substance that is luminous and that penetrates everything. The rite of the *Sūryadarshana* consists in exposing newborn children for a moment to the rays of the sun, which is an indication of the solar orb's benefic power; it is a power that can be actualized thanks to a conceptual and ritual system enabling this attitude or cult. Likewise, in North America we have seen Indians extend their arms towards the rising sun and then rub their body to imbue themselves with the strength of its rays.

[6] This parallelism between a collective earthly intention and a personal heavenly intention manifests a particular aspect of the complementarity between exoterism and esoterism.

Macrocosm, whereas the human heart is the sun of the microcosm that we are. The visible sun is but the trace of the divine Sun, yet this trace, being real, is efficacious and enables the theurgical operation thanks to a play of analogies and complementarities.

The central element of the rite is the tree, image of the cosmic axis linking earth to Heaven; the tree is the presence—necessarily vertical—of the celestial Height on the terrestrial plane; it is what allows the contact, both sacrificial and contemplative, with the solar Power. It is to this tree, chosen, felled, and set up ritually,[7] that the dancers were formerly attached by thongs hooked into their chests; in our day the only element of the sacrifice that has been retained is the fast, uninterrupted for the entire duration—some three or four days—of the Dance, which symbolically and qualitatively is sufficient when one considers that the dancers must abstain from drinking in a blazing heat, while executing the prescribed movement for hours on end.[8]

This movement is a coming and going between the central tree—bare and shorn of its lower branches—and a circular shelter, covered with branches; the dance can thus be likened to the two phases of breathing or to the beating of the heart. The entire sacred lodge, with the tree in the middle, is like a great heart whose vital phases are represented by the ebb and flow of the dance—the dancers advancing from the periphery to the center and then backwards from the center to the periphery—and this symbolism is intensified by the violent beating of the drum and by the uninterrupted singing, which recalls through its monotonous alternations the waves of the ocean. It is from the center that the dancers draw their strength: their dance, when withdrawing with back steps from the central tree towards the circular enclosure, corresponds to the phase of assimilation of the spiritual influence present in the tree.

One could ask how such a desire for spiritual realization agrees with an adventurous and warrior way of life and with the ruggedness of lifestyle resulting from it—a question that indicates an optical illu-

---

[7] See *The Sacred Pipe*, recorded and edited by Joseph Epes Brown (Norman: University of Oklahoma Press, 1953), the chapter on "The Sun Dance". See also *The Arapaho Sun Dance* (Chicago: Field Columbian Museum, 1903) and *The Ponca Sun Dance* (Chicago: Field Columbian Museum, 1905) by George A. Dorsey, studies that give an idea, at least, of the complex possibilities of the Dance with the differences of mythology and ritual that vary with each tribal tradition.

[8] It still happens, however, that Indians secretly practice the rite in the ancient manner.

sion, for life is what it is owing to its natural conditions, which means that it is a texture of things and events, of forms and destinies, in which the outer man participates, performing and undergoing them according to the laws of Nature, but of which the inner man is in principle independent and which he transcends and dominates to the extent that he realizes heroism or holiness. There is in this a fruitful combination of the veneration for impersonal Nature and the affirmation of the sacerdotal and heroic personality, and herein lies the foundation of Indian stoicism, which is the moral expression of this apparent opposition.[9]

In approaching and withdrawing with short steps from the central tree without ever turning his back to it, the sacred dancer shakes an eagle plume in each hand while blowing, to the same rhythm, an eagle-bone whistle held in the mouth; the slightly strident and plaintive sound thus produced serves as a prayer or invocation; it reminds one of the cry of the eagle soaring in the immense solitude of space towards the sun. The entire dance is accompanied by the singing of a group of men seated around a huge drum, which they beat with vehemence in an accelerated rhythm, thus emphasizing the virile character of their chant—song of victory and at the same time of nostalgia, victory over our human limitations and nostalgia for the boundlessness of the heavens.[10] At sunrise a particular rite takes place: the dancers turn their gaze towards the rising sun and greet it, while singing with both arms extended towards it in order to become penetrated with the "solar Power".

---

[9] Shinto presents the same complementarity between Nature and the hero, each of the two poles recalling in its own way the mysteries of transcendence and immanence: Nature effaces itself before the celestial Spirit while embodying it in another respect; so too the hero: he effaces himself before this Spirit while identifying himself inwardly with it; and he bows before Nature, before its inflexible laws and its generosity, because he bows before the Spirit, before its Rigor and its Mercy.

[10] Or at least a victory that is symbolic, sacrificial, and thereby virtual; but it is nonetheless also a real victory from a certain human point of view. Effective victory is a gift from Heaven and not an exploit of man.

Throughout the Dance the central tree is filled with blessings; the Indians touch it and rub their faces, bodies, and limbs; or they pray to the Great Spirit while touching the tree; healings sometimes take place, prayers are answered, and protections granted. Phenomena of various kinds have been observed, sometimes visions, but above all a sensation of freshness in the proximity of the central tree, betokening the presence of benefic powers.

This idea of "power" is crucial for the Indian: the Universe is a texture of powers all emanating from one and the same underlying and omnipresent Power, at once impersonal and personal. For the Indians, the spiritual man is united to the Universe or the Great Spirit by the cosmic powers that penetrate him, the man, and purify, transform, and protect him; he is simultaneously pontiff, hero, and magician; these powers like to manifest themselves around him through spirits, animals, and the phenomena of Nature.

The Sun Dance is meant to become a permanent inner state: a decisive contact with the sacramental Luminary has taken place; an indelible trace remains in the heart; the profane partition between ordinary consciousness and the immanent Sun is open, and the person lives hereafter under another sign and in another dimension.

The Sun Dance takes place once a year, in the summer, but it has its reflection or prolongation in the rites of the sacred pipe, which are practiced in commemoration of the Dance at each full moon; these sessions comprise, along with the use of eagle-bone whistles, prayers addressed to the four Directions of space, then to the Great Spirit, who both contains and projects this quaternity. The symbol for this metaphysics, as we have been told, is the cross inscribed in the circle: the terrestrial cross—with its North-South and East-West axes—and the celestial circle. At its extremities the horizontal cross touches Heaven; its center also touches Heaven through the form of the axis Earth-Zenith, which is precisely what the Sun Dance tree represents.

This symbolism recalls another sacral image, that of the feathered Sun, which is found painted on buffalo hides used as cloaks and occasionally as a background for ceremonies. The sun is composed of concentric circles formed of stylized eagle feathers; the resulting impression is particularly evocative in that the symbol simultaneously suggests center, radiation, power, and majesty. This symbiosis between the sun and the eagle, which is to be found again in the famous headdress of feathers formerly worn by chiefs and great warriors, brings us back to the symbolism of the sacrificial Dance of the Indians: here man is spiritually transformed into an eagle soaring towards Heaven and identifying himself with the rays of the divine Luminary; he realizes thus the motion of return and reintegration that responds to the radiation of the Sun.

Part IV

Sufism

The Religion of the Heart

In the Introduction to his "Revivification of the Religious Sciences" (*Ihyā 'ulūm ad-dīn*), Ghazali takes the theologians of his time to task, and in so doing he notes a process of exteriorization, of degradation, and even of inversion that is natural to human societies, not by right of course, but as a fact of life. On the one hand, says Ghazali, there is a growing tendency to declare lawful what is condemnable in order to justify worldly inclinations; on the other hand, and quite logically, there is an attempt to discredit any values that are contrary to this decadence, as a way to calm one's bad conscience and also to neutralize anything that might disturb the reign of lukewarmness and hypocrisy. And since it is necessarily the spiritual life with its fervor and profundity that is the principal victim of worldly defamation, Ghazali seeks to validate the fundamentally Islamic, Koranic, and Muhammadan nature of Sufism which, precisely, sums up Muslim spirituality, and which is none other than the "perfect practice" (*ihsān*) of the *Sunnah*; a "revivification of the religious sciences" thus includes above all the defense and the rehabilitation of the spiritual tradition, which represents *a priori* the profound life and the very substance of Islam. It has been said that Sufism is "sincerity" (*sidq*) of faith: indeed, if one is to be perfectly consistent this entails the transferring of religion into one's heart—seat of the divine Presence and hence of metaphysical certainty—and thereby infusing into outward religion a supernatural and deifying life.

"The spiritual essence of man", says Ghazali, "is similar to the essence of God, for God created man in His image"; and "it is because of this relationship between man and God that all men—and not only Prophets—may attain, with divine help,[1] the realization of the knowledge of God and the world", in other words, the knowledge of the Principle and its Manifestation, or of the Necessary and the Possible, or yet again of the Absolute and the Contingent; of *Ātmā* and of *Māyā*.

This means that in Islam, two "religions" meet, combine, and sometimes confront one another: the outward religion—that of Revelation and the Law—and the religion of the Heart, of Intellection, of immanent Liberty; they combine inasmuch as the outward religion proceeds from the inward religion, but oppose each other inasmuch

---

[1] *Tawfīq*; a reservation meaning: "in principle".

as the inward and essential religion is independent of the outward and formal religion. On the one hand, there is homogeneity and continuity, and on the other hand there is incommensurability and discontinuity; form proceeds from essence, yet the latter remains eminently free in regard to form. Red or green light is unquestionably light, since it illuminates, but light in itself is neither red nor green; now, the formalistic or exoteric point of view consists in affirming that such and such a color is light, and correlatively, that light is such and such a color, as if substance were accident just because the latter manifests the former.

This does not mean that Ghazali explains directly what this irreversibility of relationships consists of; nevertheless, he demonstrates in his own way that legal Islam is a projection towards the outward from the "religion of the Heart": to practice Islam with "sincerity"—hence by following the example of the Prophet—is to remove the "rust" from the heart in its state of disgrace; it is to free the immanent religion and thereby to verify the truth of Islam in the light of a certitude that is already divine because it emanates from the transpersonal Intellect. Just as beautiful actions (*husnā*)—those, precisely, that are prefigured and recommended by the *Sunnah*—purify the heart and contribute to actualizing its immanent and already celestial beauty, so, conversely, this beauty of heart will manifest itself in beautiful actions; Ghazali insists on this reciprocity, which for him is the very quintessence of Islam.[2]

Instead of "Heart", we could also say "Love"; it is not without reason that Ibn Arabi claims for himself the "religion of Love", and that Dante declares that "Love and the noble heart are one and the same thing" (*Amore e 'l cor gentil sono una cosa*). The "gentle" or "noble" heart is none other than the heart that is purified both inwardly by Intellection and contemplation, and outwardly by acts and virtues that are in conformity with Revelation; this "Love" is likewise the "Wine" of the *Khamrīyah* of Umar ibn al-Farid and of many other esoteric poems of Islam.[3] And it is moreover in this Love

---

[2] As it is of every spirituality, notwithstanding other equally possible aspects of this quintessence. "By this power of comprehension, this penetration of our being (by the Universal), our hearts will be transferred into—and united with —the Original Heart (*Amida*), which penetrates everything and which is the Heart of our hearts" (Kenryo Kanamatsu, *Naturalness* [Kyoto, 1956]).

[3] Likewise in Buddhism: Amitabha is both infinite "Light" and—as Amitayus—infinite "Life"; the divine Heart is Wisdom and Love, Clarity and Warmth.

that the spirituality of Islam and that of Christianity meet: for as soon as the emanations of the Essence enter the heart, then this heart will be situated beyond the formal order and will have become capable of detecting the divine intentions within all forms, and consequently of perceiving Unity within diversity.[4]

— ·|· —

The salvific power of Islam stems from the principle that the unicity of the truth demands the totality of faith; now, this totality involves all that we are, and thus the Heart, which sums up what we are. The one truth is that "there is no god other than the sole God"; no absolute alongside the sole Absolute.

For Christians, the only truth is that Christ alone is savior; and it is this objective unicity that requires subjective totality. Metaphysically speaking, the uniqueness of Christ means that only the *Logos* can save us, the *Logos* who created us and who is the doorway between the world and God; and basically this is a more relative way of saying that "there is no god other than the sole God", that is to say, "no good other than the sole Good". Be that as it may, man responds to the divine Unicity by his own totality, which is nothing other than the Heart or Love.

For Christianity, Love comes from Christ and it would be inaccessible and unrealizable without the Redemption, the heart of man being totally fallen; for Islam, Love is immanent in the heart, of which only the surface has been rendered blind and impotent by sin; were his downfall to be total, man would cease to be man. But once Love has been reached, the way of access through a religious denomination no longer plays any role; Love, like the "Wisdom" spoken of in the Bible, was before the world and was before man. This means that the "religion of the Heart" is independent of the religion of the Law, in principle if not in fact.

---

[4] For obvious historical and geographical reasons, this does not mean that the accomplished sage must concretely know and understand all religions besides his own. When Ibn Arabi declares that his "heart has opened to every form", it is of his own transcendent state rather than of foreign religions that he is speaking; we say "rather", for one must exaggerate neither in one direction nor the other.

This last reservation means that, if the Sufis almost always observe the concepts and practices of the revealed Religion—the exceptions being extremely rare—there are two serious reasons for this, one intrinsic and one extrinsic. The extrinsic reason is obvious: it is a question, not only of setting a good example to all the faithful, but also of not straying from the Law, which cannot take account of the Spirit outside of forms; as for the intrinsic reason, it results on the one hand from certain characteristics of human nature and on the other from spiritual opportuneness, or perhaps even from necessity. On the one hand, whatever be a man's spiritual degree, the human individual as such always remains "servant" (*'abd*); Christ was "true man and true God", and as "true man", he prayed like everyone else, notwithstanding his inward Divinity;[5] on the other hand, it is important for the "one who is delivered in this life"—the Hindu *jīvan-mukta*—to maintain, in parallel with his inward state of union with *Ātmā*, a cult of *bhakti* dedicated to a given *ishta-devatā*. Man would not be man if there were not within him two incommensurable dimensions, one for devotion and the other for union.

Nevertheless, the religious practice of one who is truly integrated into the "religion of the Heart" necessarily differs from the practice of the average man totally enclosed within the formalism of the common Law; whereas the point of view of this Law inevitably entails an individualistic and sentimental voluntarism, without forgetting a sense-bound epistemology that cuts short all "rivalry" coming from intellection,[6] the perspective of the religion of the Heart or of Love is above all intellective and thereby universal; its musical dimension pertains, not to an ideological and moral sentimentalism, but to Beauty and Love, which on the one hand remain in God and on the other hand radiate throughout both cosmic and human Manifestation.

[5] In Muslim parlance one would say: notwithstanding the penetration of his soul, inwardly, by the divine Presence.

[6] From the point of view of total truth, the sense-bound perspective is an oddly down to earth heresy, but from the point of view of religious fideism, it is morally a matter of indifference while being theologically opportune. Confessional *bhakti* is opposed to *jnāna*; Christian theologians reject Plato just as Ramanuja and other Vishnuites reject Shankara.

If, for the follower of the Heart or of Love, there is no question of abandoning religious practices, the principle of esoteric transcendence can nevertheless be manifested by a certain freedom with regard to these practices, not least by a tendency towards simplification, the whole emphasis being placed on contemplation and its direct supports; but this freedom or this objectivity will never be manifested by a dehumanization of the human, using metaphysical sublimity as a pretext, because transcendent Truth puts each thing in its place and does not mix levels. Supreme wisdom goes together with holy childlikeness.

This does not mean that the general religion, in order to have the power to save, need require the pinnacles that the religion of the Heart presents or offers—as Ghazali would no doubt have it; but it requires a sort of tendency or movement towards them, for there is not a clear demarcation line in every respect between the exoteric and the esoteric, or between the voluntaristic and the intellective domains. On the one hand, esoterism prolongs and deepens religion, or, put differently, religion adapts esoterism to a certain level of consciousness and activity; on the other hand, the two domains diverge, exoterism being form, which of necessity is particular and particularist, and esoterism on the contrary being the essence, by definition universal and universalistic, of the formal element. And this explains why Sufism on the one hand shares a common goal with religious formalism, while on the other hand transcends it, at least in principle and independently of the attitudes it adopts in fact. The form that one mistakes for the essence is one thing, and the form that expresses or serves as a vehicle for the essence, without being confused with it, is another.

In this context, we could refer to the distinction between absolute and therefore necessary Being, and contingent or merely possible being; now, the theophanic mystery of the Heart is precisely that necessary Being dwells in the center of the human microcosm, so that the metaphysical and mystical certitude proper to the religion of the Heart is the certitude that God has of Himself and which He introduces into the consciousness of man. Platonic recollection is none other than the participation of the human Intellect in the ontological certainties of the divine Intellect; this is why the Sufi is said to be *'ārif bi'Llāh*, "knower by *Allāh*", in keeping with the teaching of a famous *hadīth* according to which God is the "Eye wherewith he (the Sufi) seeth"; and this explains the nature of the "Eye of Knowledge", or of the "Eye of the Heart".

If, on the one hand, this perspective requires an equilibrium between contemplative inwardness—which is outwardly reductive and simplifying—and the necessary or opportune outward attitudes, on the other hand, it also favors trust and peace of mind, for wherever there is depth and essentiality, there is Mercy; and this indicates the natural connection between wisdom and holy childlikeness.[7]

—— ·:· ——

The religion of the Heart or of Love, from the operative point of view, is the power of interiorization. Now, Truth possesses an interiorizing quality to the extent of its loftiness; absolute Truth is absolutely interiorizing for whomsoever "hath ears to hear".

The virtues, which by their very nature bear witness to the Truth, also possess an interiorizing quality to the extent that they are fundamental; the same is true of beings and things that transmit the messages of eternal Beauty; whence the power of interiorization proper to virgin nature, to the harmony of creatures, to sacred art, to music. The aesthetic sensation—as we have often remarked—possesses in itself an ascending quality: it elicits in the contemplative soul, directly or indirectly, a recollection of the divine essences. For the "pneumatic", outward beauty, as well as moral beauty, possesses a virtue that interiorizes; it ennobles the world while separating us from the world.

If we wish to withdraw into the Heart in order to find there the total Truth and the underlying and pre-personal Holiness, we must manifest the Heart not only in our intelligence but also in our soul in general, by means of spiritual attitudes and moral qualities; for every beauty of soul is a ray coming from the Heart and leading back to it. Since ontologically the Heart comes before outward activity, its domain is nearer to Mercy than is the domain of the Law, of merits and demerits; for, in the words of the celebrated formula: "My Mercy taketh precedence over My Wrath." The religion of the Heart is the primordial Religion in time, and the quintessential Religion in the soul.

---

[7] This is the basis of quietism, whose accidental abuses could never invalidate its substantial legitimacy. Every esoterism is dangerous outside of the intellectual and moral qualifications its nature requires.

The Way of Unity

The unicity of the object demands the totality of the subject; the unique and incomparable nature of God demands totality of faith. This necessary and binding relationship proves that the Islamic thesis of salvation through sincere faith in God results from the nature of things; in other words, the acceptance of the one Truth is not an easy attitude committing us to nothing; on the contrary, it entails ultimately all that we are.

The totality of the human subject comprises two dimensions, one horizontal and the other vertical. To believe totally in God, is first of all to seek to resemble Him on the human plane; the specific deiformity of the human species obliges us to a deiformity that is freely accepted and realized; it is this vocation of horizontal perfection that is referred to by the injunction of Christ to be "perfect even as your Father in Heaven is perfect". Following this, or alongside it, comes the vocation of vertical perfection, which consists in uniting oneself in one's heart with the immanent Presence of God; a perfection that in a sense is superhuman because transpersonal. Horizontal "resemblance" or "analogy" in the first place, and this is virtue, which is manifested in attitudes and actions; then vertical "identity", and this is union which, though humanly the result of our knowledge and our effort, is fundamentally a mystery of Grace.

The unicity of the object requires the totality of the subject: this perspective, which is specifically Islamic while summarizing in its manner all integral spirituality, that is to say all spirituality that is transforming and unitive—this perspective presupposes that man be defined, not as being incapable of salvation because fundamentally corrupted by the fall, but as being capable of salvation because he is still endowed with an objective intelligence, a free will, and a perfectible soul, these properties constituting the very definition of man.[1] Now, the capacity for salvation, owing to the indestructible

---

[1] This is what explains the apparent negation, in the Koran, of the crucifixion of Christ; apparent, because the Koran affirms that "they did not kill him really (yaqīnan)". If Christ is the Intellect, it can be seen that the Fall, according to the Christian perspective, "crucified" and "killed" him by passions and sins, but at the same time—and this is the Islamic perspective—the Intellect was "raised up to God"; in other words, it remained intact in itself and God enlightened it with eternal Truth, that of saving Unity.

deiformity of man—and this is the great message of monotheism—is actualized essentially by faith in God, who is the One; the unicity of the divine object demands—and logically entails—the totality of the human subject; and it demands it in the twofold respect of individual, and therefore horizontal, perfection, and universal, and therefore vertical, perfection. This second perfection closes the circle since it opens onto the divine Subject, which is immanent, while at the same time remaining transcendent in relation to the human subject.

In other words: the discernment that allows the intelligence to distinguish between the Absolute and the relative has, as a corollary, both moral virtue and spiritual union. Virtue is the conformity of the soul to the divine Nature; and union is extinctive concentration on the immanent Self.

— ∴ —

When speaking of transcendence, what we mean generally is objective transcendence, that of the Principle, which is above us just as it is above the world; and when speaking of immanence, what we mean generally is subjective immanence, that of the Self, which is within us. Now, it is important to mention that there is also a subjective transcendence, that of the Self within us inasmuch as it transcends the ego; and likewise, there is also an objective immanence, that of the Principle inasmuch as it is immanent in the world, and not inasmuch as it excludes it and annihilates it by its transcendence.

One finds here an application of the Taoist *Yin-Yang*: transcendence necessarily comprises immanence, and immanence just as necessarily comprises transcendence. For the Transcendent, by virtue of its infinity, projects existence and thereby requires immanence; and the Immanent, by virtue of its absoluteness, necessarily remains transcendent in relation to existence.

— ∴ —

To believe in the One; this is what saves. To believe in the One, but wholly and sincerely.

Wholly: it is necessary to believe, not only that God is one, but also that this Unity carries implications for the world, since the world exists; and it exists because of the radiation that flows from Unity itself. Consequently, it is necessary to believe all that divine Reality entails, namely: the causation of the world by God; hence the connectedness of the world to God; hence the nature and vocation of man; hence Revelation and therefore the Way. To believe in the One is to believe in the implications of Unity; as is enunciated in a famous *hadīth*: "I was a hidden treasure and I wished to be known, so I created the world."

Sincerely: it is necessary to believe with our heart, and not only with our mind; it is necessary that the attestation of Unity, conceptual in the first instance, should reach and engage the will and the soul, failing which there is no "believing", no faith. There are, finally, four ways of accepting Unity: firstly, to accept its truth; then, on the cosmic and eschatological plane, to accept the truths that derive from Unity and which are necessary for salvation; then, on the affective and moral plane, to participate in the truth by means of the virtues, for if God is absolute and infinite, He is likewise perfect, which means that there is no conceivable quality of which He is not the Essence and the Source; finally, to believe in God, to believe that He is one, is to discern in Unity the mystery of Union: it is to pass from transcendence to immanence, from objective discontinuity to subjective continuity; it is to transcend the separativity subject-object in the immanent divine Selfhood, in the transpersonal depth of the Heart.

— ·:· —

It is readily affirmed that God, or the divine Essence, is absolutely indefinable or ineffable; if nevertheless we were asked which Name does justice to the divine Essence, we would say that it is "the Holy", for Holiness in no wise limits, and it includes everything that is divine; moreover, this notion of holiness transmits the perfume of the Divine in itself, and thus that of the Inexpressible.

God, being pure Holiness, is Power, Consciousness, Bliss; one could also say that He is pure Being, pure Spirit, pure Possibility. This is the meaning of the Sanskrit terms *Sat, Chit, Ānanda*, and the Arabic terms *Wujūd, Shuhūd*, and *Hayāt*, or *Qudrah, Hikmah*, and *Rahmah*. This is the supreme degree, that of the Essence, *Dhāt*, or of Unity, *Ahadīyah*; the non-supreme degree being that of the Qualities, *Sifāt*, or of Unicity, *Wāhidīyah*.

When we say that God is pure Being, pure Spirit, and pure Possibility, what is the meaning of the word "pure"? It means "absolute", or "infinite", or "perfect"; God is absolutely, infinitely, perfectly Power, Consciousness, and Bliss. The absoluteness means that nothing can equal God; the infiniteness means that nothing can limit Him; the perfection means that He lacks nothing and that every created perfection derives from the divine Nature, because God is not only the Absolute and the Infinite, but also the Good. Being absolute, God excludes everything that is not He; being infinite, He includes everything that is possible; being perfect, He projects His Goodness into existence. And He is, in each of these functions or aspects, Power, Consciousness, and Bliss; or Being, Spirit, and Possibility; this last aspect, which coincides with Radiation, being both Goodness and Beauty: expansion of Love and of Peace.

Faith is a profound and total "yes" to the One, which is both absolute and infinite, transcendent and immanent. Faith as such does not result from our mind, it is prior to it; it is even prior to ourselves. In faith, vehicled by the spiritual act, we are outside time; we are outside the ego, which is subject to time. The divine archetype of faith is the "yes" that God says to Himself; it is the *Logos* that both reflects the divine Infinity and refracts it; for this "yes" is both synthesis and refraction, receptive concentration and creative dispersal. Thus, in man faith is at once blessed unicity and blessed unlimitedness; or inwardness and radiation.

In the elementary sense of the word, faith is our assent to a truth that transcends us; but spiritually speaking, it is our assent, not to transcendent concepts, but to immanent realities, or to Reality as such; now this Reality is our very substance.

Faith may be an assent to truths that are subjectively unverifiable but objectively irrefutable, just as, on the contrary, it may be intellectual certitude regarding these same truths; it may be joined to this certitude by deepening it, just as it may be independent of intellectual constructs and surge from the heart on the basis of a symbolic and sacramental support. One could also say that faith is, not intellectual certitude in its doctrinal form, but that missing ingredient that causes intellectual certitude to become holiness; or that it is the realizational power of certitude, its *shakti*, so to speak, or again, that it is the energy that enhances certitude and becomes liberating holiness.

When faith is considered in its elementary sense, then one can say that the elect in Paradise no longer have need of it since they see God; but when the term "faith" is understood in its higher sense, then the elect necessarily have faith, since every human quality proceeds from a heavenly prototype; in this respect, faith is the "yes" of the soul to the divine Presence, this "yes" that the soul has already been able to realize on earth to the extent that it was conscious of the divine Presence. This is why the blessed, each time they taste a fruit of Paradise, remember having tasted it previously, according to the Koran. This consciousness of the Presence of God is essentially linked with the sense of the sacred, which is a contemplative and moral qualification *sine qua non*.

In other words: when one speaks of the "obscure merit of faith", the meaning is that of an effort that makes up for the absence of objective certitude: faith is a merit because we do not see God and because it is difficult for the exteriorized and passional man, who consequently is worldly in his nature, to believe in what he does not see. But when the Koran speaks of those who in Paradise are close to God and "believe in Him", it is referring to the element of approbation or fervor, or adoration, which is the very substance of the attitude of faith, and which is independent of the earthly accident that a relative ignorance represents.

What intrinsically is Being, is extrinsically Omnipotence; what intrinsically is Spirit, is extrinsically Omniscience; and what intrinsically is Bliss—the Totality of all possibilities, hence Radiation—is extrinsically Mercy. For Mercy or Generosity, or Goodness or yet Beauty, proceeds from the internal overflowing of the Divinity; "God is Love". To love God, or to be sensitive to the perfume of Holiness or to have the sense of the Sacred, is to be loved by God; he truly loves who perceives Beauty, and Beauty reveals Herself to him whom She loves. Beauty, *Jamāl*, is appeasing; it is thus close to Peace, *Salām*.

Perfect faith derives from the metaphysical evidentness of the One, and from the innate love of the Sacred or of Holiness. The sense of the Sacred, which is nothing other than a quasi-natural predisposition towards the love of God and a sensitivity towards theophanic manifestations or heavenly perfumes, essentially entails both a sense of beauty and a tendency towards virtue— beauty being so to speak outward virtue, and virtue inward beauty. The sense of the Sacred likewise entails a sense of the metaphysical transparency of things, the capacity to grasp the uncreated in the created; or to perceive the vertical ray—a messenger from the Archetype—independently from the horizontal plane of refraction, which determines the existential degree but not the divine content.

— ⋰ —

Love of God is the necessary complement of certitude, just as the Infinite is the complement of the Absolute; this is the profound meaning of faith, which combines a kernel of absoluteness with an aura of infiniteness.

The very act of faith is the remembrance of God; now "to remember", in Latin, is *recordare*, that is *re-cordare*, which indicates a return to the heart, *cor*. The act of orison, inasmuch as it is an act of faith, actualizes in fact immanent and quasi-paracletic certitude; the heart is immanent and "uncreated" faith; it coincides with this "naturally supernatural" grace that is Intellection. The mystery of certitude is our consubstantiality with all that can be known, and hence with all that is.

APPENDIX

Selections from Letters and
Other Previously Unpublished Writings

1

The human state is a central state, and consequently man's intelligence, his will, and his soul have a central character, in other words a character of totality, hence also of objectivity.

Human intelligence is total, for it can conceive of the Transcendent, the Absolute, or the Substance; and it is objective, for it can conceive the relativity, or accidentality, of the subject, hence that of its own empirical envelope. The intelligence is made for total Truth: both absolute Truth and relative truth; metaphysics and cosmology, objective as well as subjective; including degrees of absoluteness—or of relativity—in the one and in the other.

The human will is total, for it can choose the Absolute; it is objective—and thus free—for it can conquer the tendencies of the subject it belongs to; it can surmount the passional element, either in curbing it or in channeling it. The will is made for the total Good: both absolute Good and relative good; ascent and equilibrium.

The human soul is total, for it can love the Absolute, or the Infinite; and it is objective, for it can hate its own passional deviation, its own hardness. The soul is made for total Happiness: absolute, infinite Happiness and relative, limited happiness; heavenly Beatitude and earthly harmony; intrinsic Virtue and extrinsic virtue, active or passive. Happiness is synonymous with Virtue.

But there are other features—which are immediately visible—that distinguish man from the animal: first of all, his vertical posture; secondly, the gift of speech; thirdly, the creative, productive, and constructive faculty, which means art in all its degrees and in all its forms.

The distinctive features of man contain the proof of God, who is Sovereign, who speaks, and who brings forth; the proof, be it said, not because this proof is necessary, but because these features manifest the divine Nature.

The vertical posture of man proves that man is pontiff by very definition, that dignity is inherent to the human state and therefore

incumbent upon every man. Nobility of bearing is a spiritual obligation; it is not a question here of an affectation of nobility, but of a
fully conscious absence of vulgarity. Sense of aristocracy. Domination
of self. Discipline of gesture. Self-effacement and precision.

2

I. writes that there are many Christian sanctuaries in India that are
visited by Hindus. This is not surprising; it is an aspect of the Hindu
spirit, based on the *Bhagavad Gītā*: "Under whatsoever form you
worship Me", says Krishna, "it is always Me that you are worshipping." If Hindus obtain graces in such places, these are Hindu graces;
it is the Hindu Heaven that grants the prayers through one Christian
form or another.

Saint Thomas the apostle visited India, but is not buried there;
Saint Francis Xavier is buried there, but hated Hinduism and I doubt
that it is he himself who answers Hindu prayers. Christ is the founder
of a religion, therefore one cannot address him when one is not a
Christian, except if doing so on the mystical plane as Sufis do; but we
must not forget in this case that Christ is mentioned in the Koran, as
is the Virgin, and that Muslims therefore have a certain claim to him,
at least in esoterism. The Holy Virgin is not the founder of a religion,
thus her case is different from that of Christ; and since she is—in
Hindu terms—a *plenary and direct* incarnation of Sri Lakshmi, or of
the *Shakti* as such, therefore also of Saraswati and of Parvati, she can
radiate beyond forms; it is thus conceivable that she grants the prayers
of Hindus directly, given the typical attitude of Hindus, which is
based on the *Bhagavad Gītā* and other sacred Texts.

However, if, in Europe, a Hindu went to pray on the tomb of a
Christian saint, it is plausible that the saint either would not respond,
or would respond by operating a conversion to Christianity, although
it cannot be excluded that, in this case too, it would be a specific
Hindu Divinity that would be answering, precisely because of the
particular attitude of Hinduism and of the Hindus.

Islam took root in India and is very widespread; its situation is
therefore altogether particular with respect to the inter-traditional
relationships. Likewise, the case of the Sufis is a particular one: if it can
be admitted that they themselves grant Hindu prayers, this is because
of the esoteric nature of Sufism.

3

Within Western Christendom, the distinction between the "Greater" and "Lesser Mysteries" is to be found in the respective functions of Pope and Emperor: if Dante upheld the position of the latter, it was not to defend temporal power against spiritual authority, but to prevent the encroachments of one clearly defined spiritual authority on the domain of another clearly defined spiritual authority, the papacy corresponding to the "Greater Mysteries", and the empire—as heir to the priesthood of ancient Rome—to the "Lesser Mysteries"; the whole problem lies in the fact that Dante considered the Emperor, not in his political role, but in his spiritual function, which was inherited from the Roman tradition, and sanctioned by the words of Christ: "Render unto Caesar the things that are Caesar's." In a certain sense the natural exoteric complement of Christianity would be, for Dante, not the Mosaic Law, but the Roman Empire and Roman Law. The Pope, since he is unquestionably the successor of the *Pontifex Maximus* of Rome, considered himself justified in claiming the function of Emperor, either by attributing to himself an over-extended power, or by looking on the "consecration" of the Emperor as an "institution" [by the Pope]; now it was obviously not from Saint Peter that Caesar derived his authority, and this is precisely what Dante makes clear. The Emperor, since he is unquestionably the successor of Caesar and of Augustus, is thereby also the *Pontifex Maximus*, and therefore the trustee of the "Lesser Mysteries"; the situation was insoluble by reason of this confusion of powers.

4

It is clear that Catholicism, like Orthodoxy, offers the means for the highest spiritual realization; the absolute conditions for this are baptism, confirmation, first communion, and perpetual orison, that is to say, precisely, the daily invocation of the Prayer of Jesus, or of the Name of Jesus, or of the Names of Jesus and Mary.

In the spiritual life, one must know how to simplify things, which presupposes that one be acutely conscious of the essential elements of the Way. For the Christians who come to me for advice—Catholics and Orthodox—I like to repeat that one must avoid complications, and that the essential, which one must never lose sight of, is this: the discernment between the Real and the illusory, between God and the world, *Ātmā* and *Māyā*; then permanent concentration on the Real, or on the Manifestation of the Real, Jesus and Mary; and this presupposes the practice of the virtues, that is to say of the modes of conformity to the Real, for: "Be ye perfect even as your Father in Heaven is perfect." Humility is not the fixed and sentimental idea that we are worse than others—such evaluations are often conjectural—but the consciousness of our nothingness before God and then of our limitation on the human plane and with respect to other men; likewise, charity is above all the awareness that the ego of others is not less truly "myself" than our own ego. Humility and charity are above all the virtues of self-effacement and of generosity. Apart from the metaphysical significance of the virtues, there is their quasi-musical aspect: virtue is not only a question of truth, it is also a question of beauty.

In the spiritual life, outward things sometimes amount to a lot; the ambience in which we live must, as far as possible, be in conformity with the Spirit; one must live in a fragrance of *sattva*.

The Holy Virgin personifies the beauty of Heaven, she is something of the Beauty of God.

5

To be affected only by the injustices aimed at truth, not those aimed at us: this is perfect, but the truth authorizes us, and even obliges us, to draw the conclusions that we have to, all the more as our rights and those of the truth can coincide, to the very extent that we situate ourselves outside of the profane order. It would be different were the injustice no more than an impersonal and blind force, and were we but individuals subject to passions. Conversely, it goes without saying that we must accept an injustice inasmuch as it is destiny, for in that case it comes from God and cannot be unjust, but this is a new dimension that exists independently from the plane where the injustice is what it is. I would even say that we are entitled to self-defense to the very extent that we accept everything from God. Finally, to claim our legitimate right can be not only a matter of truth, but even of charity; I have always been astonished at these *malāmatiyah* who set a bad example so as to be purer before *Allāh*, as if they provided thereby some kind of service to other men.

6

First of all, sexual union is in itself a positive reality, I shall even say a divine one; Genesis says nothing to suggest the contrary, and Hinduism attributes this union to the Divinities themselves. Secondly, the cause of the Fall is not in a given aspect of nature, it is uniquely in the fact of separating all the natural aspects from their divine Source, in experiencing them outside of God, and attributing their glory and enjoyment to ourselves.

The disturbing aspects that *de facto* sexuality may contain do not come from the thing in itself, they derive from the degeneration of matter or of the flesh, and also from that of man in general; for one degeneracy leads to another. One will note also that most Westerners—unlike Hindus—do not have the innate sense of what I term "the metaphysical transparency of phenomena".

7

You ask me if this event requires a particular attitude on your part. Yes and no. When a spiritual experience is authentic and profound, it leaves a trace in us; now one must be faithful to this trace. He who has benefited from such a grace knows exactly what he must and must not do; he can no longer be exactly the same man as heretofore. He must not seek to do extraordinary things; from the point of view of the spiritual method and social comportment, nothing changes, unless there was in this comportment something abusive. What Heaven wants of us is our soul; it invites us therefore to inwardness. "The kingdom of God is within you," Christ said. "I am black, but beautiful," says the Song of Songs, and this saying is attributed to the Blessed Virgin; once again, this is about contemplative inwardness. A major spiritual event, comprising a kind of vision, cuts us off in a certain way from the world; it is as if we were living henceforth in a kind of invisible sanctuary belonging already to the hereafter; or as if we were in a small garden that is already celestial, and the happiness of which is no longer terrestrial. If we have the impression that we are unfaithful to the vision, we must make a prayer to the celestial Being come to meet us.

8

The dark color (through which the black Virgin is related, as also by her maternity, to the symbolism of Kali, "the Mother"), refers to divine Non-manifestation, of which the Virgin is the support in her capacity as Mother of the Word; the Word is the "descent", or incarnation, or manifestation of this Non-manifested.

The Virgin-Mother represents the substantial condition of the hypostatic manifestation, that is to say, she is its base which, having to support the "unique", must not be tainted by the "multiple", symbolically identified with the "flesh" which, indeed, is the domain of quantity, differentiation, and brute fact.

The soul of the contemplative who, by his spiritual act and by the ritual support of this, realizes the universal birth of the Word in his heart, must be "virgin" and "pure", or, in other words, "poor" and "empty", so as to be able to act as support for the spiritual birth of the "real Presence"; the soul must therefore carry, like the sacred image of the Virgin, the imprint of divine Non-manifestation, that is to say, darkness. On the one hand, this imprint is, in a transitory and secondary manner, the *nox profunda* and the "descent into hell", in a word, the spiritual death in which the *fiat lux* occurs; on the other hand, this imprint is, in a permanent manner, indifference or "extinction" with regard to the world, and with regard to "illusion" or the "current of forms"; this state of death is identical with "poverty of spirit" and "humility". The dark color of the black Virgin (like that of certain Hindu *pratīkas*, especially Kali, and also like the blackness of the stone set in the Kaaba) thus signifies "silence" or the absence of manifestations in the soul of the contemplative, whereas the dark color of the Child Jesus in the same image signifies divine Non-determination.

9

In authentic esoterism, it is essential to distinguish between a function that prolongs exoterism to the extent that this is possible, and another that breaks it to the extent that this is necessary; "if you want the kernel," said Eckhart, "you must break the shell." To deny this second function is to deny esoterism as such; it is also to deny that exoterism represents a limited perspective, something which it represents of necessity, since it is addressed to all men indistinctly, and not to an elite as is *Advaita Vedānta*. The "breaking" function is found fairly and squarely in Eckhart and other mystics, including a few "heretics" who basically were right.

According to Guénon, the Semitic religions are characterized by a sentimental attachment to an idea; it is obvious that esoterism, if it has any meaning, must transcend this attachment, and that it cannot be tainted by "religious nationalism", if one may so express it. It is not a question here of criticizing love for a symbol insofar as the symbol is true and lovable, it is simply a question of not falling into an idolatry of forms insofar as they are limited and exclusive; in other words, it is a question of avoiding the prejudices of denominational narcissism and of not forgetting that "there is no right superior to that of truth", according to the Hindu maxim.

Guénon was right when he wrote that "true esoterism is something completely different from outward religion, and, if there are some relationships with the latter, this can only be so insofar as esoterism finds in the religious forms a means of symbolic expression; it matters little, moreover, whether these forms be of this or that religion". And likewise: "Esoterism is essentially something different from religion, and not the 'inward' part of a religion as such, even when esoterism finds its base and its support in it."

From all of this it results that there is an esoterism *de jure* and another *de facto*: the second is all too often a metaphysico-theological amalgam in which intellectual science is combined with denominational sentimentalism, and this, let it be said in passing, is a very frequent phenomenon in Sufism; but this phenomenon—inevitable in itself—cannot prevent that *de jure* esoterism exists—be it sporadically, or in a coherent form—and this in a Christian climate as well as elsewhere; obviously it exists in India, where the contemplative mentality and the caste system permit the establishment of a rigorous sapience free from all compromise.

10

When one awakens in the morning, it often happens that one is in a dissatisfied or even in a gloomy state of mind without knowing why, and that one is then tempted to think about this or that; however, it is of essential importance for the soul first of all to resign itself to the will of God and therein to find its peace. For it is the will of God that I am there where I am; that I am now, and not yesterday or tomorrow; that I am in the situation I actually am in; and there should be no secret revolt in the soul. And there is still another part to this, namely remembering my human duty: for there is not only the will of God, which I must yield to, there is also a divine will that I must carry out, and this is the pronunciation of the supreme Name, the remembrance of God. This is what we must begin the day with, before we slip into the self-willed and restless play of the soul; and this resignation to God's will, this performing of the duty willed by God, is the fundamental condition for happiness in general.

11

"Unless ye be as children", Christ said. What is good about the state of childhood is precisely that the soul is still fresh and unspent: there is gratitude for the humblest gift of the world and of life; what is more, there is an unconscious and yet wholly real trust in God. The aging man tends to see everything in connection with a whole universe; the child, on the other hand, when he finds joy in a flower, the flower is the only thing there. Both kinds of experiences—for each has its justification—are united in the spiritual man's sense of the sacred, of his sense for celestially divine archetypes.

12

If I am told: here is *Ātmā*, there is *Māyā*; here is the Absolute, there is All-Possibility radiating out from the infinity of the Absolute; here is the Supreme Principle, God, there is Manifestation, the world; here is the archetype of Manifestation in the Divine Principle, there is the reflection of the Principle in Manifestation; here is the radiating creative *Māyā*, there is the attracting, liberating *Māyā*; and *Māyā* is nothing other than the radiation of *Ātmā*, caused by the nature of *Ātmā* to be the purest and highest Good (τò ἀγαθόν), for it is in the nature of the Good to impart itself; if one says all of this to me, then I pay attention, I understand something, I feel happy, I feel attracted to God, I attach myself to the Divine. When on the contrary I am told: a God, who owes me nothing because He is Almighty, gives me this or that command, and that my intelligence is only there to carry out this command as well as possible, and other things of this kind—when I am told this, then I do not understand anything, I feel unhappy, I do not feel attracted to religion, I no longer know what I am, nor why I am a human being. But this is what theologians all too often reduce religion to, as if they could please God thereby! They underestimate God just as they underestimate men.

However, this kind of coarsening deriving from exoterism's simplifications is more disparaging of God than of men, which does not at all mean that exoterism could not express itself differently. At all events, the difficulty lies in this: exoterism's compelling need to over-simplify things—the dogma of "one God" comes to mind—cannot do justice to the hypostatic gradations in the Divine; exoterism cannot make a distinction between Being and Beyond-Being given that it has neither the notion of the divine immanence in *Māyā* nor that of *Ātmā* transcending all of *Māyā*—even *in divinis*. If one can give the words "to create", *creare*, a totally new meaning, then one can say that Beyond-Being "creates" Being in the divine domain and endows it with: Perfection or Goodness; creative Power; All-Possibility. Being, the divine Person, receives these three hypostatic attributes from Beyond-Being, the Eckhartian "Godhead"; it receives them and has no power over them; this means that Being is the Sovereign Good and cannot be anything but the Sovereign Good; it is Creator and consequently must create, and cannot cease from doing so; it manifests All-Possibility, is almighty, but cannot escape the modalities of All-Possibility. Being has power over the form and manner, but not over the three primordial realities: the Good, Creation, and All-Possibility. It can "do" what it wills but cannot "be" what it wills, if one may express oneself thus.

I do not know why I am recapitulating all of this here for you; it is probably because I just happen to be thinking about it; because something or other has prompted me to think about it; possibly the constantly recurring confrontation with the moralistic one-sidedness of exoterism and its exaggerations, which one encounters at every turn; but which, God be praised, one can also forget.

This is the prodigious miracle of the human state, that man can even have the notion of Beyond-Being—"Godhead"—which transcends the personal God and the notion connected to it of *Māyā in divinis*; and this proves the all-diminishing and disfiguring falseness of a theology that makes of man a mere slave; far subtler is the doctrine that sees in us "children of God".

All of this is well known to the Sufism belonging to pure *ma'rifah*, otherwise it would not have coined, in the realest sense of the word "profound", the saying: "the Sufi is not created".

13

The *sophia perennis* is not an "esoterism" in itself; it can be such only in relation to an exoterism, and this is obvious, and finally it is merely a question of language. The very nature of the *sophia perennis* precludes its becoming "an exoterism in its turn", unless one means by the term "exoterism" every doctrine formulated without veils, which would be an improper usage. Once one is situated on the plane of the *sophia perennis*, the distinction between an esoterism and an exoterism is transcended; all that remains is the distinction between the true and the false. Intrinsically, esoterism is not what ought to be veiled, it is what is transcendent or quintessential, but which is veiled *de facto* in certain circumstances, without it being possible to draw absolute lines of demarcation.

EDITOR'S NOTES

Numbers in bold indicate pages in the text for which the following citations and explanations are provided.

Introduction

xiii: *Pythagoreanism* comprises the metaphysical teachings of Pythagoras of Samos (c. 569-c. 475 B.C.), one of the greatest sages of ancient Greece, whose doctrine was at once philosophical, mathematical, astronomical, and musical.

Shaivite or *Shivaite Vedānta* is the metaphysical and religious school associated with Shiva, the third God of the Hindu *trimūrti* or trinity, which emphasizes the path of knowledge (*jnāna*).

Zen is a branch of Japanese Buddhism, deriving originally from the *Ch'an* Buddhism of China.

Kabbalists are followers of the Kabbalah, a mystical stream of esoteric teachings within the Judaic tradition.

xv: The *Upanishads*, also referred to as the *Vedānta* since they were traditionally placed at the "end" of the *Veda*s and are seen by such authorities as Shankara as a synthesis of Vedic teaching, are Hindu scriptures containing metaphysical, mystical, and esoteric doctrine.

xvi: The Latin phrase *credo ut intelligam* ("I believe so that I may understand") is associated with Anselm (c. 1033-1109), Archbishop of Canterbury and one of the most important of the medieval scholastics, who prefaced his ontological argument for the existence of God with the words: "I do not seek to understand so that I may believe; but I believe so that I may understand." The author's Latin formulation *intelligo ergo credo* means, "I understand therefore I believe."

Understanding Esoterism

3: *Shankara* (788-820) is the pre-eminent exponent of *Advaita Vedānta* and regarded by the author as the greatest of Hindu metaphysicians.

Ramanuja (1017-c. 1157) is the foremost representative of *Vishishta Advaita*, the Hindu school of "qualified non-dualism", which emphasizes the personal nature of God.

5: Note 2: The German philosopher Immanuel *Kant* (1724-1804) insisted that man's knowledge is limited to the domain of sensible objects and that the idea of God is no more than a postulate of reason having no objective certainty.

7: "Neither *do men light a candle, and put it under a bushel,* but on a candlestick; and it giveth light unto all that are in the house" (Matt. 5:15).

"*Give not that which is holy unto the dogs,* neither cast ye your pearls before swine, lest they trample them under their feet, and turn again and rend you" (Matt. 7:6).

"And the *light shineth in darkness; and the darkness comprehended it not*" (John 1:5).

8: "*The rust from the mirror*": "There is a means of polishing all things by which rust is removed; that which polishes the heart is the invocation of *Allāh*" (*hadīth*); "If you find the mirror of the heart dull, the rust has not been cleared from its face" (Jalal ad-Din Rumi, *Mathnawī*, 1:34).

For the *Upanishads* see editor's note for "Introduction", p. xv.

9: For a fuller exposition of *Māyā* see the author's "Tracing *Māyā*" in *Light on the Ancient Worlds: A New Translation with Selected Letters*, ed. Deborah Casey (Bloomington, Indiana: World Wisdom, 2006), pp. 75-82.

10: *Platonism* comprises the teachings of the ancient Greek philosopher Plato (see editor's note below for "Understanding Esoterism", p. 12).

11: In the monotheistic traditions of Judaism, Christianity, and Islam the prophet *Abraham* is considered the father of both the Jews and the Arabs through his sons Isaac and Ishmael.

Vishnu, one of the supreme Gods in the Hindu *trimūrti*, is associated with the powers of cosmic maintenance and preservation.

12: *Thomas Aquinas* (c. 1225-74) was the foremost medieval scholastic philosopher and author of the monumental *Summa Theologica*.

Abu al-Hasan al-*Ashari* (873-935) was one of the most important of the early Muslim theologians. For commentary on Ashari see the author's "The Exo-Esoteric Symbiosis" in *Sufism: Veil and Quintessence: A New Translation with Selected Letters*, ed. James S. Cutsinger (Bloomington, Indiana: World Wisdom, 2006), pp. 31-33.

Moses *Maimonides* (1135-1204) was a medieval Jewish rabbi, physician, and philosopher, best known for his *Guide for the Perplexed.*

Plato (c. 427-c. 347 B.C.) was the greatest of the ancient Greek philosophers.

Plotinus (c. 205-270), founder of the Neoplatonic school of philosophy, synthesized the teachings of Plato and Aristotle in his monumental *Enneads*, a collection of discourses compiled by his disciple Porphyry (c. 232-c. 305).

Proclus (412-485), author of *The Elements of Theology* and *Platonic Theology*, was the most authoritative Neoplatonist philosopher of late Antiquity, serving as head of the Platonic Academy in Athens for nearly half a century.

"Wisdom according to the flesh": "In simplicity and godly sincerity, not with fleshly wisdom, but by the grace of God, we have had our conversation in the world" (2 Cor. 1:12).

Note 10: *Gregory Palamas* (c. 1296-1359) was an Athonite monk and later Archbishop of Thessalonica, best known for his defense of the contemplative techniques used by the Hesychast Fathers.

Socrates (c. 470-399 B.C.), proclaimed by the Delphic Oracle to be the wisest man in the world, was an Athenian philosopher and teacher of Plato.

Note 11: *Epictetus* (c. 55-135) was a Stoic philosopher and teacher of Arrian (c. 86-160).

Aristotle (384-322 B.C.), pupil of Plato, had a decisive influence on the teachings of Thomas Aquinas and other medieval Scholastics.

13: *Protagoras* of Abdera (c. 481-c. 411 B.C.) was a leading Sophist, known for his maxim that "man is the measure of all things".

Note 11 (cont.): *The "Council"* refers to the Second Vatican Council (1962-65).

Note 12: *Meister Eckhart* (c. 1260-1327), a German Dominican writer, was regarded by the author as the greatest of Christian metaphysicians and esoterists.

Abd al-Karim al-*Jili* (c. 1365-c. 1412) systematized the teachings of Ibn Arabi, notably in his most important work, *The Universal Man*, which is concerned with both cosmological and metaphysical questions.

Jalal ad-Din *Rumi* (1207-73), a Persian Sufi mystic and poet, was the founder of the Mevlevi order of "Whirling Dervishes".

Orpheus is the mythical archetype of the inspired singer; in classical mythology he played divine music in an attempt to retrieve his wife, Eurydice, from the underworld.

For *Pythagoras* see editor's note for "Introduction", p. xiii.

Orphism stems from an ancient initiatic Greek mystery religion into which *Plato* may have been initiated and about whose strict ascetical rules he writes with favor in the *Laws*.

Note 13: Muhyi al-Din *Ibn Arabi* (1165-1240), author of numerous works including *Meccan Revelations* and *Bezels of Wisdom*, was a prolific and profoundly influential Sufi mystic, known in tradition as the *Shaykh al-Akbar*, the "great master".

14: The Latin *extra ecclesiam nulla salus, "outside the Church there is no salvation"*, is a fundamental dogma of the Christian faith.

15: The doctrine of *creatio ex nihilo*, or "creation out of nothing", affirms a Creator separate from and anterior to the creation.

Note 14: Abu Hamid Muhammad al-*Ghazali* (c. 1058-1111), often regarded as the greatest religious authority in Islam after the Prophet Muhammad, was a jurist and theologian before entering upon the Sufi path.

The *story of Moses and the mysterious stranger* (= *Al-Khidr*), a righteous servant of God possessing mystic knowledge, appears in the Koran (*Sūrah* "The Cave" [18]:60-82).

Muhammad ibn al-Hasan al-*Niffari* (d. c. 970) was one of the earliest Sufi writers and the author of *The Book of Spiritual Stations* and *The Book of Spiritual Addresses*.

Note 15: Abu Mahfuz *Maruf al-Karkhi* (d. 815) was a Sufi saint who converted from Christianity.

17: In one of the miracles recounted in the Gospels, *Christ walked on the water* (see Matt. 14:22-34, Mark 6:45-53, John 6:15-21).

Note 18: *John of the Cross* (1542-91), whose mystical works include the

Ascent of Mount Carmel and the *Dark Night of the Soul*, was a Spanish priest and co-founder, with Teresa of Avila, of the Discalced Carmelites.

18: *Clement of Alexandria* (c. 150-c. 215), head of the famous Catechetical School of Alexandria and author of the treatise *On Spiritual Perfection*, taught that assimilation to God through *gnosis* is the chief aim of the Christian life and the key to human perfection.

Origen (185-252), a successor to Clement as head of the Catechetical School, is best known for his doctrine of the *Apocatastasis* ("universal salvation").

Dionysius or *Denis the Areopagite* (late fourth-early fifth century) was the greatest of all Christian masters of apophatic theology and author of several mystical works, including *The Divine Names*, *Mystical Theology*, and *The Celestial Hierarchy*.

John *Scotus Erigena* (c. 815-c. 877) was an Irish theologian, Neoplatonic philosopher, and poet.

Cardinal *Nicholas of Cusa* (1401-1464) was a German theologian, philosopher, jurist, and astronomer.

Jakob Boehme (1575-1624), known as the "Teutonic Theosopher", was a German Lutheran whose esoteric insights, often couched in Hermetic and alchemical language, appeared in such treatises as *Aurora*, *The Way to Christ*, and *Dialogue of the Supersensual Life*.

Angelus Silesius, the "Silesian Angel", was the pen-name of Johannes Scheffler (1624-1677), a Catholic priest and mystical poet greatly influenced by the teachings of Meister Eckhart.

Note 20: The *Rhinelanders* were a late medieval mystical movement influenced by the teachings of Dionysius the Areopagite, and which included Meister Eckhart, Johannes Tauler, and Henry Suso among its most prominent adherents.

Hesychasm is the spiritual practice of certain monks of the Christian East whose aim is to attain a state of *hesychia*, or inner stillness, through the practice of the Jesus Prayer or other "prayer of the heart".

Miguel de *Molinos* (1628-1696) was a Spanish mystic prominent in the religious revival known as Quietism.

Francis of Sales (1567-1622) was a leading figure in the Counter-Reformation and a noted preacher and founder of the Visitation Order. His most important spiritual writings include *An Introduction to the Devout Life* and *Treatise on the Love of God.*

20: Note 21: The Latin phrase *bilinguis maledictus*, "curse the double-tongued", appears in the Vulgate translation of *Ecclesiasticus*: "Curse the whisperer and double-tongued: for such have destroyed many that were at peace" (28:15).

The *Song of Songs* (or "Song of Solomon"), a book of the Hebrew Bible, is an allegorical love poem, traditionally interpreted by Jews and Christians to signify the mystical relationship between God and the soul.

24: The *Bhagavad Gītā*, the best known of all Hindu sacred texts and part of the much longer epic *Mahābhārata*, consists of a dialogue between the prince Arjuna and his charioteer, the *Avatāra* Krishna, concerning the different paths to God.

25: For *the Koranic denial of the Cross* see editor's note for "The Way of Unity", p. 231, Note 1.

27: The *Essenes* ("holy, pious ones") were an ancient Jewish ascetical sect, known for their communitarian life and emphasis on celibacy and simplicity.

"God became man that man might become God" is a formulation of Irenaeus (c. 130-c. 200) and Athanasius (c. 296-373), among other Church Fathers.

"My yoke is easy and my burden is light" (Matt. 11:30).

The Woman *"clothed with the sun"* (Rev. 12:1) is traditionally interpreted to be the Blessed *Virgin Mary.*

Note 26: *Amida Buddhists* are adherents of the Buddhist *Jōdo* or Pure Land sect, whose central spiritual practice is the invocation of Amida, the Buddha of "infinite light".

Note 28: Although never defined as dogma, popular recognition of the Blessed Virgin as *Co-Redemptress* dates from ancient times and can be found in both the Eastern and the Western Churches; echoing the belief of many Christians, Saint Louis Marie de Montfort writes, "Let us boldly say with Saint Bernard that we need a mediator with the Mediator himself and that the divine Mary is the one most able to fulfill this office of love" (*True Devotion to the Blessed Virgin*).

28: *"True man and true God"*: the doctrine of the "two natures" of Christ was ratified at the Council of Chalcedon in 451 and is a foundation-stone of

Christian theology.

Note 29: *Fr. Kolbe* (1894-1941) was a Polish Franciscan friar who volunteered to die in place of a stranger in the German death camp of Auschwitz.

Note 30: *Justin Martyr* (c. 100-c. 165) was an early Church Father and Christian apologist.

Heraclitus (c. 535-c. 475 B.C.) of Ephesus, the pre-Socratic philosopher best known for his aphorism that "one cannot step twice into the same river", believed nonetheless that there is a single, underlying, and unchanging order in the cosmos, which he called the *Logos*.

29: Note 31: *The* daimonion *of Socrates* was an inner guiding voice, which he understood as a gift from the gods.

The *maxim* "*Know thyself*" (*Gnothi seauton*), carved into the lintel of Apollo's Temple, is the most famous of the *Delphic* oracles.

30: *Dante* Alighieri (1265-1321) was the author of the *Divine Comedy*, one of the summits of world literature.

The Ghibellines formed one of the main political factions in Florence and other city states of northern Italy in the twelfth-thirteenth centuries; they opposed the Guelphs in the controversy about the respective powers of the Pope and the Holy Roman Emperor.

Constantine the Great (d. 337) was the first Christian Roman Emperor, whose defense and patronage of Christianity and involvement in the proceedings of the *Council of Nicaea* created the precedent for a close connection between Church and State.

Frederick II (1194-1250) was Holy Roman Emperor, King of the Romans, King of Sicily, and King of Jerusalem.

30-31: "*There is no right superior to that of truth*" is a traditional *Hindu maxim* attributed to the Maharajahs of Benares.

32: For the distinction between *heretical Gnosticism* and *gnosis* in its proper sense see the author's "*Gnosis* Is Not Just Anything" in *To Have a Center: A New Translation with Selected Letters*, ed. Harry Oldmeadow (Bloomington IN: World Wisdom, 2015), pp. 53-56.

33: "*I am black, but beautiful*, O ye daughters of Jerusalem, as the tents of Kedar, as the curtains of Solomon" (Song of Sol. 1:5).

Note 33: *Omar Khayyam* (1048-1125) was a Persian astronomer, mathematician, and poet, best known for his mystical *Rubā'iyyāt* ("quatrains").

Omar ibn al-Farid (c. 1182-1235) was a mystical poet and author of the *Khamriyah* or "Ode to Wine".

35: Note 35: The *"Night of Destiny"* (*Laylat al-Qadr*), in the year 610 A.D., is when the revelation of the Koran descended, in its entirety, into the Prophet Muhammad (see *Sūrah* "Power" [97]); the *"Night of the Ascension"* (*Laylat al-Mi'rāj*) is the miraculous "night journey" (*isrā'*) wherein the Prophet Muhammad traveled through the seven heavens to the Divine Presence (see *Sūrah* "The Night Journey" [17]:1-2).

The Mystery of the Veil

37: Note 2: For *Omar Khayyam* see editor's note for "Understanding Esoterism", p. 33, Note 33.

38: *Augustine* (354-430) was the most prolific and influential of the Western Church Fathers.

"He that loveth not knoweth not God; for *God is love*" (1 John 4:8).

42: *According to the Koran,* Ar-Rahmān *is synonymous with* Allāh: "Call upon *Allāh*, or call upon *Ar-Rahmān;* whichsoever you call upon, to Him belong the most beautiful names" (*Sūrah* "The Night Journey" [17]:110).

"Ar-Rahmān hath *revealed the Koran, created man, taught him speech*" (*Sūrah Ar-Rahmān* [55]:1-3).

43: "The *yogin* whose intellect is perfect contemplates all things as abiding in himself, and thus by the eye of knowledge he perceives that *all things are* Ātmā" (*Chāndogya Upanishad*, 6.1.4); "*Ātmā* was indeed *Brahma* in the beginning. It knew only that 'I am *Brahma*'. Therefore It became all. And whoever among the gods knew It also became That; and the same with sages and men. . . . And to this day whoever in like manner knows 'I am *Brahma*' becomes all this universe. Even the gods cannot prevail against him, for he becomes their *Ātmā*" (*Brihadāranyaka Upanishad*, 1.4.10).

44: Note 9: *God, insofar as He manifests Himself through the cosmos, being called "the Outward"* (Az-Zāhir) *in the Koran:* "He (God) is the First and the Last, and the Outward and the Inward" (*Sūrah* "Iron" [57]:3).

45: *"Nothing is like unto Him"* (*Sūrah* "Consultation" [42]:11).

46: "*God is the Light of the Heavens and the earth*" (*Sūrah* "Light" [24]:35).

For *Ibn Arabi* see editor's note for "Understanding Esoterism", p. 13.

Seth was the third son of *Adam*, brother of Cain and Abel, and father of Enoch (see Gen. 4:26-28).

48: *The sin of Eve and Adam* leading to *the Fall* is recounted in Genesis: "And unto Adam he [God] said, Because thou hast hearkened unto the voice of thy wife, and hast eaten of the tree, of which I commanded thee, saying, Thou shalt not eat of it: cursed is the ground for thy sake; in sorrow shalt thou eat of it all the days of thy life; Thorns also and thistles shall it bring forth to thee; and thou shalt eat the herb of the field; In the sweat of thy face shalt thou eat bread, till thou return unto the ground; for out of it wast thou taken: for dust thou art, and unto dust shalt thou return" (Gen. 3:17-19).

The Latin *intrate per angustam portam*, "enter ye in at the strait gate", appears in the Vulgate translation of the New Testament: "Enter ye in at the strait gate: for wide is the gate, and broad is the way, that leadeth to destruction, and many there be which go in thereat: Because strait is the gate, and narrow is the way, which leadeth unto life, and few there be that find it" (Matt. 7:13-14; cf. Luke 13:24).

49: The Latin *fiat lux*, "let there be light" (Gen. 1:3), appears in the Vulgate translation of the Old Testament.

The Latin *dies irae*, "day of wrath", appears in the Vulgate translation of the Old Testament: "That day (of the judgment) is a day of wrath, a day of tribulation and distress, a day of calamity and misery, a day of darkness and obscurity, a day of clouds and whirlwinds, a day of the trumpet and alarm against the fenced cities, and against the high bulwarks" (Prophecy of Sophonius 1:15-16).

Hindu tradition tells of the *Avatāra Krishna* enthralling the adoring *gopīs*, or cowherd girls of Vrindavan, with the music of his flute and stealing their *saris* (clothes).

51: Note 22: Paramahamsa *Ramakrishna* (1834-86), a *bhakta* of the Hindu Goddess *Kali*, was one of the great Hindu saints of modern times. See the author's "*Vedānta*" in *Spiritual Perspectives and Human Facts: A New Translation with Selected Letters*, ed. James S. Cutsinger (Bloomington, Indiana: World Wisdom, 2007), pp. 124-126.

52: The doctrine of *Apocatastasis*, universal salvation, was expounded by the

Church Father Origen (185-252). Esoterically the doctrine is linked with the recovery, through sleepless attention, of man's primordial unity in God.

53: The woman "*clothed with the sun,* and the moon under her feet, and upon her head a crown of twelve stars" (Rev. 12:1) is traditionally interpreted to be the *Blessed Virgin* Mary.

"Beauty is *the splendor of the true*" is an axiom attributed by the author to Plato.

"I am *black, but beautiful,* O ye daughters of Jerusalem, as the tents of Kedar, as the curtains of Solomon" (Song of Sol. 1:5).

Note 24: The story of *Herod* the Great (74-4 B.C.), the Jewish king at the time of the birth of Jesus, and *Salomé,* the daughter of Herodias, is recounted in the New Testament (Matt. 14:3-11, Mark 6:17-29).

The encounter between the *Queen of Sheba* and King *Solomon* is recounted in 1 Kings 10:1-13 (cf. Matt. 12:42, Luke 11:31) and also in the Koran (*Sūrah* "The Ants" [27]:20-44, *Sūrah* "Sheba" [34]:15-19).

The priest *Zacharias,* or Zechariah, was father of John the Baptist and husband of Elizabeth.

54: For the *divine Mary* see editor's note for "Understanding Esoterism", p. 27, Note 28.

Note 26: The Latin *nigra sum sed formosa,* "I am black but beautiful", appears in the Vulgate translation of the Old Testament: "I am black, but beautiful, O ye daughters of Jerusalem, as the tents of Kedar, as the curtains of Solomon" (Song of Sol. 1:5).

55: Note 27: *Vishnu* is the second god of the Hindu trinity (*trimūrti*), Brahmā being the first and Shiva the third. Vishnu is the maintainer, preserver, and protector of the created or

Shiva is the third god of the Hindu trinity (*trimūrti*) and is associated with the powers of generation and destruction.

Hypostatic and Cosmic Numbers

60: "*Beauty is the splendor of the True*" is an axiom attributed by the author to Plato.

61: Note 6: *The monogram of Jesus* is a combination of letters that forms an abbreviation for the name of Jesus. The Greek letters I H S—that is, *iota, êta,* and *sigma*—are an abbreviation for ΙΗΣΟΥΣ, or *IÊSOUS,* the Name of Jesus; elsewhere the author writes in this regard, "The cipher of the Greek Letters I H S, signifying *Iesous,* but interpreted in Latin as *In Hoc Signo* ['By this sign (you shall conquer)'] or as *Jesus Hominum Salvator* ['Jesus is the Savior of men'] and often written in Gothic letters, can be analyzed in its primitive form into three elements—a vertical straight line, two vertical lines linked together, and a curved line—and thus contains a symbolism at once metaphysical, cosmological, and mystical; there is in it a remarkable analogy, not only with the name *Allāh* written in Arabic, which also comprises the three lines of which we have just spoken (in the form of the *alif,* the two *lams,* and the *hā*), but also with the Sanskrit monosyllable *Aum,* which is composed of the three *mātrās* (A U M), indicating a 'rolling up' and thereby a return to the Center. All of these symbols mark, in a certain sense, the passage from 'coagulation' to 'solution'" (*Stations of Wisdom* [Bloomington, Indiana: World Wisdom, 1995], pp. 131-32n).

63: Note 10: The *Kaaba* is a cube-shaped construction located in the Great Mosque of Mecca, the most sacred site of Islam and destination of the *hajj* or pilgrimage.

64: The *four Archangels* of Semitic monotheism are Gabriel, Michael, Raphael, and Azrael. For a more detailed treatment of this subject see the author's "*An-Nūr*" in *Dimensions of Islam* (London: George Allen & Unwin, 1969), pp. 102-120.

66: For a more detailed exposition of the *mystical cosmology* of the American Indians see the author's "A Metaphysic of Virgin Nature" and "The Shamanism of the Red Indians" in *The Feathered Sun: Plains Indians in Art and Philosophy* (Bloomington Indiana: World Wisdom, 1990), pp. 14-43.

67: "*My Mercy taketh precedence over My Wrath*" (*hadīth qudsī*).

68: *The seal of Solomon* comprises two superimposed equilateral triangles, one with its apex pointing upward, the other downward.

69: The *Book of Tobit* is accepted as a canonical Biblical text in the Catholic and Orthodox traditions but regarded by Protestants as apocryphal.

For *Zacharias* see editor's note for "The Mystery of the Veil", p. 53.

The Primordial Tree

71: "And the Lord God planted a garden eastward in Eden; and there he put the man whom he had formed. And out of the ground made the Lord God to grow . . . the *tree of life* also in the midst of the garden, and the *tree of knowledge of good and evil*" (Gen. 2:8-9).

For *the sin of Adam and Eve* see editor's note for "The Mystery of the Veil", p. 48.

72: *Asharite theology* is an early school of speculative Islamic theology, based on the teaching of Abu al-Hasan al-Ashari (see editor's note for "Understanding Esoterism", p. 12). It claims that anthropomorphic descriptions of God in the Koran should not be interpreted as metaphors, but accepted at face value, that is, "without asking any questions" or "without asking how" they apply to God.

Note 2: The *Theologica Germanica* ("German Theology") is an anonymous mystical treatise of the late fourteenth century.

73: *The idea that the knowledge of Good and Evil is the privilege of God*: "And the Lord God commanded the man, saying, Of every tree of the garden thou mayest freely eat: But of the tree of the knowledge of good and evil, thou shalt not eat of it" (Gen. 2:16-17).

For the *Apocatastasis* see editor's note for "The Mystery of the Veil", p. 52.

74: *Made in the image of God*: "And God said, Let us make man in our image, after our likeness" (Gen. 1:26).

76: The building of the *Tower of Babel* and the confounding of human language are recounted in Gen. 11:4-9.

Moses smashed the first tablet of stone inscribed with the Ten Commandments when he saw the Israelites worshipping *the golden calf* (Exod. 32:15-19).

"And when the woman (Eve) saw that the tree was good for food, and that it was pleasant to the eyes, and a tree to be desired to make one wise, she took of the fruit thereof, and did eat, and gave also unto her husband (Adam) with her; and he did eat. And the eyes of them both were opened, *and they saw that they were naked*; and they sewed fig leaves together, and made themselves aprons" (Gen. 3:6-7).

77: God's *placing cherubim armed with swords at the gateway of Paradise* is recounted in Gen. 3:24.

The symbolism of Janus, the Roman god of change and time, derives from his two faces, one facing the past, the other the future.

Note 10: *Clothing is a divine revelation, and this accords with the biblical story.* "Unto Adam also and to his wife did the Lord God make coats of skins, and clothed them" (Gen. 3:21).

78: For *Plato* see editor's note for "Understanding Esoterism", p. 12.

Lucifer, literally the "shining one", is the Angel of the Morning Star whose *fall* from heaven is recounted in Isaiah 14:12-15.

Note 13: For *Plotinus* see editor's note for "Understanding Esoterism", p. 12.

79: *Manicheism* is a dualistic and syncretistic religion that originated in the Persian Empire in the second century A.D. It is based on the heretical Gnostic idea that spirits from a transcendent realm of light have become imprisoned in the darkness of matter and can be liberated from their bondage only by agents sent by the "Father of Light", versions of whom include Zoroaster, the Buddha, the prophets of Israel, Jesus, and the founder of the sect itself, Mani (c. 216-76).

For the *Kabbalah* and *Kabbalists* (Note 18) see editor's note for "Introduction", p. xiii.

82: The words of an ancient liturgical hymn for Holy Saturday—"O truly necessary sin of Adam, which by the death of Christ is done away! O happy fault *(felix culpa)*, which merited such and so great a Redeemer!"—are traditionally ascribed to *Augustine* (see editor's note for "The Mystery of the Veil", p. 38).

The Triple Nature of Man

86: The term *rational animal* (Latin: *animal rationale*), while originating with scholasticism, is associated with Aristotle (see editor's note for "Understanding Esoterism", p. 12), who identified reason or the "rational principle" as what distinguishes man from the animals (*Nicomachean Ethics*, 1098a).

Made "in the image of God": "And God said, Let us make man in our image, after our likeness" (Gen. 1:26).

90: "*Be ye therefore perfect, even as your Father in Heaven is perfect*" (Matt. 5:48).

91: "*The Kingdom of God is within you*" (Luke 17:21).

92: "He that loveth not knoweth not God; for *God is love*" (1 John 4:8).

The Virtues in the Way

93: Made "*in the image of God*": "And God said, Let us make man in our image, after our likeness" (Gen. 1:26).

97: For how to "*see God everywhere*" see the author's "Seeing God Everywhere" in *Gnosis: Divine Wisdom: A New Translation with Selected Letters*, ed. James S. Cutsinger (Bloomington, Indiana: World Wisdom, 2006), pp. 87-100.

"He that loveth not knoweth not God; for *God is love*" (1 John 4:8).

99: Platonic "*recollection*" refers to the doctrine, notably presented in the dialogues *Phaedo* and *Meno*, according to which real knowledge is inscribed in human intelligence from eternity and needs merely to be "recollected" (*anamnesis*) through intellectual intuition.

The Latin phrase *ex toto corde*, "with all (thy) heart", appears numerous times in the Vulgate translation of the Old and New Testaments, as for example: "And thou shalt love the Lord thy God with all thy heart, and with all thy soul, and with all thy might" (Deut. 6:4-5; cf. Matt. 22:37, Mark 12:30, Luke 10:27).

For *Aristotle* see editor's note for "Understanding Esoterism", p. 12.

101: "*One thing needful*": "One thing is needful: and Mary hath chosen that good part, which shall not be taken from her" (Luke 10:42).

102: "God is a Spirit: and they that worship Him must worship Him *in spirit and in truth*" (John 4:24).

Note 4: *Shinto*, the "way of the gods", is the indigenous religion of Japan.

103: "God became what we are, in order that we might *become what He is*": the essential teaching expressed by this Patristic formula is common to many Church Fathers, including Irenaeus (c. 130-c. 200).

Editor's Notes

The Nature and Role of Sentiment

110: Note 1: "My *Mercy* taketh *precedence over* My *Wrath*" (*hadīth qudsī*).

Note 2: *Mencius* (c. 391-c. 308 B.C.), known as the "Second Sage" after Confucius, was one of the most influential of early Confucian philosophers.

112: "He that loveth not knoweth not God; for *God is love*" (1 John 4:8).

113: "*Much will be forgiven her, for she loved much*" (Luke 7:47).

"*Blessed are they that mourn, for they shall be comforted*" (Matt. 5:4).

Note 5: For *Umar ibn al-Farid* see editor's note for "Understanding Esoterism", p. 33.

What Sincerity Is and What It Is Not

116: *Boethius* (c. 480-c. 524) was a Christian philosopher, statesman, and master of the seven liberal arts, who was canonized as "Saint Severinus" for his martyrdom.

For *Augustine* see editor's note for "The Mystery of the Veil", p. 38.

117: Note 1: "Unto *the pure all things are pure*: but unto them that are defiled and unbelieving is nothing pure; but even their mind and conscience is defiled" (Tit. 1:15).

119: Note 2: *Hate thy soul*: "If any man come to me, and hate not his father, and mother, and wife, and children, and brethren, and sisters, yea, and his own soul also, he cannot be my disciple" (Luke 14:26).

The Problem of Sexuality

122: "*Sin of the flesh*": "Now the works of *the flesh* are manifest, which are these; Adultery, fornication, impurity, licentiousness, idolatry, witchcraft, hatred, variance, emulations, wrath, strife, seditions, heresies, envyings, murders, drunkenness, revellings" (Gal. 5:19-21).

Paul (c. 5-c. 67), formerly Saul of Tarsus before his conversion to Christianity on the road to Damascus (see Acts 9:1-22), was the Apostle to whom are attributed fourteen of the twenty-seven books of the New Testament.

123: For *the sin of Adam* see editor's note for "The Mystery of the Veil", p. 48.

The wedding *at Cana*, where *Christ consecrated or blessed marriage* and *changed the water into wine*, is recounted in John 2:1-10.

Note 5: The immaculate conception is the Roman Catholic dogma that, from the first moment of her conception, the Virgin *Mary* was free from all *stain of original sin.*

124: *Jacob* was the grandson of Abraham, the son of Isaac and Rebecca, the younger twin brother of Esau, and the husband of *Rachel* and Leah (see Gen. 25-50).

For the *Song of Songs* see editor's note for "Understanding Esoterism", p. 20.

The parable of the ten virgins is recounted in Matt. 25:1-13.

Man must not put asunder what God has joined together, Christ said in condemning divorce: "And [Jesus] answered and said unto them, What did Moses command you? And they said, Moses suffered to write a bill of divorcement, and to put her away. And Jesus answered and said unto them, For the hardness of your heart he wrote you this precept. But from the beginning of the creation God made them male and female. For this cause shall a man leave his father and mother, and cleave to his wife; and they twain shall be one flesh: so then they are no more twain, but one flesh. What therefore God hath joined together, let not man put asunder" (Mark 10:3-9).

125: For *Krishna* see editor's note for "The Mystery of the Veil", p. 49.

David (c. 1040-970 B.C.) was the second king of Israel and Judah, the composer of the *Psalms*, and, according to Christian tradition, an ancestor of Jesus Christ; he had several wives and concubines (see 2 Samuel 5:13).

Solomon (r.c. 970-931 B.C.), who succeeded his father David as the King of Israel, "had seven hundred wives, princesses, and three hundred concubines" (1 Kings 11:3).

126: Note 9: For *Ramakrishna* see editor's note for "The Mystery of the Veil", p. 51.

127: "*It is not good that man should be alone; I shall make for him a help meet like unto him*" (Gen. 2:18).

For *Eve* see editor's note for "The Mystery of the Veil", p. 48.

"*God created man in His* own *image,* in the image of God created He him; *male and female created He them*" (Gen. 1:27).

128: Note 13: The *Yoga-Vāsistha,* attributed to the sage Valmiki, is an Advaitic dialogue between a human spiritual master, Vasistha, and his divine disciple, Rama, concerning the relationship between consciousness and Reality and including the story of the realized *Queen Chudala, guru* to *her husband, King Shikhidhwaja.*

For *Shankara* see editor's note for "Understanding Esoterism", p. 3.

129: Note 14: *Shinran* (1173-1262) was the *founder* of the *Jōdo-Shinshū* or "True Pure Land school" of Japanese Buddhism.

Honen Shonin (1133-1212), founder of the *Jōdo* or "Pure Land school" in

Japan, taught that everyone without exception, whether *celibate* or *married,* can be reborn into Amida's paradise simply by faithful repetition of his Name.

130: For *Ramanuja* see editor's note for "Understanding Esoterism", p. 3.

131: For *Krishna's flute* see editor's note for "The Mystery of the Veil", p. 49.

Note 16: For *Dante* see editor's note for "Understanding Esoterism", p. 30. The passage quoted by the author translates as: "Whatever melody most sweetly sounds / on earth, and to itself most draws the soul, / would seem a cloud that, torn by lightning, thunders, / if likened to the music of that lyre / which sounded from the crown of that fair sapphire, the brightest light that has ensapphired heaven" (Dante, *Paradiso* XXIII, 97-102).

Note 17: "Therefore shall a man leave his father and his mother, and shall cleave unto his wife: and they shall be *one flesh* (Gen. 2:24; cf. Mark 10:8); "And the Lord God caused a deep sleep to fall upon Adam, and he slept: and he took one of his ribs, and closed up the flesh instead thereof; And the rib, which the Lord God had taken from man, made he a woman, and brought her unto the man. And Adam said, This is now *bone* of my *bones,* and *flesh of* my *flesh*: she shall be called Woman, because she was taken out of Man" (Gen. 2:21-23).

132: According to *Meister Eckhart* (see editor's note for "Understanding Esoterism", p. 13), "if someone were as well prepared for ordinary nourishment as he is for the holy *sacrament* [the Eucharist], he would receive God in this nourishment just as fully as in the sacrament itself" (quoted in

Christianity/Islam: Perspectives on Esoteric Ecumenism: A New Translation with Selected Letters, ed. James S. Cutsinger [Bloomington, Indiana: World Wisdom, 2008], p. 21).

132-33: The "*lesser mysteries*" of Western Antiquity, secondary to the "*greater mysteries*", were secret cultic rites associated with the Greek city of Eleusis.

133: For a fuller commentary on the *patristic argumentation against the Greeks* see the author's "The Dialogue between Hellenists and Christians" in *Light on the Ancient Worlds: A New Translation with Selected Letters*, ed. Deborah Casey (Bloomington, Indiana: World Wisdom, 2006), pp. 45-57.

134: In *Mahāyāna* tradition, Dharmakara was an ancient king who renounced his throne and became a monk, devoting himself to good deeds and the service of others and vowing, were he to become a Buddha, to establish a perfect world, a Pure Land, for all those who invoked his Buddha name, *Amitabha* (Sanskrit) or Amida (Japanese).

For Angelus *Silesius* see editor's note for "Understanding Esoterism", p. 18.

135: Note 20: The Angelical Salutation—otherwise known as the *Ave Maria* or "Hail Mary"—describes the *Virgin Mary* as *gratia plena*, "*full of grace*" (cf. Luke 1:28, 42).

136: *Sita*, an incarnation of the goddess *Lakshmi*, was abducted by the demon king *Ravana* and taken from India to the island of Lanka, where she was eventually rescued by her husband, *Rama*, the seventh *Avatāra* of the Hindu god Vishnu; after rescuing her, however, Rama began to doubt her fidelity and ordered her banished to the forest and killed; spared by the executioner, she was finally able to convince Rama of her devotion, though her own heart was now broken.

137: Note 25: The *Rāmāyana*, a Hindu epic tale attributed to the sage Valmiki, recounts the story of Rama, the seventh *Avatāra* of Vishnu, and his wife Sita.

Dimensions of the Human Vocation

141: *Dominion over all other earthly creatures*: "And God blessed them, and God said unto them, Be fruitful, and multiply, and replenish the earth, and subdue it: and have dominion over the fish of the sea, and over the fowl of the air, and over every living thing that moveth upon the earth" (Gen. 1:28).

142: The Latin phrase *credo quia absurdum est* ("I believe because it is absurd") comes from an apologetic work, *On the Flesh of Christ*, by Quintus Septimius Florens *Tertullian* (c. 160-c. 225), an early Church Father and ascetical writer.

Note 3: For the Latin phrase *credo ut intelligam* and *Anselm* see editor's note for "Introduction", p. xvi.

The Supreme Commandment

143: The *Torah* is the written foundation of Jewish law, consisting of the Pentateuch or first five books of the Old Testament and revealed to Moses on Sinai.

144: "The *letter* killeth, but the *spirit* giveth life" (2 Cor. 3:6).

Note 3: *The Pauline interpretation of circumcision*: "For in Jesus Christ neither circumcision availeth any thing, nor uncircumcision; but faith which worketh by love" (Gal. 5:6); "For he is not a Jew, which is one outwardly; neither is that circumcision, which is outward in the flesh: But he is a Jew, which is one inwardly; and circumcision is that of the heart, in the spirit, and not in the letter" (Rom. 2:28-29).

Note 4: *Hasidism* is a current of Jewish Kabbalah (see editor's note for "Introduction", p. xiii) founded in the eighteenth century in Eastern Europe by Israel ben Eliezer (1700-60), widely known as the Baal Shem Tov.

Note 5: The *Psalms* is a book of the Hebrew Bible and the Christian "*Old Testament*", comprising songs in praise of the Lord and attributed to the prophet-king David (see editor's note for "The Problem of Sexuality", p. 125).

For the *Song of Songs* see editor's note for "Understanding Esoterism", p. 20.

145: Note 7: "*The world is false; Brahma is true; the soul is not other than Brahma*": this summation of *Advaita Vedānta* is traditionally ascribed to Shankara (see editor's note for "Understanding Esoterism", p. 3).

Note 8: "The *yogin* whose intellect is perfect contemplates all things as abiding in himself, and thus by the eye of knowledge he perceives that *all things are* Ātmā" (*Chāndogya Upanishad*, 6.1.4); "*Ātmā* was indeed *Brahma* in the beginning. It knew only that 'I am *Brahma*'. Therefore It became all. And whoever among the gods knew It also became That; and the same with sages and men. . . . And to this day whoever in like manner knows 'I am *Brahma*' becomes all this universe. Even the gods cannot prevail against him, for he becomes their *Ātmā*" (*Brihadāranyaka Upanishad*, 1.4.10).

145-46: "*Judge not that ye be not judged*" (Matt. 7:1).

146: "He that is not with me is against me; and *he that gathereth not with me scattereth abroad*" (Matt. 12:30).

"If any man come to me, and *hate* not his *father*, and *mother*, and wife, and children, and brethren, and sisters, yea, and his own soul also, he cannot be my disciple" (Luke 14:26).

147: Note 10: *Vincent de Paul* (1581-1660) was a French priest who founded the Sisters of Charity to the serve the poor.

The *Curé d'Ars* was Jean-Baptiste-Marie Vianney (1786-1859), a French parish priest and much sought-after confessor from the French village of Ars, who was widely known for his gift of reading souls.

148: Note 13: "*Hear, O Israel, the Lord our God is one Lord*" (Deut. 6:4); these words were repeated by Jesus when asked by the scribes which was the most important commandment of all (see Mark 12:28-29).

149: Note 14: The *Decalogue* refers to the Ten Commandments given by God to Moses on Mount Sinai (see Exod. 20

The True Remedy

151: The "*kingdom of God is within you*" (Luke 17:21).

152: "He that is not with me is against me; and *he that gathereth not with me scattereth abroad*" (Matt. 12:30).

"*The Church must scrutinize the signs of the times and interpret them in the light of the Gospel*" is from the *encyclical Gaudium et spes* ("Pastoral Constitution on the Church in the Modern World"), promulgated by Pope Paul VI on December 7, 1965.

"*Seek ye first the kingdom of God and His righteousness and all these things shall be added unto you*" (Matt. 6:33).

The words of Christ to the rich young man: "If thou wilt be perfect, go and sell that thou hast, and give to the poor, and thou shalt have treasure in heaven:

and come and *follow me*" (Matt. 19:21).

The example of Mary takes precedence over that of Martha: "Now it came to pass, as they went, that [Jesus] entered into a certain village: and a certain woman named Martha received him into her house. And she had a sister called Mary, which also sat at Jesus' feet, and heard his word. But Martha was cumbered about with much serving, and came to him, and said, Lord, dost thou not care that my sister hath left me to serve alone? bid her therefore that she help me. And Jesus answered and said unto her, Martha, Martha, thou art careful and troubled about many things: But one thing is needful: and Mary hath chosen that good part, which shall not be taken from her" (Luke 10:38-42).

153: "*Hardness of heart*": "He hath blinded their eyes, and hardened their heart; that they should not see with their eyes, nor understand with their heart, and be converted, and I should heal them" (John 12:40; cf. Exod. 7:13, Deut. 2:30, 2 Chron. 36:13, Isa. 63:17 passim); "For the hardness of your heart [Moses] wrote you this precept" (Mark 10:5).

"But when ye pray, use not vain repetitions as the *heathen* do" (Matt. 6:7).

The new "pastoralism" refers to the modernizing changes brought about in the Catholic Church by the Second Vatican Council (1962-65).

Note 2: "Give not that which is holy unto the dogs, neither *cast* ye your *pearls before swine*, lest they trample under their feet, and turn again and rend you" (Matt. 7:6).

154: For the *Divine Comedy* see editor's note for "Understanding Esoterism", p. 30.

155: For *Dante* see editor's note for "Understanding Esoterism", p. 30.

Pope Celestine V ruled for five months in 1294 before becoming the first pope to abdicate. He was previously known as *Pier* (or Pietro) *Angelerio from Murrhone* (Morrone) and founded the *Celestine Order* as *a branch of the Benedictines.*

Nicholas IV (1227-1292) was born Girolamo Masci and was Pope from 1288-92.

Charles II (1254-1309) was King of Naples from 1285-1309.

Boniface VIII (1230-1303) was Pope from 1294-1303.

Note 5: The *Benedictines* belong to the Order of Benedict of Nursia (480-543), whose "Rule" provided the foundation for monastic life in Western Christendom.

156: *Clement V* (1264-1314) was Pope from 1305-14.

Esau was the son of Isaac and *the brother of Jacob.*

Diocletian, Roman emperor from 284-305, promoted the last great wave of persecution against the early Church.

The *spirituali* were a reform group within the Catholic Church who believed that spiritual renewal would come about through more intense study of the Scriptures and through "justification by faith".

157: *The eagle of Florence,* an epithet for Dante, alludes to the statue of the poet created by Enrico Pazzi to celebrate the sixth centenary of the poet's birth; the sculptor placed an eagle at Dante's feet.

Ancient gnostic terminology distinguishes between three types of human beings: the *pneumatic* (*pneumatikos*), who is centered upon the spirit (*pneuma*); the psychic (*psychikos*), who is centered upon the soul (*psyche*); and the hylic (*hylikos*) or somatic (*somatikos*), who is centered upon matter (*hyle*) or the body (*soma*).

For *Thomas Aquinas* see editor's note for "Understanding Esoterism", p. 12.

Note 8: *Anastasius II* was Pope from 496-98.

Photinus (d. 376) was a bishop of the early Church who denied the divinity of Christ.

The Monophysite heresy claimed that there is only one *physis*, or "nature", in Christ—namely, his Divinity—whereas Monothelites, acknowledging the existence of two natures, teach that they are united in a single *thelema*, or "will".

158: Note 9: *Valentinus* (second century A.D.), the most influential of the early Gnostics, taught that the material world was created by an inferior deity and is therefore intrinsically evil and that redemption depends on a saving knowledge (*gnosis*) of this cosmogonic myth.

159: *The cultural revolution of the Medici and the Borgias* refers to the patronage of these powerful families towards the movement of the Italian Renaissance.

Editor's Notes

The "*motionless mover*", or Unmoved Mover, is the classic expression of *Aristotle* (see editor's note for "Understanding Esoterism, p. 12), for the divine Principle, as in *Metaphysics*, 1072b.

"*One thing necessary*": "One thing is needful: and Mary hath chosen that good part, which shall not be taken from her" (Luke 10:42).

Criteria of Worth

165: Note 1: "*Wolves in the fold*": "For I know this, that after my departing shall grievous wolves enter in among you, not sparing the flock" (Acts 20:29).

Foundations of an Integral Aesthetics

171: For *Platonic recollection* see editor's note for "The Virtues of the Way", p. 99.

For *Plotinus* see editor's note for "Understanding Esoterism", p. 12.

Note 2: For *Pythagoras* see editor's note for "Introduction", xi.

For *Plato* see editor's note for "Understanding Esoterism", p. 12.

172: "God created man in His own image, in *the image of God* created He him; male and female created He them" (Gen. 1:27).

In his famous "Simile of the Sun" (*Republic*, VI:507-509), *Plato* refers to *the eye* as "*the most solar of instruments*" (508b).

Plotinus comments on Plato's "Simile of the Sun" in the treatise "On Beauty" (*Enneads*, I.6.9).

Note 5: "He (God) *has prescribed for Himself Mercy*" (*Sūrah* "Cattle" [6]:12; cf. 6:54)

173: For *Shankara* see editor's note for "Understanding Esoterism", p. 3.

175: Note 8: For *Ramakrishna* see editor's note for "The Mystery of the Veil", p. 51.

For "*seeing God everywhere*" see editor's note for "The Virtues in the Way", p. 97.

The Degrees of Art

177: *Ars sine scientia nihil* (est), or "Art without knowledge is nothing", is a saying attributed to the medieval architect Jean Mignot.

Note 1: Peter Paul *Rubens* (1577-1640) was an influential Flemish painter in the Baroque style.

Giovanna Tornabuoni was one of the subjects and patrons of the Italian Renaissance painter Domenico *Ghirlandaio* (1448-94).

178: According to Catholic tradition, *Veronica* was a pious woman of Jerusalem who wiped the brow of Jesus with a cloth as he carried the cross to Golgotha. The cloth—"the veil of Veronica"—was miraculously impressed with the *Holy Face* of Jesus.

Christian tradition considers the apostle *Luke*, one of the four evangelists or ascribed authors of the canonical Gospels, as well as the author of the Acts of the Apostles, as the first iconographer.

Shiva, the third god of the Hindu *trimūrti*, is associated with the powers of destruction and transformation. In the form of *Natarāja*, or "Lord of the Dance", he is represented as *dancing* upon the vanquished demon of chaotic matter.

In Tibetan Buddhism, *Tara*, the "Mother of all the Buddhas" or "Mother of Compassion", is the female counterpart of the *bodhisattva* Avalokiteshvara.

Note 1 (cont.): Ogata *Korin* (1658-1716) was a Japanese painter and designer, best known for his folding screens.

182: For the *Mahābhārata* see editor's note for "Understanding Esoterism", p. 24.

The *Bhāgavata Purāna*, or *Srīmad Bhāgavatam*, includes narrations of the life of *Krishna* (see editor's note for "The Mystery of the Veil", p. 49), among other *Avatāras* of Vishnu.

For *Rama* and the *Rāmāyana* see editor's note for "The Problem of Sexuality", p. 137, Note 25.

The Latin *spiritus* (*autem*) *ubi vult spirat*, "The wind [Spirit] bloweth where it listeth" (John 3:8), is from the Vulgate translation of the New Testament.

For the *Bhagavad Gītā* see editor's note for "Understanding Esoterism", p. 24.

Editor's Notes

For the *Upanishads* see editor's note for "Introduction", p. xv.

183: *"Suffer the little children to come unto me and forbid them not; for of such is the Kingdom of Heaven"* (Matt. 19:14, Mark 10:14, Luke 18:16).

184: For *Orphism* see editor's note for "Understanding Esoterism", p. 13.

For *Platonism* see editor's note for "Understanding Esoterism", p. 10.

187: *Paracelsus* (1493-1541) was a Swiss-German physician, botanist, astronomer, and esoterist.

188: *Bernard* of Clairvaux (1090-1153) was a Cistercian monk and author of numerous homilies on the *Song of Songs*. He insisted that churches of his Cistercian Order should be plain in character and that vestments and ornaments should not be made of precious materials.

Girolamo *Savonarola* (1452-98), a Dominican friar, reformer, and apocalyptic preacher, was known for his condemnations of corruption among the clergy and for his denunciation of Pope Alexander VI and his dissolute court.

189: The proverb, "Tell me whom thou frequentist and I shall tell thee who thou art" (*de dime con quién andas, decirte he quién eres*) is spoken by Sancho Panza in the Spanish novel *Don Quixote* (chap. 23) by Miguel de Cervantes (1547-1616).

The Role of Appearances

193: *Louis* IX (1214-70) was King of France from 1226.

Louis XIV (1710-74), King of France from 1743 until his death, led a scandalous and ostentatious personal life and contributed greatly to the decline of royal authority.

194: Note 1: *Clovis* (c. 466-511), the first king to unite all the Frankish tribes under one ruler, and *Charlemagne* (c. 742-814), the first Emperor of the Holy Roman Empire, were alike in extending their lands through numerous conquests and wars.

The Function of Relics

199: *The Holy Tunic*, "the coat without seams", is venerated as the garment Jesus wore shortly before his Crucifixion; it is kept at *Treves*, now known as

Trier, in south-west Germany.

200: *Cyril of Jerusalem* (c. 313-386) was a bishop and doctor of the early Church.

For the *Kaaba* see editor's note for "Hypostatic and Cosmic Numbers", p. 63.

James the Greater (d. 44) was one the twelve apostles of Jesus, the brother of John, and perhaps the first apostle to be martyred.

Note 2: For *Abraham* see editor's note for "Understanding Esoterism", p. 11.

201: Note 3: The author's *Logique et transcendence* (Paris: Éditions Traditionnelles, 1970) appeared in English as *Logic and Transcendence* (Bedfont: Perennial Books, 1975; Bloomington, Indiana: World Wisdom, 2009); the chapter "*Le symbolisme du sablier*" is rendered as "The Symbolism of the Hourglass". The author's *Forme et substance dans les religions* (Paris: Dervy Livres, 1975; Paris: L'Harmattan, 2012) appeared in English as *Form and Substance in the Religions* (Bloomington, Indiana: World Wisdom, 2002); the chapter "*Les cinq Présences divines*" is rendered as "The Five Divine Presences".

203: Note 9: The remains of *Philomena* (d. fourth century) were purportedly discovered in a Roman catacomb in 1802 and moved to a newly built church in Mugnano del Cardinale in Italy in 1805. A number of *miracles* were performed with the saint's intercession, notably in the town of *Ars* in France. In 1961 she was *declassified* from the revised version of the Roman Martyrology.

204: *Hanbalism*, one of the four traditional Sunni schools of Islamic jurisprudence, is named after Ahmad Ibn Hanbal (d. 855), who accentuated a literal interpretation of the Koran.

Wahhabism, an *extreme* form of *Hanbalism*, is named after the eighteenth-century preacher and activist, Muhammad ibn Abd al-Wahhab (1703-92).

For a summary of the author's views on *Protestantism* see "Christian Divergences" in *In the Face of the Absolute: A New Translation with Selected Letters*, ed. Harry Oldmeadow (Bloomington, Indiana: World Wisdom, 2014), pp. 49-66.

An Elementary Criteriology of Celestial Apparitions

206: The Latin phrase *quaerite et invenietis*, "seek, and ye shall find", appears in the Vulgate translation of the Gospel of Matthew: "Ask, and it shall be given you; seek, and ye shall find; knock, and it shall be opened unto you" (Matt. 7:7).

Note 1 (cont.): For *credo ut intelligam* see editor's note for "Introduction", p. xvi.

Note 2: "*Heresy resides in the will and not in the intelligence*": According to Thomas Aquinas "Heresy is a species of unbelief", and "unbelief resides in the will and not in the intellect" (*Summa Theologica*, Part 2-2, Quest. 11, Art. 1; Quest. 10, Art. 2). In defense against charges of heresy, Meister Eckhart responded, "I can be in error, but I cannot be a heretic, for the first belongs to the intellect, the second to the will."

"*To err is human but to persevere in error is diabolical*" is a saying attributed to the Stoic philosopher Seneca (c. 4 B.C.-65 A.D.).

208: For *Hesychasm* see editor's note for "Understanding Esoterism", p. 18.

209: Note 4: *Sister* Mary *Consolata* (1903-46), an Italian Capuchin nun who was granted the blessing of numerous conversations with Christ over the course of many years, is best known for her "act of love", received from Christ himself and consisting of the mantric formula, "Jesus, Mary, I love you! Save souls!"

Note 5: For Immanuel *Kant* see editor's note for "Understanding Esoterism", p. 5.

Swami *Siddheswarananda* (1897-1957) was a monk of the Ramakrishna Order, a popularizing writer and lecturer on religious ecumenism, and the founder, in 1937, of a Vedanta Center near Paris.

210: "*And behold the angel of the Lord appeared unto him in a dream, saying, Joseph, thou son of David, fear not to take unto thee Mary thy wife. . . . Then Joseph being raised from sleep did as the angel of the Lord had bidden him*" (Matt. 1:20, 24).

"*Behold the angel of the Lord appeareth to Joseph in a dream, saying, Arise, and take the young child and his mother, and flee into Egypt. . . . When he arose, he took the young child and his mother by night, and departed into Egypt*" (Matt. 2:13-14).

Note 7: For Shankara, or *Shankaracharya*, see editor's note for "Understanding Esoterism", p. 3.

211: Note 9: Praying before a statue of the Blessed Virgin nursing (*lactatio*) the Child Jesus, *Bernard* of Clairvaux (see editor's note for "The Degrees of Art", p. 188) continually besought her to "show that you are a mother"; the statue miraculously came alive, and the Virgin pressed her breast, causing a stream of milk to come forth and wet the lips of Bernard, dry from singing her praises.

212: "He that loveth not knoweth not God; for *God is love*" (1 John 4:8).

The Latin phrase *a fructibus eorum cognoscetis eos*, "by their fruits ye shall know them", appears in the Vulgate translation of the Gospel of Matthew: "Ye shall know them by their fruits. Do men gather grapes of thorns, or figs of thistles? Even so every good tree bringeth forth good fruit; but a corrupt tree bringeth forth evil fruit" (Matt. 7:16-17).

The Sun Dance

216: For the *Kaaba* see editor's note for "Hypostatic and Cosmic Numbers", p. 63.

217: Note 3: "*Have dominion over the earth*": "And God blessed them, and God said unto them, Be fruitful, and multiply, and replenish the earth, and subdue it: and *have dominion* over the fish of the sea, and over the fowl of the air, and over every living thing that moveth upon the earth" (Gen. 1:28).

218: Note 4: For *Shinto* see editor's note for "The Virtues in the Way", p. 102, Note 4.

Note 5: *Saura*s are Hindu worshippers of Surya, the Vedic solar deity.

"The Sun has filled the Heaven and the Earth. . . . He is *the soul of things that move as well as of those that are still*" (*Rig Veda*, I.115.1).

219: Note 7: *Joseph Epes Brown* (1920-2000), recorder and editor of *The Sacred Pipe: Black Elk's Account of the Seven Rites of the Oglala Sioux*, was one of the most authoritative non-native commentators on the spiritual heritage of the American Indians.

George A. Dorsey (1868-1931) was an ethnographer and anthropologist who worked at Harvard University and at the Field Museum of Natural History in Chicago.

Editor's Notes

The Religion of the Heart

225: For *Ghazali* see editor's note for "Understanding Esoterism", p. 15.

226: *To remove the "rust" from the heart in its state of disgrace*: "There is a means of polishing all things by which rust is removed; that which polishes the heart is the invocation of *Allāh*" (*hadīth*).

For *Ibn Arabi* see editor's note for "Understanding Esoterism", p. 13.

Amore e'l cor gentil sono una cosa—"Love and the noble heart are one and the same thing"—is the first line of a poem in *Dante's* (see editor's note for "Understanding Esoterism", p. 30) *La Vita Nuova*, "The New Life".

For *Umar ibn al-Farid* see editor's note for "Understanding Esoterism", p. 33.

Note 2: *Kenryo Kanamatsu* (1915-86) was a Japanese author, translator, and practitioner of *Jōdo-Shinshū* or "Pure Land" Buddhism.

227: The first part of the *Shahādah*, or "Testimony" of faith in Islam, consists of the words, *"There is no god other than the sole God"*.

"No good other than the sole Good": "Why callest thou me good? There is none good but one, that is, God" (Matt. 19:17, Mark 10:18; cf. Luke 18:19).

The "Wisdom" spoken of in the Bible was before the world and was before man: "The Lord possessed me (Wisdom) in the beginning of His way, before His works of old. I was set up from everlasting, from the beginning, or ever the earth was" (Prov. 8:22-23).

Note 4: *"My heart is open to every form*: it is a pasture for gazelles and a cloister for Christian monks, a temple for idols, the Kaaba of the pilgrim, the tables of the Torah, and the book of the Koran. I practice the religion of Love; in whatsoever direction His caravans advance, the religion of Love shall be my religion and my faith" (*Ibn Arabi, Tarjumān al-ashwāq*). For a commentary on these verses see the author's *Understanding Islam: A New Translation with Selected Letters*, ed. Patrick Laude (Bloomington, Indiana: World Wisdom, 2011), pp. 30-31.

228: According to the Definition of Chalcedon, promulgated by the fourth of the Ecumenical Councils (451 A.D.), Christ the *Logos* is at once *"true man and true God"*.

Note 6: For *Plato* see editor's note for "Understanding Esoterism", p. 12.

For *Ramanuja* see editor's note for "Understanding Esoterism", p. 3.

For *Shankara* see editor's note for "Understanding Esoterism", p. 3.

230: "*Hath ears to hear*": "He that hath ears, let him hear" (Matt. 11:15).

For the "*pneumatic*" see editor's note for "The True Remedy", p. 157.

"*My Mercy taketh precedence over My Wrath*" (*hadīth qudsī*).

The Way of Unity

231: "Be ye *perfect even as your Father in Heaven is perfect*" (Matt 5:48).

Note 1: *The apparent negation, in the Koran, of the crucifixion of Christ*: "They did not kill him nor crucified [him], but it appeared so unto them. . . . They did not kill him truly. God raised him to Himself" (*Sūrah* "Women" [4]:157-58). On the subject of the crucifixion, the author writes elsewhere: "As for the apparent denial of the crucifixion by the Koran, we have always held that this is a question of theology rather than history, and we have encountered the same point of view in a work of Massignon ('Le Christ dans les Evangiles selon al-Ghazzali'): 'Abu Hatim, basing himself on the opinion of one of his masters (who is not named), declares that the beginning of the Koranic verse (4:157) in no way denies the crucifixion and that it must be interpreted after taking account of its ending, "and they did not kill him truly (*yaqīnā*). God raised him to Himself", and, since Jesus died a martyr, remembering the verses (2:154; cf. 3:169) on the death of martyrs: "Do not say of those who have been killed on the way of God that they are dead: but that they are living; although you are not aware of it"'" (*Gnosis: Divine Wisdom: A New Translation with Selected Letters*, ed. James S. Cutsinger [Bloomington, Indiana: World Wisdom, 2009], p. 7n).

235: *The blessed, each time they taste a fruit of Paradise, remember having tasted it previously, according to the Koran*: "And give glad tidings (O Muhammad) unto those who believe and do good works; that theirs are Gardens (of Paradise) underneatwhich rivers flow; whensoever they are given a fruit therefrom for provision, they say: This is what was given us aforetime; and they were given a likeness of it" (*Sūrah* "The Cow" [2]:25).

"*Obscure merit of faith*": "The merit of faith consists in this, that man through obedience assents to things he does not see" (Thomas Aquinas, *Summa Theologica*, Part 3, Quest. 7, Art. 3).

"He that loveth not knoweth not God; for *God is love*" (1 John 4:8).

Selections from Letters and Other Previously Unpublished Writings

239: Selection 1: "The Book of Keys", No. 504, "Of the Human State".

240: Selection 2: Letter of June 22, 1970.

"Under whatsoever form you worship Me, it is always Me that you are worshipping; for, O Partha (Arjuna), on all sides, men tread paths leading to Me" (*Bhagavad Gītā*, 4:11).

The apostle *Thomas* is said to have traveled to *India* around 50 A.D. to preach the Gospel.

Francis Xavier (1506-52) was a co-founder of the Society of Jesus and a Christian missionary in Asia.

Lakshmi, the consort of Vishnu, is the Goddess of good fortune and the embodiment of beauty; *Saraswati*, the consort of Brahma, is the Hindu Goddess of music, art, and learning; and *Parvati*, the consort of Shiva, is the Goddess of fertility, love, and devotion, as well as of divine strength and power.

241: Selection 3: "Christic Mysteries", *Études Traditionnelles*, July-August 1948.

For the *"Greater"* and *"Lesser Mysteries"* see editor's note for "The Problem of Sexuality", pp. 132-33.

For *Dante* see editor's note for "Understanding Esoterism", p. 30.

"Render unto Caesar the things that are Caesar's, and unto God the things that are God's" (Mark 12:17; cf. Matt. 22:21, Luke 20:25).

Julius *Caesar* (100-44 B.C.) was the Dictator of Rome from 49-44 B.C.

Augustus (63 B.C.-14 A.D.) was the first Roman Emperor, ruling from 27 B.C.-14 A.D.

Peter (d.c. 64-68) was one of the twelve apostles of Jesus and the first pope of Rome.

Selection 4: Letter of May 4, 1971.

242: *"Be ye perfect even as your Father in Heaven is perfect"* (Matt 5:48).

Selection 5: Letter of August 3, 1971.

243: Selection 6: Letter of August 4, 1973.

Selection 7: Letter of July 6, 1977.

"Behold, *the kingdom of God is within you*" (Luke 17:21).

"*I am black, but beautiful*, O ye daughters of Jerusalem, as the tents of Kedar, as the curtains of Solomon" (Song of Sol. 1:5).

For the *Song of Songs* see editor's note for "Understanding Esoterism", p. 20.

244: Selection 8: "The Black Virgin of Czestochowa", *Études Traditionnelles*, May 1940.

Kali is the destructive and transformative manifestation of the Hindu Goddess Parvati, consort of Shiva.

For the *Kaaba* see editor's note for "Hypostatic and Cosmic Numbers", p. 63.

Selection 9: "Concerning *An Introduction to Christian Esoterism*", unpublished, c. 1980.

For Meister *Eckhart* see editor's note for "Understanding Esoterism", p. 13.

245: René *Guénon* (1886-1951) was a French metaphysician and one of the formative authorities of the perennialist school. For some commentary by the author see *René Guénon: Some Observations*, ed. William Stoddart (Hillsdale, New York: Sophia Perennis, 2004).

"*True esoterism is something completely different from outward religion, and, if there are some relationships with the latter, this can only be so insofar as esoterism finds in the religious forms a means of symbolic expression; it matters little, moreover, whether these forms be of this or that religion*" (René *Guénon, The Esoterism of Dante* [Hillsdale, New York: Sophia Perennis, 2001], p. 3).

"*Esoterism is essentially something different from religion, and not the 'inward' part of a religion as such, even when esoterism finds its base and its support in it*" (René *Guénon, Perspectives on Initiation* [Ghent, New York: Sophia Perennis, 2001], p. 20).

Selection 10: Letter of January 5, 1983.

246: Selection 11: Letter of June 11, 1983.

"*Unless ye be as children*": "Verily I say unto you, Except ye turn, and become as little children, ye shall in no wise enter into the kingdom of Heaven" (Matt. 18:3).

Selection 12: Letter of June 11, 1983.

247: Meister Eckhart distinguished between *Gott* ("*God*"), which is *Being* or the Divine insofar as it expresses itself as a person, and *Gottheit* ("*Godhead*"), which is *Beyond-Being* or the transpersonal divinity of the Absolute as such.

248: "Blessed are the peacemakers, for they shall be called *the children of God*" (Matt. 5:9).

Selection 13: Letter of November 1, 1987.

GLOSSARY OF FOREIGN TERMS AND PHRASES

'Abd (Arabic): "servant" or "slave"; as used in Islam, the servant or worshiper of God in His aspect of *Rabb* or "Lord".

Ādi-Buddha (Sanskrit): in Buddhist cosmology, the universal or primordial Buddha, in whom is personified supreme suchness or emptiness, and from whom come forth both the *Dhyāni-Buddha*s and the historical Buddhas, including Siddhartha Gautama.

Advaita (Sanskrit): "non-dualist" interpretation of the *Vedānta*; Hindu doctrine according to which the seeming multiplicity of things is regarded as the product of ignorance, the only true reality being *Brahma*, the One, the Absolute, the Infinite, which is the unchanging ground of appearance.

A fortiori (Latin): literally, "from greater reason"; used when drawing a conclusion inferred to be even stronger than the one already put forward.

Ahadīyah (Arabic): the supreme Divine Unity of the pure Absolute; see also *Wāhidīyah*.

Āl (Arabic): "family", especially the family of Muhammad, the Prophet of Islam.

Alter ego (Latin): literally, "the other I".

Amor (Latin): love.

Ānanda (Sanskrit): "bliss, beatitude, joy"; one of the three essential aspects of *Apara-Brahma*, together with *Sat*, "being", and *Chit*, "consciousness".

Andros (Greek): the male; see also *Anthropos*.

Anima (Latin): the "soul" (feminine) as the breath of life or vital principle of the physical body; see also *Corpus* and *Spiritus*.

Anthropos (Greek): the human being, male or female; see also *Andros*.

Apara-Brahma (Sanskrit): the "non-supreme" or penultimate *Brahma*, also called *Brahma saguna*; in Schuon's teaching, the "relative Absolute".

Apocatastasis (Greek): "restitution, restoration"; among certain Christian theologians, including Clement of Alexandria, Origen, and Gregory of Nyssa, the doctrine that all creatures will finally be saved.

A posteriori (Latin): literally, "from after"; subsequently; proceeding from effect to cause or from experience to principle.

A priori (Latin): literally, "from before"; in the first instance; proceeding from cause to effect or from principle to experience.

'Ārif bi 'Llāh (Arabic): literally, "knower by God"; in Sufism, one who has attained supreme spiritual knowledge, or *ma'rifah.*

Ars sine scientia nihil est (Latin): "art without knowledge is nothing."

Artifex (Latin): literally, "maker or producer of art"; artist, craftsman.

Asmā' (Arabic, singular *ism*): literally, "names"; in Islam, the Divine Names of God, traditionally numbered at ninety-nine, and including the supreme Names of the Essence (*Dhāt*) and the non-supreme Names of the Qualities (*Sifāt*).

Ātmā or *Ātman* (Sanskrit): the real or true "Self", underlying the ego and its manifestations; in the perspective of *Advaita Vedānta*, identical with *Brahma.*

Avatāra (Sanskrit): a divine "descent"; the incarnation or manifestation of God, especially of Vishnu in the Hindu tradition.

Ave Maria (Latin): "Hail, Mary"; traditional prayer to the Blessed Virgin, also known as the Angelic Salutation, based on the words of the Archangel Gabriel and Saint Elizabeth in Luke 1:28 and Luke 1:42.

Avyakta (Sanskrit): literally, "unmanifested"; latent, hidden; see also *Vyakta.*

Barakah (Arabic): "blessing", grace; in Islam, a spiritual influence or energy emanating originally from God, but often attached to sacred objects and spiritual persons.

Barzakh (Arabic): as used in the Koran, a "barrier" or "separation" between paradise and hell, or this life and the next, or the two seas (fresh and salt); in the interpretation of Sufism, an "isthmus" connecting different planes of reality.

Basmalah (Arabic): traditional Muslim formula of blessing, found at the beginning of all but one of the *sūrah*s of the Koran, consisting of the words *Bismi 'Llāhi 'r-Rahmāni 'r-Rahīm,* "In the Name of God, the Clement (*Rahmān*), the Merciful (*Rahīm*)".

Glossary

Bast (Arabic): "dilation"; the expansion of the soul through spiritual hope or joy; see also *Qabd.*

Bhakta (Sanskrit): a follower of the spiritual path of *bhakti*; a person whose relationship with God is based primarily on adoration and love.

Bhakti or *bhakti-mārga* (Sanskrit): the spiritual "path" (*mārga*) of "love" (*bhakti*) and devotion; see also *Jnāna* and *Karma.*

Bodhisattva (Sanskrit, Pali): literally, "enlightenment-being"; in *Mahāyāna* Buddhism, one who postpones his own final enlightenment and entry into *Nirvāna* in order to aid all other sentient beings in their quest for Buddha-hood.

Brahma or *Brahman* (Sanskrit): the Supreme Reality, the Absolute.

Brahma nirguna (Sanskrit): *Brahma* considered as transcending all "qualities", attributes, or predicates; God as He is in Himself; also called *Para-Brahma.*

Brahma saguna (Sanskrit): *Brahma* "qualified" by attributes and predicates; God insofar as He can be known by man; also called *Apara-Brahma.*

Buddhi (Sanskrit): "Intellect"; the highest faculty of knowledge, to be contrasted with *manas*, that is, mind or reason.

Bushidō (Japanese): literally, the "way of the warrior"; in Japan, the exacting code of conduct of the military samurai class, strongly influenced by Buddhist, Shinto, and Confucian ideals.

Chit (Sanskrit): "consciousness"; one of the three essential aspects of *Apara-Brahma*, together with *Sat*, "being", and *Ānanda*, "bliss, beatitude, joy".

Corpus (Latin): body; one of the three constituent elements of the human microcosm along with the soul and spirit; see also *Anima* and *Spiritus.*

Creatio ex nihilo (Latin): literally "creation out of nothing"; the doctrine that God Himself is the sufficient cause of the universe, needing nothing else; often set in contrast to emanationist cosmogonies.

Credo quia absurdum est (Latin): "I believe because it is absurd."

Credo ut intelligam (Latin): "I believe so that I may understand."

Darshan or *Darshana* (Sanskrit): a spiritual "perspective", point of view, or school of thought; also the "viewing" of a holy person, object, or place; more

285

generally, the visual assimilation of celestial qualities or the contemplation of the Divine in nature or in art.

De facto (Latin): literally, "from the fact"; denoting something that is such "in fact", if not necessarily "by right".

De jure (Latin): literally, "by right"; an expression often used in contradistinction with *de facto*.

Deva (Sanskrit): literally, "shining one"; in Hinduism, a celestial being; any of the gods of the *Vedas*, traditionally reckoned as thirty-three.

Devadāsī (Sanskrit): literally, "servant of God"; a female temple dancer and courtesan married to the god of the temple and skilled in the erotic arts.

Dhāt (Arabic): the supra-personal Divine Essence; see also *Ahadīyah*.

Distinguo (Latin): literally, "I mark or set off, differentiate", often used in the dialectic of the medieval scholastics; any philosophical distinction.

Esse (Latin): literally "to be"; the divine Principle as pure Being; see also *Posse*.

Ex-voto (Latin): literally, "from the vow", a shortened form of *ex voto suscepto*, "from the vow made"; an object offered to a saint or to a divinity in fulfillment of a vow.

Faqīr (Arabic, plural *fuqarā'*): literally, the "poor one"; in Sufism, a follower of the spiritual path, whose "indigence" or "poverty" (*faqr*) testifies to complete dependence on God and a desire to be filled by Him alone.

Gnosis (Greek): "knowledge"; spiritual insight, principial comprehension, divine wisdom.

Gopī (Sanskrit): literally, "keeper of the cows"; in Hindu tradition, one of the cowherd girls involved with Krishna in the love affairs of his youth, symbolic of the soul's devotion to God.

Gratia plena (Latin): literally, "full of grace"; part of the Angelical Salutation, or "Hail Mary" (*Ave Maria*) (cf. Luke 1:28, 42).

Grosso modo (Italian): "roughly speaking".

Guru (Sanskrit): literally, "weighty", grave, venerable; in Hinduism, a spiritual master; one who gives initiation and instruction in the spiritual path and in whom is embodied the supreme goal of realization or perfection.

Glossary

Hadīth (Arabic, plural *ahādīth*): "saying, narrative"; an account of the words or deeds of the Prophet Muhammad, transmitted through a traditional chain of known intermediaries.

Hadīth qudsī (Arabic): "divine, holy narrative"; an extra-Koranic saying in which God Himself speaks through the mouth of the Prophet.

Hāl (Arabic): in Sufism, a passing spiritual state; contrasted with a permanent spiritual degree or station (*maqām*).

Haqīqah (Arabic, plural *haqā'iq*): "truth, reality"; in Sufism, esoteric or metaphysical knowledge of the supremely Real; also the essential reality of a thing.

Hayāt (Arabic): the Divine "Life"; see also *Shuhūd* and *Wujūd*.

Hic et nunc (Latin): "here and now".

Hijāb (Arabic): veil, curtain.

Hikmah (Arabic): the Divine "Wisdom"; see also *Qudrah* and *Rahmah*.

Homo (Latin): the human being, male or female; see also *Vir*.

Homo faber (Latin): literally, "man the artisan"; man as creator or producer.

Homo sapiens (Latin): literally, "wise man"; the human species.

Hypostasis (Greek, plural *hypostases*): literally, "substance"; the transcendent form of a metaphysical reality, understood to be eternally distinct from all other such forms; in Christian theology, a technical term for one of the three Persons of the Trinity.

Ihsān (Arabic): "excellence, perfection"; in Islam, virtuous or beautiful action; spiritual excellence.

In divinis (Latin): literally, "in or among divine things"; within the divine Principle; the plural form is used insofar as the Principle comprises both *Para-Brahma*, Beyond-Being or the Absolute, and *Apara-Brahma*, Being or the relative Absolute.

Intelligo ergo credo (Latin): "I understand therefore I believe."

Ipso facto (Latin): by that very fact.

Ishta-devatā (Sanskrit): in Hinduism, the "chosen deity" to which a worshiper is devoted.

Īshvara (Sanskrit): literally, "possessing power", hence master; God understood as a personal being, as Creator and Lord; manifest in the *Trimūrti* as Brahmā, Vishnu, and Shiva.

Isrā' (Arabic): literally, "night journey"; see *Mi'rāj*.

Istikhārah (Arabic): in Islam, a prayer for divine guidance in times of uncertainty.

Jalwah (Arabic): spiritual radiation or exteriorization; see also *Khalwah*.

Jīvan-mukta (Sanskrit): one who is "liberated" while still in this "life"; a person who has attained a state of spiritual perfection or self-realization before death; in contrast to *videha-mukta*, one who is liberated at the moment of death.

Jnāna or *jnāna-mārga* (Sanskrit): the spiritual "path" (*mārga*) of "knowledge" (*jnāna*) and intellection; see also *Bhakti* and *Karma*.

Jnānī or *Jnānin* (Sanskrit): a follower of the path of *jnāna*; a person whose relationship with God is based primarily on sapiential knowledge or *gnosis*.

Jōdo (Japanese): "pure land"; the untainted, transcendent realm created by the Buddha Amida (Amitabha in Sanskrit), into which his devotees aspire to be born in their next life.

Jōdo-Shinshū (Japanese): "true pure land school"; a sect of Japanese Pure Land Buddhism founded by Shinran, the disciple of Honen, based on faith in the power of the Buddha Amida and characterized by use of the *nembutsu*.

Kali-Yuga (Sanskrit): in Hinduism, the fourth and final *yuga* in a given cycle of time, corresponding to the Iron Age of Western tradition and culminating in a *pralaya* or the *mahāpralaya*; the present age of mankind, distinguished by its increasing disorder, violence, and forgetfulness of God.

Kalpa (Sanskrit): in Hinduism, a "day in the life of Brahmā", understood as lasting one thousand *mahāyuga*s or fourteen *manvantara*s.

Karma (Sanskrit): "action, work"; one of the principal *mārga*s or spiritual "paths", characterized by its stress on righteous deeds (see *Bhakti* and *Jnāna*); in Hinduism and Buddhism, the law of consequence, in which the present is explained by reference to the nature and quality of one's past actions.

Glossary

Karma-mārga, karma-yoga (Sanskrit): the spiritual "path" (*mārga*) or method of "union" (*yoga*) based upon right "action, work" (*karma*); see *Bhakti* and *Jnāna*.

Karma-yogī (Sanskrit): a practitioner of *karma-yoga*, or the "way of works".

Khalīfah (Arabic, plural *khulafā'*): literally, "successor"; a representative or vicar, often used in reference to the successors of the Prophet Muhammad; in Sufism, every man is in principle a *khalīfah* of God.

Khalwah (Arabic): spiritual retreat or interiorization; see *Jalwah*.

Kōan (Japanese): literally, "precedent for public use", case study; in Zen Buddhism, a question or anecdote often based on the experience or sayings of a notable master and involving a paradox or puzzle which cannot be solved in conventional terms or with ordinary thinking.

Kosha (Sanskrit): literally "envelope", sheath; the *Vedānta* teaches that *Ātmā* manifests itself through a (descending) series of embodiments: *ānandamaya-kosha* ("sheath of bliss"), *vijnānamaya-kosha* ("sheath of intellect"), *mano-maya-kosha* ("sheath of mind"), *prānamaya-kosha* ("sheath of vital breath"), and *annamaya-kosha* ("sheath of nutriment").

Koubba (French): in Islam, and especially in North Africa, the tomb or monument of a venerated saint or marabout.

Lex (Latin): law.

Logos (Greek): "word, reason"; in Christian theology, the divine, uncreated Word of God (cf. John 1:1); the transcendent Principle of creation and revelation.

Mahāpralaya (Sanskrit): in Hinduism, the "great" or final "dissolving" of the universe.

Mahāyuga (Sanskrit): in Hindu tradition, a "great age", comprising four lesser ages (*yugas*) or periods of time, namely, *krita-yuga* (the "golden" age of Western tradition), *tretā-yuga* ("silver"), *dvāpara-yuga* ("bronze"), and *kali-yuga* ("iron").

Malāmatiyah (Arabic): literally, "the blameworthy"; a Sufi sect that accentuated self-reproach and endeavored to conceal virtue behind a façade of ignoble action.

Mantra (Sanskrit): "instrument of thought"; a word or phrase of divine origin, often including a Name of God, repeated by those initiated into its proper use as a means of salvation or liberation.

Manvantara (Sanskrit): in the Hindu theory of cosmic cycles as derived from the *Mānava-Dharma-Shāstra*, a period of seventy-one *mahāyugas*; see *Mahāyuga* and *Yuga*.

Maqām (Arabic): "place", "station"; in Sufism, the permanent spiritual degree or station reached by a practitioner of the path; contrasted with a passing spiritual state (*hāl*).

Ma'rifah (Arabic): "knowledge"; in Sufism, the spiritual way based upon knowledge or *gnosis*, analogous to the Hindu *Jnāna-mārga*.

Materia prima (Latin): "first or prime matter"; in Platonic cosmology, the undifferentiated and primordial substance serving as a "receptacle" for the shaping force of divine forms or ideas; universal potentiality.

Māyā (Sanskrit): universal illusion, relativity, appearance; in *Advaita Vedānta*, the veiling or concealment of *Brahma* in the form or under the appearance of a lower, relative reality; also, as "productive power", the unveiling or manifestation of *Ātmā* as "divine art" or theophany. *Māyā* is neither real nor unreal, and ranges from the Supreme Lord to the "last blade of grass".

Mi'rāj (Arabic): literally, the "ascension"; the miraculous "night journey" (*isrā'*) of the Prophet Muhammad from Mecca to Jerusalem, from where, after praying with his fellow prophets at the Al-Aqsa Mosque on the Temple Mount, he ascended through the seven heavens to the Divine Presence.

Mitzvoth (Hebrew, sing. *mitzvah*): the outward precepts, prescriptions, and commandments in the Hebrew Bible, traditionally numbered at 613, relating to the religious and moral conduct incumbent upon the Jews.

Moksha (Sanskrit): "release" or "liberation" from *samsāra*; according to Hindu teaching, the most important of the aims of life, attained by following one of the principal *mārga*s or spiritual paths (see *Bhakti*, *Jnāna*, and *Karma*).

Mors (Latin): "death".

Mutatis mutandis (Latin): literally, "those things having been changed which need to be changed".

Nembutsu (Japanese): "remembrance or mindfulness of the Buddha", based upon the repeated invocation of his Name; same as *buddhānusmriti* in Sanskrit and *nien-fo* in Chinese.

Glossary

Nihil obstat (Latin): literally, "nothing hinders"; in the Roman Catholic Church, a certification by an official censor that a book is not objectionable on doctrinal or moral grounds.

Nirvāna (Sanskrit): literally, "blowing out" or "extinction"; in Indian traditions, especially Buddhism, the extinction of suffering and the resulting, blissful state of liberation from egoism and attachment; extinction in relation to universal manifestation.

Nous (Greek): intellect; the highest faculty in man, by which truth can be directly known.

Nox profunda (Latin): literally, "deep night"; in the spiritual path, the experience of loss and darkness accompanying the death of the ego.

Nuditas sacra (Latin): sacred nudity.

Nūr Muhammadī (Persian): the "Muhammadan Light"; the pre-existential or uncreated nature of the Prophet Muhammad, before the creation of Adam.

Para-Brahma (Sanskrit): the "supreme" or ultimate *Brahma*, also called *Brahma nirguna*; the Absolute as such.

Paramahamsa (Sanskrit): literally, "highest flyer" or "supreme swan"; in Hinduism, a title given to certain great saints and renunciates, who have attained the supreme state of *moksha*.

Paramātmā (Sanskrit): the "supreme" or ultimate Self; see *Ātmā*.

Petitio principii (Latin): literally, "assuming the initial point"; circular reasoning; a logical fallacy or begging of the question where the premise assumes the truth of the conclusion.

Philosophia Perennis (Latin): "Perennial Philosophy".

Pneuma (Greek): the spirit that predominates over the soul and the body (cf. 1 Thess. 5:23; 1 Cor. 2:14-15).

Pontifex (Latin): "bridge-maker"; man as the link between heaven and earth.

Pontifex Maximus (Latin): "supreme pontiff"; a phrase claiming for the Bishop of Rome (Pope) the right of universal jurisdiction over the entire Church both East and West.

Posse (Latin): literally, "to be able"; the divine Principle as infinite Possibility;

see *Esse*.

Prājna (Sanskrit): the state of deep sleep; in *Vedānta*, one of the four states of consciousness; see also *Vaishvārana, Taijasa, Turīya*.

Prajnā (Sanskrit): "wisdom, intelligence, understanding"; in Hinduism, the self-awareness of *Ātmā*; knowledge of things as they truly are; in Buddhism, one of the six *pāramitās* or virtues of the *Bodhisattva*.

Pralaya (Sanskrit): "dissolution"; Hindu teaching that all appearance is subject to a periodic process of destruction and recreation; see *Mahāpralaya*.

Prakriti (Sanskrit): literally, "making first" (see *materia prima*); the fundamental, "feminine" substance or material cause of all things; see *Purusha*.

Prapatti (Sanskrit): "seeking refuge"; pious resignation and devotion to God.

Pratīka (Sanskrit): "symbol"; image.

Principium individuationis (Latin): the "principle of individuation".

Psyche (Greek): the soul; one of the three constituent elements of the human microcosm along with the body and spirit; see *Pneuma, Soma*.

Purusha (Sanskrit): literally, "man"; the informing or shaping principle of creation; the "masculine" demiurge or fashioner of the universe; see *Prakriti*.

Qabd (Arabic): "contraction"; the soul in a state of spiritual fear; see *Bast*.

Qudrah (Arabic): the Divine Power; see also *Hikmah* and *Rahmah*.

Quinta essentia (Latin): literally, "the fifth essence"; the ether; also, a perfect embodiment of something.

Quod absit (Latin): literally, "which is absent from, opposed to, or inconsistent with"; a phrase commonly used by the medieval Scholastics to call attention to an idea that is absurdly inconsistent with accepted principles.

Rahīm (Arabic): see *Basmalah*.

Rahmah (Arabic): "compassion, mercy"; in Islam, one of the Names of God, who is supreme Compassion, Mercy, and Clemency; see *Basmalah, Hikmah*, and *Rahmah*.

Rahmān (Arabic): see *Basmalah*.

Glossary

Rajas (Sanskrit): in Hinduism, one of the three *gunas*, or qualities, of *Prakriti*, of which all things are woven; the quality of expansiveness, manifest in the material world as force or movement and in the soul as ambition, initiative, and restlessness.

Rāsa-līlā (Sanskrit): literally, "dance-play"; the circular dance of the *gopīs* in the company of their beloved, Kris*Rasūl* (Arabic): "messenger, apostle"; in Islam, one whom God sends with a message for a particular people.

Religio (Latin): religion.

Religio perennis (Latin): the "perennial religion".

Rūh (Arabic): "Spirit"; in Sufism, either the uncreated Spirit of God or the spirit of man; see *Pneuma*.

Salāt 'alā 'n-Nabī (Arabic): a formula of blessing upon the Prophet Muhammad; in Sufism, often recited as part of a rosary during devotional worship.

Samsāra (Sanskrit): literally, "wandering"; in Hinduism and Buddhism, transmigration or the cycle of birth, death, and rebirth; also the world of apparent flux and change.

Sat (Sanskrit): "being"; one of the three essential aspects of *Apara-Brahma*, together with *Chit*, "consciousness", and *Ānanda*, "bliss, beatitude, joy".

Sat-Chit-Ānanda or *Saccidānanda* (Sanskrit): "being-consciousness-bliss"; the three essential aspects of *Apara-Brahma*, that is, *Brahma* insofar as it can be grasped in human experience.

Satori (Japanese): in Zen Buddhism, the sudden experience of enlightenment; a flash of intuitive insight often gained through the employment of a *kōan* during *zazen* or "sitting meditation".

Satsanga (Sanskrit): literally, "company of the good"; the frequenting of men or women of spiritual or ascendant tendency.

Sattva (Sanskrit): in Hinduism, one of the three *gunas*, or qualities, of *Prakriti*, of which all things are woven; the quality of luminosity, manifest in the material world as buoyancy or lightness and in the soul as intelligence and virtue.

Shahādah (Arabic): the fundamental "profession" or "testimony" of faith in Islam, consisting of the words *Lā ilāha illā 'Llāh, Muhammadan rasūlu 'Llāh*: "There is no god but God; Muhammad is the messenger of God."

Shakti (Sanskrit): creative "power" or radiant "energy"; in Hinduism, expressed tantrically as the consort or feminine complement of Shiva.

Shekhinah (Hebrew): in Judaism, the dwelling-place or presence of God in the world; the Divine immanence, often personified in female form.

Shinshū (Sanskrit): see *Jōdo-Shinshū*.

Shuhūd (Arabic): "perception, consciousness"; often in reference to the Sufi doctrine of *wahdat ash-shuhūd*, "the unity of perception"; see *Wujūd*.

Sifāt (Arabic, singular *Sifah*): the Divine Qualities; see *Asmā'*, *Dhāt*.

Sine qua non (Latin): an indispensable or essential condition.

Soma (Greek): the body; one of the three constituent elements of the human microcosm along with the soul and spirit; see *Pneuma*, *Psyche*.

Sophia (Greek): "wisdom"; in Jewish and Christian tradition, the Wisdom of God, often conceived as feminine (cf. Prov. 8).

Sophia Perennis (Greek): "Perennial Wisdom"; the eternal, non-formal Truth at the heart of all orthodox religious traditions.

Spirituali (Latin): a reform group within the Catholic Church who believed that spiritual renewal would come about through more intense study of the Scriptures and through "justification by faith".

Spiritus (Latin): "spirit"; the supra-individual principle of the human microcosm, with its seat in the heart.

Sunnah (Arabic): "custom, way of acting"; in Islam, the norm established by the Prophet Muhammad, including his actions and sayings (see *Hadīth*) and serving as a precedent and standard for the behavior of Muslims.

Sūrah (Arabic): one of the one hundred fourteen divisions, or chapters, of the Koran.

Taijasa (Sanskrit): the dream state; in *Vedānta*, one of the four states of consciousness; see also *Prājna*, *Turīya*, *Vaishvānara*.

Tamas (Sanskrit): in Hinduism, one of the three *gunas*, or qualities, of *Prakriti*, of which all things are woven; the quality of darkness or heaviness, manifest in the material world as inertia or rigidity and in the soul as sloth, stupidity, and vice.

Glossary

Tanzīh (Arabic): "remove, declare to be incomparable"; in Islam, the assertion that God is pure and free of all imperfections, hence utterly unlike His creatures; a perspective stressing divine distance and rigor.

Tashbīh (Arabic): "compare, assimilate"; in Islam, the assertion that God must have some similarity to His creatures, anthropomorphic descriptions of Him in the Koran being analogically accurate; a perspective stressing divine nearness and mercy.

Tawfīq (Arabic): in Islam, the divine aid or help.

Torah (Hebrew): "instruction, teaching"; in Judaism, the written law of God, as revealed to Moses on Sinai and embodied in the Pentateuch (Genesis, Exodus, Leviticus, Numbers, Deuteronomy).

Trimūrti (Sanskrit): literally, "having three forms"; in Hindu tradition, a triadic expression of the Divine, especially in the form of Brahmā, the creator, Vishnu, the preserver, and Shiva, the transformer.

Turīya (Sanskrit): "the fourth"; in *Vedānta*, the highest state of consciousness, identified with *Brahma*; see also *Prājna, Taijasa, Vaishvānara*.

Unio mystica (Latin): "mystical union"; in Christianity, the final stage of the spiritual path.

Upāya (Sanskrit): "means, expedient, method"; in Buddhist tradition, the adaptation of spiritual teaching to a form suited to the level of one's audience.

Vaishvānara (Sanskrit): the waking state; in *Vedānta*, one of the four states of consciousness; see also *Prājna, Taijasa, Turīya*.

Vāsanā (Sanskrit): literally, "impression, longing"; mental impressions or desires, habitual ways of understanding.

Veda (Sanskrit): "knowledge"; in Hinduism, the body of sacred knowledge held to be the basis of orthodoxy and right practice.

Vedānta (Sanskrit): "end or culmination of the *Vedas*"; one of the major schools of traditional Hindu philosophy, based in part on the *Upanishads*, esoteric treatises found at the conclusion of the Vedic scriptures; see *Advaita*.

Vir (Latin): male; see *Homo*.

Vyakta (Sanskrit): literally, "the perceivable"; that which has been brought into manifestation; see *Avyakta*.

Wāhidīyah (Arabic): the non-supreme Divine Unicity of the "relative Absolute"; see *Ahadīyah*.

Wujūd (Arabic): "being"; often in reference to the Sufi doctrine of *wahdat al-wujūd*, "the unity of being"; see *Shuhūd*.

Yantra (Sanskrit): literally, "instrument of support"; a geometrical design, often representing the cosmos, used in Tantric Hinduism and Tibetan Buddhism as a visual support or focus for meditation.

Yin-Yang (Chinese): in Chinese tradition, two opposite but complementary forces or qualities, from whose interpenetration the universe and all its diverse forms emerge; *yin* corresponds to the feminine, the yielding, the moon, liquidity; *yang* corresponds to the masculine, the resisting, the sun, solidity.

Yoga (Sanskrit): literally, "yoking, union"; in Indian traditions, any meditative and ascetic technique designed to bring the soul and body into a state of concentration.

Yuga (Sanskrit): an "age" in Hinduism; one of the four periods into which a cycle of time is divided.

Zāhir (Arabic): "the Outward"; God insofar as He manifests Himself in and through the cosmos; contrasted with the divine Name *Al-Bātin*, "the Inward".

For a glossary of all key foreign words used in books published by World Wisdom, including metaphysical terms in English, consult: www.DictionaryofSpiritualTerms.org. This on-line Dictionary of Spiritual Terms provides extensive definitions, examples, and related terms in other languages.

INDEX

'abd, 41, 67, 68, 228, 283
Abraham, 11, 200, 250, 264, 274
Absolute, the, 3, 10, 11, 23, 27, 37,
    38, 39, 40, 43, 55, 57, 58, 70,
    73, 75, 85, 90, 92, 97, 98, 105,
    106, 128, 141, 145, 148, 161,
    170, 171, 172, 215, 225, 232,
    234, 236, 239, 246, 274, 281,
    283, 285, 287, 291
abstention, 98, 153, 189
abstinence, 122, 126
Adam, 46, 48, 71, 72, 73, 76, 77,
    78, 81, 82, 123, 135, 257, 260,
    261, 264, 265, 291
Ādi-Buddha, 134
Advaita Vedānta, 245, 249, 267,
    284, 290
aestheticism, 169
aesthetics, 109, 169, 173
Ahadīyah, 233, 283, 286, 296
Ajanta frescoes, the, 182
Ali, 68
Allāh, 37, 39, 42, 125, 229, 242,
    250, 256, 259, 277
All-Possibility, 73, 246, 247
Amaterasu, 218
American Indians, the, 126, 188,
    189, 217, 218, 259, 276
Ānanda, 58, 59, 60, 61, 68, 87, 89,
    92, 112, 172, 233, 283, 285,
    293
angels, 159, 200, 208
Angelus Silesius, 18, 134, 253, 266
Anglican schism, the, 124
anima, 59, 131
Anselm, 142
Apocatastasis, 52, 73, 80, 253, 257,
    260, 283

archetypes, the, 43, 59, 171
Aristotle, 12, 13, 99, 159, 251, 261,
    262, 271
art, xvi, 19, 22, 45, 89, 101, 109,
    132, 146, 169, 170, 172, 183,
    184, 185, 186, 188, 189, 190,
    191, 198, 199, 203, 230, 239,
    257, 269, 273, 279, 284, 286,
    290; Balinese, 182; extra-
    liturgical, 178, 180, 181, 182;
    Hindu, 182; non-traditional,
    183; profane, 76, 177, 178, 180;
    sacred, 45, 89, 146, 170, 172,
    177, 178, 179, 180, 182, 185,
    189, 203, 230; Taoist, 45, 182;
    traditional, 177, 179, 185
Aryan mythologies, the, 217
Ashari, al-, 12, 73, 250, 260
Asharite theology, 72, 260
Ātmā, 9, 11, 27, 28, 37, 38, 40, 42,
    43, 51, 52, 55, 58, 61, 63, 64,
    69, 75, 92, 112, 138, 145, 172,
    225, 228, 242, 246, 247, 256,
    267, 268, 284, 289, 290, 291,
    292
Augustine (of Hippo), 38, 48, 82,
    116, 256, 261, 263
Augustus, 241, 279
avarice, 100, 153
Avatāra(s), xvi, 28, 40, 54, 55, 67,
    68, 79, 106, 130, 208, 254,
    257, 266, 272, 284
average man, the, 8, 186, 228
avidity, 99
avyakta, 43

barakah, 133, 173, 203
Baroque, the, 198, 203, 272

Index

Tradition, xi, 149, 193, 200
transcendence, 3, 10, 13, 14, 34, 45,
    46, 59, 61, 70, 85, 86, 93, 96,
    102, 142, 175, 190, 212, 215,
    220, 229, 232, 233, 274
tree of Life, the, 71, 77
trial(s), 48, 49, 139, 140, 141, 151
triviality, 102, 126
Truth, the, 3, 8, 25, 26, 95, 116,
    149, 230; total, xi, xiv, 7, 9,
    105, 134, 152, 154, 193, 228,
    230, 239
Turīya, 42, 292, 294, 295

ugliness, 169, 173, 174, 175, 196,
    198, 211, 212
Unconditioned, the, 37, 38, 40
unio mystica, 11
Union, 27, 233
Unity, 62, 70, 74, 148, 227, 231,
    232, 233, 254, 278, 283
Upanishads, xv, 8, 24, 249, 250,
    273, 295

Vaishvānara, 42, 294, 295
Vedānta, xiii, 12, 27, 42, 208, 210,
    245, 249, 257, 267, 283, 284,
    289, 290, 292, 294, 295
veil, the, 7, 37, 38, 40, 41, 44, 45,
    46, 47, 49, 50, 51, 52, 53, 54,
    102, 120, 191, 212, 213, 256,
    259, 260, 261, 263, 264, 265,
    271, 272
Veronica, 178
vigilance, 66, 98, 99, 101
Vincent de Paul, 147
Virgen del Pilar, 218
Virgin, the, 27, 28, 39, 53, 82, 135,
    178, 201, 203, 204, 212, 218,
    240, 244, 264, 266, 276
Virgin-Mother, 244
virility, 40, 124, 126

virtue, 9, 12, 14, 15, 19, 20, 22, 25,
    29, 31, 38, 39, 45, 48, 49, 50,
    52, 53, 54, 55, 65, 70, 74, 76,
    86, 87, 88, 89, 90, 91, 93, 95,
    96, 97, 98, 100, 101, 102, 103,
    104, 105, 106, 107, 115, 116,
    118, 125, 135, 137, 142, 153,
    161, 162, 164, 165, 170, 171,
    174, 175, 185, 193, 205, 215,
    230, 231, 232, 236, 239, 242,
    289, 293
Vishnu, 11, 50, 55, 125, 130, 250,
    258, 266, 272, 279, 284, 288,
    295
Vishnuism, 10, 17
Vishnuite miniature, 181
vision(s), 13, 23, 25, 33, 44, 74, 81,
    94, 205, 206, 207, 210, 211,
    212, 221, 243
volition, 88, 94, 210
vyakta, 43

Wahhabism, 204, 274
Wāhidīyah, 233, 283, 296
waking state, the, 209, 210, 295
Western Christendom, 159, 194,
    241, 270
will, the, xiv, xv, xvi, 3, 4, 5, 6, 8,
    9, 22, 24, 27, 33, 34, 43, 44,
    48, 51, 54, 57, 61, 62, 65, 66,
    73, 75, 76, 77, 81, 85, 87, 88,
    89, 90, 91, 92, 93, 94, 95, 97,
    99, 102, 109, 111, 112, 113,
    116, 117, 118, 122, 127, 129,
    130, 132, 135, 139, 141, 142,
    144, 145, 147, 148, 151, 152,
    158, 161, 162, 165, 173, 180,
    185, 190, 195, 198, 199, 202,
    204, 205, 206, 207, 208, 209,
    211, 226, 227, 229, 231, 233,
    239, 243, 246, 263, 270, 275,
    284

BIOGRAPHICAL NOTES

Frithjof Schuon

Born in Basle, Switzerland in 1907, Frithjof Schuon was the twentieth century's pre-eminent spokesman for the perennialist school of comparative religious thought.

The leitmotif of Schuon's work was foreshadowed in an encounter during his youth with a marabout who had accompanied some members of his Senegalese village to Basle for the purpose of demonstrating their African culture. When Schuon talked with him, the venerable old man drew a circle with radii on the ground and explained: "God is the center; all paths lead to Him." Until his later years Schuon traveled widely, from India and the Middle East to America, experiencing traditional cultures and establishing lifelong friendships with Hindu, Buddhist, Christian, Muslim, and American Indian spiritual leaders.

A philosopher in the tradition of Plato, Shankara, and Eckhart, Schuon was a gifted artist and poet as well as the author of over twenty books on religion, metaphysics, sacred art, and the spiritual path. Describing his first book, *The Transcendent Unity of Religions*, T. S. Eliot wrote, "I have met with no more impressive work in the comparative study of Oriental and Occidental religion", and world-renowned religion scholar Huston Smith said of Schuon, "The man is a living wonder; intellectually apropos religion, equally in depth and breadth, the paragon of our time". Schuon's books have been translated into over a dozen languages and are respected by academic and religious authorities alike.

More than a scholar and writer, Schuon was a spiritual guide for seekers from a wide variety of religions and backgrounds throughout the world. He died in 1998.

Harry Oldmeadow was, until his recent retirement, the Coordinator of Philosophy and Religious Studies at La Trobe University Bendigo, in southeast Australia. A widely respected author on the *sophia perennis* and the perennialist school, his publications include *Traditionalism: Religion in the Light of the Perennial Philosophy* (2000) and *Frithjof Schuon and the Perennial Philosophy* (2010). He has edited several anthologies for World Wisdom, the most recent being *Crossing Religious Frontiers* (2010), and has contributed to such journals as *Sophia* and *Sacred Web*. In addition to his studies of perennialism, he has written extensively on the modern encounter of Eastern and Western traditions in works such as *Journeys East: 20th Century Western Encounters with Eastern Religious Traditions* (2004) and *A Christian Pilgrim in India: The Spiritual Journey of Swami Abhishiktananda* (2008).